'Peter Wilson has found a way of both practising and describing a version of psychotherapy with young people that is entirely intelligible and accessible, inspired and inspiring, tentative and confident, humorous and compassionate. With no jargon, and no grandiose claims. Psychoanalysis with young people as a most appealing improvisation, not the earnest routine ideology of virtue that it is all too often presented as being.'

Adam Phillips, *Child & Adult Psychoanalytic Psychotherapist, essayist, author and literary critic*

'This timely and compassionate book draws deeply on the author's extensive experience of working with young people. It stands as an accessible and much-needed corrective to today's trend toward manualised approaches and prescriptive action. Instead, the book advocates for open listening, honest self-awareness, and the importance of working as an ally to the developing "self" of the young person who is experiencing conflict. Such work is less about delivering treatment—less about "doing"—and more about being alongside: showing interest, recognition, and respect for the natural maturational processes the author so insightfully explores.

Unique in its depth and perspective, this is an essential and scholarly resource on adolescence.'

Paul van Heeswyk, *Consultant Child & Adolescent Psychotherapist*

'Wilson describes the experience of being and working with adolescence in a unique and compelling way which will resonate with all who work with this age group.'

Professor Jeremy Holmes, *Psychiatrist and Psychotherapist*

The Adolescent and the Psychotherapist

This work of collected essays brings together the clinical, theoretical and educational wisdom of one of the foremost child psychoanalytic psychotherapists in the United Kingdom, Peter Wilson.

Wilson offers a clear, accessible understanding of adolescence from a psychoanalytic perspective and highlights the importance of working dynamically. While guiding the reader through work with multiple behavioural and psychic difficulties often presented in the clinical space, he highlights the importance of the therapist not always having the answers. He encourages reflection and exploration, showing the importance of working through the process with one's adolescents in therapy.

This book is an invaluable resource for psychoanalysts, therapists, psychiatrists, psychologists, occupational therapists and teachers, as well as young people and their parents.

Peter Wilson is a Consultant Child and Adolescent Psychoanalytic Psychotherapist based in London, United Kingdom.

Independent Psychoanalytic Approaches with Children and Adolescents series
Series Editors: Ann Horne and Teresa Bailey

For more information about this series, please visit: www.routledge.com/ Routledge-Handbooks-in-Religion/book-series

The Adolescent and the Psychotherapist

Why 'I Don't Know' Matters

Peter Wilson

Routledge
Taylor & Francis Group

LONDON AND NEW YORK

Designed cover image: Photodisc & ImageDJ / Design Master

First published 2026
by Routledge
4 Park Square, Milton Park, Abingdon, Oxon OX14 4RN

and by Routledge
605 Third Avenue, New York, NY 10158

Routledge is an imprint of the Taylor & Francis Group, an informa business

For Product Safety Concerns and Information please contact our
EU representative GPSR@taylorandfrancis.com. Taylor & Francis
Verlag GmbH, Kaufingerstraße 24, 80331 München, Germany.

British Library Cataloguing-in-Publication Data
A catalogue record for this book is available from the British Library

ISBN: 978-1-041-15630-7 (hbk)
ISBN: 978-1-041-15629-1 (pbk)
ISBN: 978-1-003-68043-7 (ebk)

DOI: 10.4324/9781003680437

Typeset in Times New Roman
by codeMantra

Contents

About the authors

Peter Wilson is a consultant child and adolescent psychoanalytic psychotherapist. His first working experience was as an unattached youth worker. He trained as a social worker at the London School of Economics and then moved to New York, United States, to work in a residential treatment centre, The Hawthorne Cedar Knolls School, run by the Jewish Board of Guardians. After three years, he applied to the Hampstead Course and Clinic in London for a place on the child and adolescent psychoanalytic training run by Anna Freud. He was interviewed for this in New York by Augusta Alpert and Marianne Kris, colleagues of Anna Freud.

He qualified as a child and adolescent psychoanalyst in 1971. For the next twenty years, he worked in the Hoxton, Brixton and Camberwell Child Guidance Clinics and in the Brent Consultation Service for adolescents. He held senior positions as a Principal Child Psychotherapist in Camberwell Health Authority, as a Senior Clinical Tutor in the Institute of Psychiatry, as the Director of the Brandon Centre (a psychotherapy service for young people) and as a Consultant Psychotherapist in the Peper Harow Therapeutic Community for adolescents.

He later co-founded YoungMinds, a national charity promoting child and adolescent mental health, and served as its Director for 12 years. Later, he served as a Clinical Adviser to the Place2Be, a national counselling organisation based in schools. Following his retirement, he supervises child and adolescent psychotherapists and teaches on the IPCAPA (the Independent Psychoanalytic Child and Adolescent Psychotherapy Association – part of the British Psychotherapy Foundation) course, the Tavistock M34 course and in IATE, the Institute for Arts in Therapy and Education.

He has written widely and is the author of *YoungMinds in Our Schools*, published by YoungMinds in 2003.

Preface

Adam Phillips

When the Independent Group analyst Peter Lomas suggested that the neurotic was somebody who couldn't bear being an ordinary person, he forgot to mention that the psychoanalyst too might find his own ordinariness a problem. The question in psychoanalysis – and this is particularly salient, as Wilson's remarkable book shows, in child and adolescent psychotherapy – has always been, what is special, what is different about the psychotherapist? What is the therapist authoritative about, if anything? What kind of authority does the therapist have, and what kind of authority does he want to have? After all, patients of the child psychotherapists are young people in the process, hopefully, of becoming the kind of adults they want to be, and so dependent on the adults having something they need (what they don't usually need, in Wilson's view, is the bad faith and spurious authority of so-called psychiatric diagnosis). How does child and adolescent psychotherapy avoid being either parenting or teaching, or merely pathologising; how does it become the distinctive thing it is, and must be, in order to make a good difference? This is the book, quite unlike any other in the field, that is actually able to address these questions, and in an utterly compelling way.

What kind of expertise, what kinds of special knowledge, then, do those people in the so-called helping professions for young people need to have, and how is psychological and emotional help different from other kinds of help? These are the questions Wilson implicitly asks, and wants us to consider, and be intrigued by, in this unusual and unusually evocative book. After all, our relationship to help – which is fundamentally our relationship to dependence – is what psychotherapy is about. So among so many other things, this book is an extraordinary and radical account of what it is for one person to help another person, and especially to help them with their difficulties in living. And how this requires the acknowledgement of a shared ordinariness, a shared vulnerability and unconsciousness, that is the best thing about us as dependent, and sometimes rational, animals. 'What I set out to do' in treating adolescents, Wilson writes, 'was to meet them rather than to judge them… I did not seek to chivvy them along, hurry them up, make them see the folly of their ways'. He does not, that is to say, impose anything on them; he allows for them doing things in their own way, and in their own time. He assumes that they have good reasons for what they do, even if what they do may endanger them. This is a book, that is to say, of great wisdom, with no pretension to wisdom. A book of great subtlety with no pretension to superior insight. What Wilson clearly knows about – and it is a rarer gift than it might seem, and is an essential kind of wisdom – is how to talk to children; without patronising them, without coercing them, without charming them, and without needing to impress them. He shows what it is to be, as he puts it, 'alongside them', what it might be, in the fullest sense, to meet them. In other words, there is a real sense in which this book might be, not solely, for people who work with children, but for anyone who has children, or, indeed, was once a child.

When Jacques Lacan famously said that the analyst is someone 'supposed to know' – that the patient attributes his own unconscious self-knowledge to the analyst – what was left out was that the analyst, and especially the child psychotherapist, does actually know something, something quite important about the psycho-biological development of the child; there is the unconscious – how it is assumed to work, and to work on us, and between us – and there is the life-cycle inspired and informed, depending on one's allegiances, by instinctual life and/or the need for relationship in the service of development. There is the appetite for life, so intense in children and adolescents, and the kind of life this can make possible. But development is the object of desire, and what needs to be understood is all the ways, subtle and not so subtle, that the growing child has of sabotaging and actually attacking his development. It is the child – and also of course his adults – as potentially his own worst enemy that Wilson is attentive to, but also allows for; as well as the child drawn irresistibly to the enjoyments and possibilities of his life. Indeed what comes through in this book, between the lines as it were, is the extent to which Wilson can imagine and back the child's pleasures.

It is very rare in the so-called psychoanalytic literature to get a sense, as one does again and again in Wilson's writing, of how much people can enjoy each other's company (what perhaps really needs to be understood in a therapeutic treatment are the obstacles created by both the therapist and the patient, to their really being able to enjoy each other's company). And one of the obstacles to such enjoyment – and indeed to a sense of new possibility – is the therapist's idealisation of theory, and method and technique. So much depends, Wilson writes, on 'the very personality of the psychotherapist as an actual individual... ultimately it is the nature of my personality rather than the quality of my theoretical persuasion that affects the quality of the therapeutic experience between me and the adolescent'. Persuasion as about both his theoretical affiliations and commitments, and about his resistance to persuading the patient. And 'personality' cannot be taught; it can only be nurtured; it is, Wilson writes, and it should be noted, the 'very' personality of the therapist that matters. In a scientific ethos of so-called evidence-based research – an ethos Wilson is interested enough in, but undogmatically and intelligently sceptical about (what, he asks pertinently, are we to count as evidence, and as evidence of what?) – method is always privileged over personality (it is worth recalling here Camus's suggestion that only those without character need methods). For Wilson, anything tantamount to an impersonal therapy is a contradiction in terms, and his eloquent ferocity in this book about the many misdemeanours committed in the name and profession of mental health – not least the flight, by the medical professions, into statistics and diagnosis and drug treatments – is a salutary warning. There is, that is to say – and it is surprisingly unusual among the strong-est psychoanalytic writers – no inner superiority in the kind of therapist Wilson is, no narcissistic certainties or pronouncements – narcissism being one of the many things that Wilson is particularly acute about in this book.

Wilson has managed to take the very best of the Anna Freudian tradition, to do with instincts and their vicissitudes in relation to what she called 'develop-mental lines', and made it easily compatible, if not actually complimentary to, the object-relations theories of Winnicott and his followers. And what both these traditions have in common – and here Wilson is both exemplary and unique – is a radical suspicion and suspension of dogma, and of the determined knowing best that mars a good deal of child psychotherapy, in practice and in theory. It is curios-ity, in both the therapist and his patient that Wilson puts his money on. 'I believe', Wilson writes, 'that all psychotherapists need to work within a broad theoretical framework of an understanding of human beings – their nature, their emotional and social development and what it is that drives them and causes them to worry'. A broad theoretical framework of an understanding of human beings does not involve a restrictive or restricted bibliography (or an assumption of self-sufficiency on the part of the psychotherapy profession). It allows, as I say, for wide-ranging curiosity, something Wilson clearly fosters in the children he sees, and the thera-pists he teaches (in the many fortunate years of supervision I had with Wilson as a newly qualified child psychotherapist I learnt a version of psychoanalysis that was inspiring and practicable, and that I could love). Wilson's whole approach implies that the only real authority comes out of collaboration. And an imaginative understanding of development and its vicissitudes. The risk, he writes, for psycho-analysts is that 'they treat [adolescents] not as adolescents but more assuredly as mini-adults, which I strongly believe they are not'. It is treating people as they are, not as what they should be, that Wilson makes such an eloquent case for.

Indeed, Wilson manages to make uncertainty and not knowing at once delightful and revelatory. You will, that is to say, find none of the omniscience in Wilson's work, that it has become all too easy to associate with psychoanalysis, and despite the ironic fact that the most omniscient schools of psychoanalysis – the Kleinians and Lacanians – have the most telling critiques of omniscience in psychoanalysis (only the omniscient want to critique omniscience as part of their omniscience). Wilson has found a way of both practising and describing a version of psycho-therapy with young people that is entirely intelligible and accessible, inspired and inspiring, tentative and confident, humorous and compassionate. With no jargon, and no grandiose claims. Psychoanalysis with young people as a most appealing improvisation, not the earnest routine ideology of virtue that it is all too often pre-sented as being.

There is the kind of uncommon common sense in this book that psychotherapy has never really articulated and needs: the common sense born of being able and willing to listen, with a view to saying things at once useful and kind, and without militant competence, and without knowing beforehand how everyone should live, and the common sense that comes from a profound sense of what we might actually have in common, and so of what we might realistically do for each other.

Adam Phillips is a British child, adolescent and adult psychoanalytic psychotherapist, essayist, author and literary critic.

Acknowledgements

This book has been built on a variety of experiences that I have gone through in many different places during the course of my professional life. Within them all, there have been some remarkable people who have made particular impressions on me as I have, as it were, 'grown up'. There are of course too many to crowd into this brief space.

Some, however, stand out. A long time ago, in the 1960s, when I worked in a residential treatment centre for emotionally disturbed children and adolescents, one man stands out – Frank Farinella, a social work manager who was in charge of the running of the centre. His capacity to be tough and no-nonsense in his approach whilst, at the same time, compassionate and endearingly sensitive showed me the way to be a man in what has been a predominately female caring and therapeutic environment.

Beyond him, in my child and adolescent psychoanalytic training, Anna Freud impressed me with the clarity of her thinking, her wry humour and careful attention to detail. Subsequently, Moses Laufer provided me, in his psychotherapy centre for young people, the kind of 'apprenticeship' that I needed in working psychotherapeutically with adolescents – together with the opportunity to think psychoanalytically with a range of psychoanalysts and colleagues. Their influence remained as I then went on to run the Brandon Centre, a similar service for young people, with staff such as Olivia Amiel and Olivia Harvard-Watts.

Melvyn Rose, Penny Jones and David Kelly next made a lasting impression on me in the way they thought, in working with very troubled adolescents in Peper Harow, a leading therapeutic community. Similarly, all those who worked with me, notably Dinah Morley and Steve Flood, in the extraordinary undertaking of building YoungMinds which became a leading charity in promoting services in the field of child mental health. I ended my working life in an organisation, in The Place2Be and learnt so much of the lives of children in primary school and especially of the headteachers and teachers who served them. Benita Refson, Niki Cooper and Kelly Swain-Cowper made a particular impression on me whilst I was there.

Throughout all this time, I read as much as I could, though sadly never enough. My reading ranged wide and far, from let's say Antony Trollope to Phillip Roth, and psychoanalytically from Freud, of course, through to Ferenczi, Winnicott, Ogden, Greenberg and Kohut. I should add some mention of music which has played such a large part of my personal and professional life. Among many others,

Stephen Sondheim rings most true: and Gabriel Latchin, an excellent pianist, has done so much to teach me the music of jazz piano.

Special thanks go to Michael Tait, Onel Brooks, Paul Van Heeswijk, Wallace Hamilton, John Coleman, Matthew Audley, Dee Ingham and Jane Blom-Cooper, all of whom have shared with me, in their own unique ways of thinking, their views of the curiosities and the idiosyncrasies of the bewildering world of psychotherapy at large and much else besides.

At the end of it all, three people remain for whom I am the most grateful. The first is Adam Phillips. He and I have met regularly through a large part of our lives. We have gone through life's mysteries, amusements and challenges and done our best to make sense of it all. He is in my view the most inspiring, fresh, independent and original writer and psychoanalyst of our time. I am particularly grateful for his writing the preface to this book. Ann Horne is the second person for whom I am most thankful. Without her, this book would simply not have happened. Her intelligence, psychotherapeutic nous, humour and sheer skill in knowing how to write and publish are nothing less than a delight. The last person of course is my wife, Jil, a senior child and adolescent psychotherapist herself and mother of our three dear children, Emma, Samuel and Jessica. She and I have been married for a very long time and throughout she has been supportive, encouraging and critical in the very best sense. Her love and, let's face it, endurance has been simply vital for me.

I am grateful to Bloomsbury Academic, an imprint of Bloomsbury Publishing Plc, and the editors for permission to publish Chapter 1 'What evidence works for whom?' Originally published by Palgrave in S Campbell, D Morley & R Catchpole (eds.) (2016) *Critical Issues in Child and Adolescent Mental Health.*

I am also grateful to Routledge and the editors for permission to publish Chapter 2 'Latency and certainty' which first appeared in the *Journal of Child Psychotherapy* 15(2) (1989); and Chapter 5 Delinquency which first appeared as chapter 21 pp.311–327 in M Lanyado & A Horne (eds.) (1999) *The Handbook of Child and Adolescent Psychotherapy: Psychoanalytic Approaches.*

I am also grateful to Elsevier (Churchill Livingstone) and the editor for permission to publish Chapter 4 'Psychotherapy with adolescents' originally published as chapter 19 pp.443–467 in J Holmes (ed.) (1991) *A Textbook of Psychotherapy in Psychiatric Practice.*

I am also grateful to John Wiley & Sons (Whurr Publications Ltd) and the editors for permission to publish Chapter 6 'Narcissism and adolescence' which first appeared as chapter 5 pp.51–63 in J Cooper & N Maxwell (eds.) (1995) *Narcissistic Wounds: Clinical Perspectives.*

I am also grateful to Jessica Kingsley and the editors for Chapter 9 'People meet in a classroom and say "Hello"' which was originally published as chapter 9 pp.153–164 in David Colley and Paul Cooper (eds.) (2017) *Attachment and Emotional Development in the Classroom; Theory and Practice.*

Chapter 3 'I don't know' was originally published as a Clinical Paper in a Special Section on Psychotherapy with Adolescents in the *Journal of the British Association of Psychotherapists* 2001 39 (2). The journal is no longer published, and the BAP has merged to become part of the British Psychotherapy Foundation, so permissions have not been able to be obtained.

Chapter 7 'Me loves me' was presented at a conference organised by Limbus Foundation, Dartington, Devon, UK, November 9, 2019.

Chapter 8 'The adolescent, the psychoanalyst and the working alliance' was presented in London at the Winter Conference of IPCAPA (the Independent Psychoanalytic Child and Adolescent Psychotherapy Association – part of the British Psychotherapy Foundation) in 2021.

Chapter 10 'Why can't an adolescent be more like an adult? The relationship between adolescent and adult psychoanalytic psychotherapist was presented at a conference jointly organised by Brent Centre for Young People and Westminster School 17 June 2023, an earlier version having previously been given at Brent Centre for Young People's International Online Seminar 2005. I am grateful for the invitations and the ensuing discussions.

Introduction

I qualified as a child and adolescent psychoanalytic psychotherapist at the Hampstead Child Therapy Course and Clinic, run by Anna Freud, in London in 1971. Since then, I have worked in three Child Guidance Clinics (now known as Child and Adolescent Mental Health Services, CAMHS), two adolescent services and a therapeutic community (Peper Harow). Following on from these activities, I have worked as the Founder and first Director of a national child mental health charity, YoungMinds, and as Clinical Adviser in a national school counselling service, The Place2Be. Whilst carrying out this work, I have maintained a small private practice. As time has gone on, I have developed what I think is a particular style of psychotherapy which is both personal and drawn from a psychoanalytic framework of understanding human nature. This book brings together a selection of those papers that I have written at various points in my life that I have taken a fancy to and that have highlighted what I have cared about and thought to be important during this time.

I have worked most of my life one way or another with young people – youth worker, social worker, psychotherapist, psychoanalyst. I have often questioned why I should have devoted so much interest to them. I can't say I am entirely clear about the answer. No doubt something in my own past (whether accomplished or unsorted) has excited my interest in them and has furthered my usefulness in their psychotherapy. But, for sure, their vitality has been undoubtedly a draw, so too their many potentialities and possibilities for the future. It may also be their sheer unpredictability that has been an attraction – the periodic nature of their emotional turmoil that they have had to contend with as a result of whatever may have cropped up for them, out of the blue as they have grown up.

The word 'adolescence' derives from the Latin, 'adolescere', meaning to grow up. It is a time of an odd but normal transition in life from childhood to adulthood – the teen years and early twenties. This is a baffling time for many as they face the challenges of two major developmental tasks – one, of coming to terms with the extraordinary biological revolution of puberty, and two, of going through the complicated business of becoming separate from childish dependencies and forging new kinds of individual identity. With all this in mind, as a psychotherapist, I

DOI: 10.4324/9781003680437-1

have viewed adolescence as an optimum time of life for making a significant difference to their immediate lives and to what might come about for them in later life.

Mysteriousness

Both things, 'adolescence' and 'psychotherapy', are complex, elusive, varied, changing, intangible, ethereal – and so much seemingly beyond reach. The sheer phenomena of adolescence in itself is a mysteriousness – 'a quality or state of being impossible to know, understand or explain' (Merriam-Webster definition).

Synonyms abound: 'baffling', 'enigmatic', 'mystifying', 'obscure', 'perplexing', 'weird'. There are of course many young people who do not merit such vivid expressions; they do not reveal themselves in such outlandish ways. Some manage to find a way of living throughout it all, more or less well enough – usually, the more 'healthy', the better backed up and better settled by their parents in their childhoods and their current lives. These are those who have found a way of being buoyed and lifted by their adolescent stirrings; they have been able to pass on, ready to face their limitations and find accomplishments with the passage of time. Others have somehow bypassed their adolescence, rendering themselves strangely inert, whether through compliance, fear, denial, inhibition or fatigue.

But the majority in my view parade their inner confusions in all kinds of dramatic ways for all to see and enjoy and endure, not least themselves. Many of the adolescents in whose lives I have been involved have been undoubtedly troubled, some close to mental illness, driving those around them as mad as they feel. Tormenting thoughts of suicide, hatred of their bodies, fearful of other people, lost in forlorn isolation and withdrawal, negation of their abilities or prospects have all been in the mix. They have indeed been confused in the midst of their human transition from the relative order and innocence of childhood to the awesome and strange ogre of adulthood – whatever semblance of adult life may be on offer or deemed appropriate in the society which surrounds them. As they make their way forward, they appear to have got stuck, entrenched and overwhelmed by the emotional disturbances and traumas of their infancy and childhood which have impinged on their current lives – and ultimately unprepared and unable to let go and overcome the feelings that have haunted them. It is very much the purpose of psychoanalytic psychotherapy to enable adolescents to be less dominated by their anxieties, less defeated in how they see themselves and more free to pursue their interests and desires without unnecessary constraints.

Psychotherapy

Some adolescents find their own possibilities of improvement, whilst others may well seek help, whether of their own volition or cajoled by others, not least parents. For the most part, they find psychotherapy of one kind or another. The world of psychotherapy is indeed a bewildering place and it is difficult for anyone to get the hang of it all. There are those psychotherapies that focus on changing the specific problematic behaviour and symptomatology, without necessarily worrying about the causes of such problems. They lean heavily on their scientific evidence for the effectiveness of what they do; they are predominantly guided by the findings of such evidence. Others, by contrast, are significantly less focused in this way and show much greater interest in how their adolescents' difficulties have come about and how they and their families have encountered and responded to them in the best way they could. These psychotherapists are propelled much more by their own convictions about the nature of personality and by their own particular ways of approaching adolescents whether it be through talking or art or music or other forms of expression. By and large, their interest is predominantly on feelings rather than cognitions. It is of course very much in the evaluative spirit of our times that questions abound as to which approach is the best for whom, whose evidence is the best and which psychotherapies are the most cost effective.

Controversies forever thicken. However, I place myself unequivocally in the latter approach, in psychoanalytic psychotherapy. I believe that all psychotherapists need to work within a broad theoretical framework of an understanding of human beings – their nature, their behaviour and emotional and social development. There are indeed many ways of making sense of human behaviour. For me, psychoanalysis has provided me with the framework I have needed and which has 'held' me together – in the sense of equipping me with a range of ideas and concepts to make sense of who I am and who am I facing and trying to help; and in the sense of enabling me to receive, countenance and withstand the full force of feeling that is inherent in any psychotherapeutic encounter, and especially so with disturbed adolescents.

Psychoanalysis of course carries many meanings for different people. The purist adult psychoanalyst is devout in his or her following of Freud and later psychoanalysts and addresses him or herself very much in the transference to the unconscious. At the other end of the spectrum is the cynic, the critic who dismisses psychoanalysis as absurdly fanciful, precious and unscientific. I dwell in the midst of all this but with a much greater leaning towards the former. What matters for me is the emphasis that I place on what I understand to be going on in the whole personality, as best as I can encompass it with all its irrationality and changeability. I have seen the life of the adolescent as being driven both by desires and passions, sexual and aggressive in nature and also by narcissistic sensibilities in relation to the preservation of self-respect. These I can see are all modulated according to the demands of reality, family and culture in which the adolescent grows. It is the emotional inner world of the adolescent that takes my interest and which predominates in the adolescent experience. It is a world that I see as riven by conflict both within and in relation to the outside world. The past always prevails, whether it be expressed in behavioural terms or through a reliving in present relationships.

Psychotherapy and the actuality of the individual psychotherapist

Psychoanalytic knowledge constitutes in and of itself the essential framework without which any psychotherapy of a psychoanalytic persuasion cannot proceed. However, much depends on how this knowledge is translated and conveyed in any psychotherapeutic encounter with an adolescent – and this in turn depends very much in my view on the very personality of the psychotherapist as an actual individual. This is a factor in the course of any psychotherapy that tends to be underemphasised and often ignored in favour of a preoccupation with the dynamics of transference and counter transference. If I take my own experience for example, I am aware that, in all probability, the psychotherapy that an adolescent might receive from me may be different, and in many cases very different, from what he or she may receive from a colleague or other practitioner of similar theoretical persuasion. This in no way is intended to suggest that my way is better or worse; just different, as indeed I am a different person from others. There have been numerous influences in my life which have shaped my distinctive way of doing things – through reading, both theoretical and literary, through identifications with those I have admired and through the many family and cultural experiences that have led to the kind of person I am.

These are all uniquely personal experiences and it is these that I believe have such a strong and pervasive effect on the kind of psychotherapy I practice with adolescents. Ultimately, it is the nature of my personality rather than the quality of my theoretical persuasion that affects the quality of the psychotherapeutic experience between me and the adolescent. When I look further into my own experience, I really don't think I practice the same kind of psychotherapy now that I used to when I was young. At that time, I think I was perceived very differently from the way I am now. Over time, as I grew older, I was seen less as an older brother and more as a father and later as a grandfather. I think too that my perception and expectations of adolescents changed as I became older. The same psychoanalytic framework prevailed but was applied differently and experienced differently. Transferences of course made their impact but were fashioned according to my changing ages and my developing personality.

It is the nature of the psychotherapist's personality which is notoriously difficult to capture – and something which confounds the efforts of empirical research in its attempts to gain access to the quality and effectiveness of the psychotherapeutic experience. It is this factor – the psychotherapist's actual personality – that is undoubtedly necessary if we are to really understand what works and what doesn't in any particular interchange between adolescent and psychotherapist. In my own case, for example, I find myself encountering all kinds of difficulties in defining who I am. Self-analysis ideally might be a way of discovering this. However, my own conceits and self-doubts too often blur the picture. Similarly, if I look to other people, their idealisations or envies cloud the vision. A glance at the *DSM V* disappoints too, so inadequate in its categorisations and 'disordered' in its psychiatric focus. I am thus left looking for something more general to embrace the more elusive nature of my personality – as the American Psychological Association puts it, the 'enduring characteristics and behaviour that comprise a person's unique adjustment to life; including major traits, interests, drives, values, self-concepts, activities and emotional patterns' (APA 2018).

Numerous theories abound relating to personality but none can capture the whole story nor satisfy me in my quest for a fuller understanding. However, I am finding that McGilchrist's writings, based on his research into the functioning of the brain, go some way to describing certain aspects of my personality which I think have particular relevance to what kind of psychotherapist I am and have been over the years (2009, 2012) He highlights for example a fundamental division that exists in the brain between its two hemispheres, the right and the left. Both are necessarily inter-related, combining to ensure adequate balance and cohesion in the individual's overall functioning. However, McGilchrist points to the fact that each hemisphere performs different functions, and, according to which hemisphere – the left or the right – is dominant in different individuals, major differences arise in how they experience the world and how they go about dealing with it. At the risk of oversimplifying this difference, the left hemisphere focuses narrowly on preciseness, the specific, the explicit, the minute detail. The right hemisphere, on the other hand, takes a broader more flexible view with greater reliance on the implicit, on the gestalt, on reflection, imagination and intuition.

I find the qualities that McGilchrist highlights in the right hemisphere by and large fit my own view of my personality, and indeed the views of those who generally support me – that I am a warm and easy-going person, thoughtful and flexible and funny at times (albeit occasionally impulsive, self-absorbed and quick tempered). And so, with all this mind, I see myself as a person and as a psychotherapist, ready to enter into the subjective world of the adolescents I see – to be attentive, receptive, intrigued. By and large, I am not threatened by their sheer irrationality, their not making sense to themselves or to anyone else. I am happy to live within the life and living paradoxes of their adolescence – the paradoxes that reside for example in the wish to be independent but not too much, to be free but within restraints, to know it all but know nothing, to be grown up but as a child and so forth. For me, this is very much in the general nature of humanity, though amplified strenuously in adolescence. I hold my ground as best I can as an adult and yet become almost as absorbed as they are in their current engagements, whether they be in sport, music, politics or academia or whether they be lost in devotion to themselves or to a particular person, male or female, idealised or actual. I always keep in mind their histories and the activities that are filling their daily lives but I don't delve needlessly and intrusively into what they may prize as personal or special. The daily life of our therapeutic sessions may well be quite ordinary, not particularly revelatory or lifted through interpretation. Many adolescents can at times be quite mundane, a far cry from the more romantic revelations of psychoanalysis.

What matters is the growing trust in the flow of the therapeutic relationship, the to and fro, the back and forth of the interchange that throws up from time to time a new feeling or a fact or a dream or a new insight or awareness. Without labouring the point, I try to make the most of these moments with the adolescent that over time can accumulate into the forming of a personal wisdom. I am, amongst other things, a moderately good jazz pianist and I very often liken the way I practice psychotherapy as I do playing music – finding the tune, the right key, the right rhythm, the right phrasing, the right chords – and above all forever improvising, exploring, finding out, repeating, back and forth, time for resting and so forth. It is above all a subjective and creative experience – and something that gives expression to the kind of person I think I am, which, for want of a better way of putting it, is decidedly right hemisphered in nature.

This psychoanalytic psychotherapy resides in the substance of this relationship between adolescent and psychotherapist. It is this that constitutes the essential psychoanalysis in psychotherapy with adolescents – on a similar but different level to the more conventional psychoanalysis that is carried out with adults through the formal interpretation of the unconscious. Inevitably, in the developing professional closeness in my psychoanalytic relationship with an adolescent, my feelings, whether positive or negative, become involved, which I have to acknowledge and refrain from acting out. They are a necessary part of the process, not least in throwing light on what is being brought to life through the reliving in this relationship of what has gone in the past of the adolescent – a new realisation to which I may draw the adolescent's attention.

This of course is a far cry from my being influenced by a predominance of left hemisphere functioning. In this respect, I am far removed from those psychotherapists who do appear to be led much more by their left-brain hemisphere. These are those who are drawn to a more focused therapeutic approach, a preoccupation with the most immediate, discrete and rational ways of thinking. They pride themselves on their objectivity and on their reliance on evidence which is built on a disciplined, measured and methodical analysis of observed behaviour. Out of such devotion, a form of psychotherapy has arisen and has taken precedence in the public sphere over the last 60 years or so – a form well known as cognitive behaviour therapy (CBT). It has much to recommend it, not least because of its practicality and declared short-term effectiveness – different from psychoanalytic psychotherapy which necessarily tends to be longer term. This is a world, however, which I find alien, not so much because of my theoretical orientation (I simply fail to see how CBT can possibly work with the more disturbed and tormented adolescents that I have seen) but because of my sheer inability or disinclination to do it. It just doesn't suit me, whether that be because of my right hemisphere of my brain or not. I just don't 'get it', much the same as many of those with the dominance of the left hemisphere don't 'get' what I do. I have simply been uninterested in confining my attention on adolescents' 'symptoms' or behavioural details. I have been unable to set aside my abiding interest in the past and living lives of the adolescents I have seen and to find ways of exploring their irrationality, their ambiguity, the idiosyncratic meanings they attach to what they do and feel. I have had no capacity or interest to fill in questionnaires, to draw up goals and outcomes to make any kind of reliable measure or to comprehend algorithms.

'I don't know'

All that I have written so far relates fundamentally to the issue of my personality, my actual capabilities and sensibilities as a person, rather than of myself as a practitioner of any declared theoretical rationale I might make. Psychotherapy is in my view a profoundly individual idiosyncratic activity – no one psychotherapist can claim to be the one who is right, or is the only one who knows how to do it. It is here of course that I reach my own personal paradox: I can say quite assertively that I do know what I am talking about at the same time as I am sighing 'I don't know'. The gnawing fact is that whatever I have gained through my reading, teaching, supervising, practicing and experiencing has only ever been partial. I can never know the full picture – and hence the resounding title of this book, 'I don't know'. There is clearly a conundrum here, a confusion that revolves around the dangers of extremity, of belief in absolute knowledge and thus of absolute certainty.

'I don't know'. Three little words. How repeatedly we use them in our every-day speech, how ubiquitous and how familiar – as we draw breath, as it were, to find the right word or thought. We find ourselves at a loss, notwithstanding that we do know some things and very often a lot of things. 'I don't know' is not a denial or dismissal of what we know, nor in any way a glorification of ignorance or a retreat into stupidity. It is simply an honest affirmation of our partial knowledge. We live through patches of 'I don't know', our view forever blinkered or incomplete. There is always something yet to know, and, further, more that is the unknown known – aspects of ourselves about which we think we know, but don't know – things kept hidden from conscious knowledge through inner repression or external oppression in the unconscious.

Numerous philosophers, novelists and psychoanalysts have over time encountered and mused upon their observations of not knowing. Socrates was one of the first:

> 'I am wiser than this man; it is likely that neither of us knows anything worthwhile, but he thinks he knows something when he does not, whereas when I do not know, neither do I think I know, so I am likely to be wiser than he to this small extent, that I do not think I know what I do not know'.
>
> (Plato, 1954. Apology, line 21d)

He later added to this, that 'awareness of ignorance is the beginning of wisdom'. Elizabeth Strout, an award-winning contemporary novelist, sums up the final words of her elderly central heroine in *Olive, Again* (2019): 'I do not have a clue who I have been. Truthfully, I do not understand a thing'. And amongst psychoanalysts, Bion is perhaps the most remarkable for his distinctive writings about the psychoanalytic process and the possibility of cure. He maintained that the only way an individual can pursue cure is through tolerance of doubt and intimacy with the unknown:

> The purest form of listening is to listen without memory or desire. Every session must have no history and no form ... Out of darkness and formlessness something emerges.
>
> (Bion 1965)

More recently, in 2024, Rory Stewart, a writer, philosopher, broadcaster and former politician, has produced a BBC Radio 4 series on 'The Long History of Ignorance'. This provides a comprehensive account of the importance of recognising the vital contribution of ignorance to the development of ideas and to learning in general. As he puts it, the 'boundary between knowledge and ignorance is never static'. He makes a clear argument that there is considerable creative potential in the frank acknowledgement of not knowing. If, for example, in any given conversation I make it clear that of course 'I know' (implicitly for sure), the likely consequence is that the conversation will dry up, there being no opening for a dialogue. Similarly, I know of a well-renowned and expensive solicitor who was once consulted over a particularly vexatious legal matter. Before his client had finished his concerns, the solicitor precipitously interrupted and merrily declared he didn't know. He then cried out: 'so let's find out' and proceeded to carry out research into the problem. In other words, parading a definitive knowledge can foreclose on discovery; not knowing opens up new possibilities.

In the psychotherapy world, this virtue of not knowing carries with it a particular resonance as we encounter the unique mysteriousness of adolescent minds. The adolescents, by the very nature of their self-experimentation and destructiveness, are at risk. Their parents in turn, so often are at their wits end, clamour for definition and immediate solutions. Compelling pressure preys upon the competence of the professionals to come up 'with the answers'. Invariably, there are no easy answers as the adolescent lives through what he or she has to – and all that can reasonably be expected is for the psychiatrist or psychotherapist to help hold the anxiety for the parents and keep a line open with the adolescents. All too readily, however, many professionals fall into the trap of believing they have the very ingredients that are being called for. In effect, it seems to me, their narcissism is touched and they claim knowledge which in truth they do not possess. All too often, they stray from what can only be a modest acknowledgement of their partial knowledge to the self-important assertion of absolute knowledge – 'I, for sure, know'. Without restraint, whether externally imposed or internally driven, their assertions of sureness are likely to rebound and indeed confound those they are trying to help.

These dangers are clearly of concern at a clinical level. They are also of concern at a broader professional level. There is for example a clear divide between those psychotherapists who are predominately in the thrall of their scientific evidence and those who draw conviction from their psychoanalytic theories. However much they may at times overlap, both protest their own respective identities. They are in competition – and inevitably, both claim their superiority and entrench themselves in their own certainties and moral rectitudes. Arrogance springs up on all sides – 'We know – and you don't'. On the more psychoanalytic side, there tends to be the lofty belief that 'we alone' have a monopoly on the unconscious and that all else fails in superficiality. On the more 'scientific' side, there is the abiding faith in the truth of the metric and that all else is fanciful and merely 'anecdotal'. Increasingly, there is a loss of humility on all sides and of a simple acknowledgement of 'I don't know'. However much some may cling on to the anchors of the unconscious or of rationality, there is so much bewildering irrationality and variability in the lives of people, especially adolescent people, that the quest to know more is infinite. It is important that none of us alienates each other whom we condemn for not acceding to our superiority, much to the disservice of the young people we serve.

These matters are of particular concern when it comes to considering the public provision of contemporary adolescent mental health services and commissioners (as in British Child and Adolescent Mental Health Services) or insurers of psychotherapy services (as in the United States and Australia) who are characteristically preoccupied with cost-effectiveness. They naturally seek reassurances that what they spend their money on will be well spent – and look for the 'evidence' to support their decision making. It can be of no surprise that they favour cognitive behavioural therapy and other comparable 'evidence-based' psychotherapies. The evidence for the more psychoanalytic therapies is necessarily less concrete and tangible. This increasing preference of course flourishes within the context of what can best described as the scientific hegemony of our time. It is 'the science', as we are all told, that knows. Of course, science in many fields has had a powerful effect on so many areas of our lives. However, it doesn't know everything and certainly not in the field of psychotherapy with adolescents. The 'evidence' that is so heavily relied upon is, as far as I can see, far from being as reliable or as conclusive as it is made out to be. At best, it points to the likelihood of psychotherapy effectiveness being only with those suffering 'mild' to 'moderate' levels of disorder. Its science is so reliant on dispassionate observation that I cannot imagine how it can catch the essence of irrationality, turmoil and ambiguity of so many of the very disturbed minds of adolescents that I have seen or know about – far more severe than just 'mild' and 'moderate'. It is a world that is seemingly unable to comprehend that degree of adolescent emotional disturbance, and is merely responding to a managerial imperative to increase 'throughput'. Greater pressure is being placed on the need for Child and Adolescent Mental Health Services to carry out more assessments and to diagnose them accordingly upon criteria which are ill-defined and seemingly very limited in scope. In the clear medical tradition, it follows that 'treatment' should then be indicated. This is beginning to take place in a manualised form of psychotherapy, all too often with the aid of AI and the use of apps. It is a world that I view as naive, reductive and diminishing of the psychoanalytic nature of psychotherapy – and simply blind to the mysteriousness of the adolescent condition. It is regrettable that it prospers so well at present in the public sphere to the cost of the psychoanalytic psychotherapies which I value and which are becoming increasingly dismissed and arrogantly sidelined.

The chapters of this book

The chapters that follow highlight in various ways the value of 'I don't know' and of doubt and uncertainty. The first 'What evidence works for whom' is a take-off of the numerous scientific studies that are vigorously carried out into what works clinically with whom. The chapter questions the nature of such evidence and challenges the biased claims that are made on its behalf by the so-called objective researchers. It is revealing to note that, despite appearing in an important book, *Critical Issues in Child and Adolescent Mental Health* (Campbell et al. 2016), it met with la belle indifference from the scientific community.

The next chapter focuses on latency, that period of life, the childhood years, which optimally is a time of significant cognitive development. At best, it is also a time of internal emotional and social consolidation characterised generally by a careful sense of orderliness. Without this, things do not bode well for the disruptive arrival of puberty in adolescence. It is for this reason that this chapter has its place in this book. There is also another reason for its inclusion and that is about the whole issue of certainty. All children try to make sense of the world in which they live, not least in a world that is confusing and difficult to understand. This chapter is entitled 'Latency and Certainty'; it illustrates something of the desperate demand for certainty in an uncertain world. It shows the struggle of an ordinary latency-aged boy, trying to make sense and find some order in the midst of a family secret in which basic truths about family members have been hidden. There is rather touching innocence in the way he sought to find clarity, relying as much as he could on what Piaget describes as 'concrete operational thinking' (1954), a notable characteristic of a latency-aged child. In many respects, such thinking is akin to the functioning of the left-brain hemisphere to which I have earlier referred. In Ian McEwan's novel, *Enduring Love* (Jonathan Cape 1997), the leading character, Joe, a scientist, is trying to comprehend a grotesque accident that he had witnessed and which had traumatised him. He is dutifully diligent and meticulous in his detailed preoccupations with the accident. His wife, Clarissa, however, watching him struggling to understand in his own way, says to him, 'You're such a dope. You're so rational sometimes. You're like a child'.

The next chapter 'I don't know' is a paper that was hewn out of years of my therapeutic experience, sitting in rooms with numerous adolescents who invariably, in response to the ubiquitous therapist question 'How are you feeling' (whether explicit or implied), can do no better than come up with 'I don't know'. Initially, I was cross with these adolescents, seemingly so entrenched in resistance to my therapeutic efforts. Gradually, however, I grew to fundamentally appreciate that there was more to this phrase than met the eye. The adolescent was being honest when he said, 'I don't know', true to his experience and unwilling to come up with something false or compliant. This realisation freed me up to be more respectful of the complexity of the adolescent experience. It also reflected my own unknowingness which clearly became the inspiration for this book and its title.

The next two chapters, four and five, are perhaps the least modestly unknowing in the book. They were written respectfully for a textbook and a handbook with a requirement, as I read it, to write something decidedly informative and instructive. They were written, too, in my mid-life when I was perhaps the least modest and overly assured in my adherence to psychoanalysis. 'Psychotherapy with Adolescents' covers as methodically as possible the basic elements of psychotherapeutic practice with adolescents. Despite its air of certainty, it does end with an entreaty to all psychotherapists to bear their own uncertainties, not least in relation to often baffling paradoxes of the adolescent experience – so infuriating, so tormenting and so more than enough to leave everyone with the sigh of 'I don't know'.

I have chosen to include the chapter 'Delinquency' because in my view, transgressing the law in its broad sense is not an uncommon feature of adolescent behaviour. So caught up in the wish to defy authority and to differentiate themselves from the dominance of their parents that they are drawn to the forbidden and to the pursuit of all kinds of possibilities that run the risk of breaking the rules, whether of the law or of the family. The chapter highlights the difficulties and confusions of the psychotherapist in dealing with the unfathomable ambivalence of many adolescents towards psychotherapy and the prospect of change. There is much, too, in the nature of delinquency that I believe is a response to the fear that is building up within adolescents and their puzzlement at what they perceive as uncaring in their environment. In narcissistic retreat, it is as if they are seeking something definitive to dispel the confusion of 'I don't know'. For example, at the time of writing this chapter, In 1996 I wrote a review of Winnicott's seminal paper on the 'The Anti-Social Tendency' for the *Journal of Child Psychotherapy*. I would like to quote my first paragraph of that review to convey the sheer unknowingness of it all and the self-assertion they set to guard against uncertainty:

'The awesome characteristic of delinquency is its obduracy: for the time that it lasts, it is stubborn and impenitent. Paradoxically, in its very act of wrongdoing, it carries with it an unswerving sense of rightness. In the moment of stealing, there is a mark of justification - 'it's mine'. In the strike of violence, there is a sound of vindication: 'that settles it'. And in the course of deception, there is a note of defiance – 'why not?' The delinquent act, in other words, has purpose. It is making a statement, standing up for something and not letting be.' Each act of delinquency carries the mark of self certainty in protest against the confusion and lack of affirmation from the environment. With this mind, rules will be broken and those who uphold them, confounded. It is no surprise the delinquent is a thorn in the side of the reformer and therapist; by definition, non-compliant: in effect, destructive: and for the most part, seemingly lacking remorse or inclination to change'. They sigh: 'I don't know.'

The following two chapters, six and seven, take on the lead of the last one in particular and both pursue my interest in the whole phenomenon of narcissism, It is a difficult concept to harden down, not least because it can be applied to pretty well all of us one way or another; after all, we must love ourselves in order to develop and take care of ourselves. However, it does carry with it a sharp ring of disapproval when it becomes applied to describe those people who are excessively consumed with their own importance, as seen so painfully in so many of the political and corporate leaders of our time. Basically, I see narcissism as a very powerful general force in human behaviour, almost as strong as the sexual drive. I take it to be particularly so as a key factor in the emotional life of adolescents, as they contend with their essential vulnerability, caught between the loss of childhood and the challenge of finding a way of becoming an adult. A retreat into a kind of cocoon of self-insulation and omnipotence as a defence against these anxieties and of not knowing is a central theme.

Both chapters give several illustrations of different kinds of narcissistic behaviour in adolescents. Their behaviour was baffling, beyond the wits of their parents, indeed beyond their own self-understanding and finally much to the dismay of their psychotherapist, me. Throughout it all, they shrieked the song of 'Me, me, me', which seemed to me to be a desperate attempt to define themselves and hold themselves together against the overbearing frustrations and thwartings of their everyday life. Psychotherapy proceeded very much in the dark but I found that through basic processes of meeting, listening and affirming – such undervalued and underemphasised ingredients in the psychotherapy process – these proved effective in establishing some degree of trust. So too did clarifying and interpreting as best I could what I thought was making them so afraid and how they were trying to protect themselves from further hurts. There was improvement in all the cases, though of course partial and incomplete as they continued with their adolescence.

The last three chapters of the book are my latest pieces of writing. It is perhaps of no surprise that that they look more closely at the very nature of communication between the adolescent and the adult. The first (Chapter 8) and the last (Chapter 10) focus in particular on the relationship between the adolescent and the adult psychoanalytic psychotherapist. I find myself at the end of my professional life wondering about some basic questions about how we as adult psychoanalytic psychotherapists go about our business. Can we as adult psychotherapists comfortably assume that we are on the same page with most adolescents – that we are actually in an 'alliance' with them much of the time? And, more fundamentally, do we think we are sufficiently in tune with the remarkable basic bodily forces of puberty and their impact on mental life? These chapters illustrate the extraordinary happenings during adolescence which can only but intensify their sense of bewilderment and not knowing – as indeed ours. It again highlights the confusions and misunderstandings that occur in the broad field of communication between the old and the new, whether in the therapeutic situation or indeed more generally.

It is in Chapter 9 that I take a broader view outside the psychoanalytic psychotherapy field. I have had for many years a close association with the education world and in particular with the relationships between adolescents and adult teachers. In this chapter, I focus on a not untypical tension that can arise in a classroom situation between the adult teacher and the adolescent student. It traces the lives of two separate people, one old, one young; one, the teacher, one the student; and in this case, one, the middle class and privileged; the other, the more working class and less privileged. As a result of their own upbringings and personal characteristics, they build up in their minds particular views of the other which are in my respects inaccurate; accordingly, they over-react defensively in relation to the other. The process of learning in the classroom is thus disrupted. The purpose of the chapter is not to suggest that psychotherapy be introduced as a solution, but more that greater acknowledgement by both of the ways they misrepresent each other may lead to better understanding and consequent modification in their attitudes and behaviour. The psychoanalytic concept of transference is essentially being used to inform the situation. The chapter ends with four typical forms of relating in the classroom, called 'hello's, in which children and adolescents anticipate and greet the teacher according to their experiences in their own families.

Conclusion

The theme that has thread its way through this Introduction and throughout the whole book is – 'I don't know'. This is not a cry of despair and resignation: much more a plea for greater honesty and humility. The danger is always the proclamation of absolute knowledge and certainty – whether that be assertion of professional superiority or the premature false definition of the self. It is very much in the explorative nature of psychoanalytic psychotherapy that there is always the possibility of further discovery.

References

American Psychological Association. (2018) *Dictionary of Psychology*, Available: https://dictionary.apa.org/.

Bion, W (1965) Memory and desire. In E. Bott Spillius (1988, ed) *Melanie Klein Today volume 2: Mainly Practice,* London: Routledge.

McEwan, I. (1997) *Enduring Love*, London: Jonathan Cape.

McGilchrist, I. (2009) *The Master and His Emissary: The Divided Brain and the Making of the Western World*, New Haven CT and London: Yale University Press.

McGilchrist, I. (2012) *The Divided Brain and the Search for Meaning*, New Haven CT & London: Yale University Press.

Piaget, J. (1954) *The Construction of Reality in the Child*, New York: Basic Books.

Plato (691–697). (1954) 'The Apology of Socrates'. In H Tredennick (ed. & translator) *The Last Days of Socrates*, Harmondsworth: Penguin Classics.

Stewart, R. (2024) *The Long History of Ignorance*, BBC Radio 4 and iPlayer.

Strout, E. (2019) *Olive, Again*, New York & London: Random House.

Wilson, P. (1996) 'The anti-social tendency. A review of Winnicott's paper of the same title', *Journal of Child Psychotherapy* 22(3): 394–397.

Wilson, P. (2016) 'What evidence works for whom'. In S. Campbell, D. Morley and R. Catchpole (eds) *Critical Issues in Child and Adolescent Mental Health*, London: Palgrave: 1–13.

Chapter 1

What evidence works for whom?

*Previously published in S. Campbell, D. Morley &
R. Catchpole (eds) Critical Issues in Child and
Adolescent Mental Health (2016)*

I am a psychodynamic psychotherapist. I have been one for over 40 years, working primarily with children and adolescents, having trained with Anna Freud at
the Hampstead Child Therapy Course and Clinic (now the Anna Freud Centre) at
a time when it was a centre of excellence in the training of child psychoanalysts.

I want to state this from the beginning of this chapter to give some indication of
who I am and from where I come. Mine is, as is everybody's, a partial view – one
amongst many that makes claim to its value in the broad field of psychotherapy. For
the most part, I am reasonably tolerant, respectful of these many others and, for the
most part, curious about them. However, there is one particular view which simply
bemuses and exasperates me, if for no other reason that I see it as so intolerant of
mine. I find myself sitting uncomfortably in the midst of what can only be described
as a predominating scientific hegemony that seems intent to assert its supremacy in
the world of psychotherapy on the basis of certain 'scientific' procedures, not least of
which are randomised controlled trials (RCTs) and meta-analyses. Out of this strong-
hold, a firm belief has arisen that insists that psychodynamic psychotherapies are less
effective than others which are supposedly better supported by 'the evidence'. Such a
belief is increasingly being held by academics and policy makers. As Shedler (Shedler
2010) observes, 'With each repetition, its apparent credibility grows. At some point,
there seems little need to question or revisit it because "everyone" knows it to be so'.

I am of course wearily aware of what 'everyone' knows. Under the sway of this
prevailing belief, I have felt from time to time inevitably buffeted and dismissed,
both as someone who does not follow the ordained path and who, as a psychotherapist, persists in practicing his own way of doing things. However, in recent
years, in large part emboldened by those engaged in critical psychiatry and psychotherapy such as Sami Timimi (Timimi 2002, 2007, 2013, 2015) and Del Loewenthal (Loewenthal and Samuels 2014; Loewenthal 2015), I have come to look more
closely at the preferential claims made by scientists for certain psychotherapies
over others that I favour. I have increasingly taken exception to the false certainties
that lie behind these claims. In particular, I have discovered something obvious but
so well camouflaged – that these claims carry the same kind of irrational bias and
entrenched conviction of which I am accused.

DOI: 10.4324/9781003680437-2

As we all know, there are many pathways to the ever-elusive 'truth' about the psychotherapies. There is a voluminous literature giving expression to all manner of psychotherapeutic ideas and approaches. All of them claim to be in one way or another useful and effective – and they all present their versions of evidence to substantiate their claims. The simple question then arises for me: what kind of evidence? There are of course many answers, some persuasive, others less so. But as far as I am concerned, what matters above all else is to know how far the evidence that is produced rings true for me – how far can I trust it to take into account the kind of psychotherapy I carry out. What I do is a highly personal emotional occupation – and I look to research that understands this and seeks to explore some of the intricacies and effects of what I and others do. Of course, I know that I am at risk of only looking for whatever it might be that confirms that what I am doing is alright. But equally, within my own psychodynamic domain and through enquiries that are made within it, I find greater relevance to my own learning and development than bowing to the pronouncements of a scientific high ground that seems quite alien.

Choosing What's Best for You

In November 2007, the CAMHS Evidence-Based Practice Unit of University College London and Anna Freud Centre published a small booklet entitled 'Choosing What's Best for You; what scientists have found helps children and young people who are sad, worried or troubled' (CAMHS 2007). Its intention was to inform young people about 'what scientists have found out so far, after comparing different ways of helping a large number of people'. It was widely distributed and is currently available and accessible on the website. I have no reason to believe its message has significantly changed since its publication. I have chosen to base this chapter on my criticism of this booklet since I believe it carries so forthrightly the fundamental values and assumptions of a dominant scientific community that is antithetical to the psychodynamic approach that I follow.

It is a lively publication, full of colour, bright cartoon images of smiling young people and, more, smiling doctors/scientists in white coats. It is well designed to capture the interest of young people and no doubt many others (including practitioners and commissioners – it is easy and quick to read!). So far, so good – here is a genuine attempt to reach out and disseminate the knowledge gained about 'what works'. However, once inside the covers, we begin to encounter in its structure and content a distinct flavour of partiality both in terms of its orientation and selected findings.

Its first two sections describe the different types of mental health difficulty that young people may have and the different types of help that may be available. Unavoidably in such a small booklet, the descriptions are very brief, so much so that they border on caricature. The typology of mental health problems clearly derives from the well-known systems of psychiatric diagnostic classification. The main sections of the booklet are headed with several of these types in turn followed by guidance on which kind of help works best with each condition. Presumably, to heighten the popular appeal of the booklet, different kinds of help are star rated – three stars for those types of help that 'are very likely to help'; two stars for those 'likely to help' and one star for those that 'might help'.

If we count up all the stars for all the conditions, we discover that medication is the most star rated, ahead of cognitive behaviour therapy and way ahead of behaviour therapy and systemic family therapy. Other therapies hardly get a look in with very few stars. Psychodynamic psychotherapy scores just 3–2 for depression and 1 for eating disorders.

It may well be churlish to criticise this booklet. It was produced in the commendable spirit of a wish to share information gained from research with the wider public and especially young people. It drew on work contained in the second edition in 2006 of a publication called 'Drawing on the Evidence' (CAMHS 2006) again produced by the CAMHS Evidence-Based Practice Unit, designed to provide 'advice for mental health professionals working with children and adolescents'. This in turn had been greatly influenced by a comprehensive review of the evidence published in the book *What Works for Whom? A Critical Review of Treatments for Children and Adolescents* (Fonagy et al. 2002)

There can be no doubt about the thoroughness of those who produced this work. Nor can it be said that they were unaware of the limitations of the evidence they were reviewing. They could see for example that different kinds of evidence show some treatments to be well backed by evidence whilst other therapies to be less so. Throughout the booklet, there are several 'reminders' to this effect. In so many ways, the writers of this booklet strove not to be prescriptive or directive.

And yet, despite their worthy endeavours, we have to ask ourselves whether or not they succeeded? Beyond their words and caveats, did they really convey the openness and fairness they sought to achieve? Did they manage to give a balanced view based on a wide range of evidence? Many thought that they did. But many too, including myself, simply greeted their publication with dismay and outrage. We could not comprehend how this booklet could be so narrow and one sided in its disregard for so much thinking at that time in building a comprehensive multi-disciplined national child and adolescent mental health service. Not surprisingly, long established psychoanalytic staff at the Anna Freud Centre, in which the CAMHS Evidence-Based Practice Unit is based, were appalled to find that psychodynamic psychotherapy had been so minimally represented.

There were many other objections. Some were very concerned that a number of psychotherapies were not mentioned at all, e.g. the creative therapies (music, dance, art), solution focused therapy, play therapy, not to mention the whole world of counselling. Some thought their forms of psychotherapy were poorly described or even demeaned as having no therapeutic value. Others objected to the rating system which they thought was crass, needless and unfair. Others thought some of the findings failed to fit in any way with their everyday experience.

Can it really be the case that this booklet was produced in the spirit of true impartiality, unaffected by emotional bias and irrational hostility towards the nature of psychodynamic therapy, at whatever level of consciousness?

The medical model: diagnosis

Beyond all these various concerns, there is a more fundamental criticism of this booklet which relates to the values and beliefs that underlay its thinking – values and beliefs derived from medical practice. Throughout, there resides in its writing an unqualified commitment to the medical model of understanding mental health problems. Foremost in its structure is a basic focus on diagnosis and treatment. Clearly, from a medical point of view, this makes sense, ordering symptoms in such a way as to establish a basis for comparative analysis and to determine appropriate direction for treatment. Such an approach has served a useful purpose in the physical side of medicine. There are, however, many reservations when it is applied to psychotherapeutic practice. The question arises as to how relevant and appropriate it can be to apply such a model to the realities of everyday clinical practice carried out by a variety of helpers, the majority of whom are not medical practitioners.

For all the time and effort that has been put in over the years to the definition of psychiatric diagnoses in *DSM* (American Psychiatric Association 1952–2022) and *ICD* (World Health Organization), diagnostic labels remain by and large mystifying to many non-medical practitioners in the broad field of child and adolescent mental health. The ever-growing world of 'disorders' may make sense to psychiatrists and clinical psychologists, but for the most part, it bewilders and confuses others so that they come to believe that there is something physically wrong with the children who worry them. The fact is that most of these diagnoses lack any clear 'discernible physical basis, any association with particular physical or biological tests' (Timimi 2013). Psychiatrists base their diagnoses primarily on subjective judgement and evaluation of observable symptoms and behaviours – rather than on the basis of any physical evidence. There is a clear issue of reliability here; it is not at all uncommon for different psychiatrists to make quite different diagnoses based on similar behaviour.

Many worry that the effect of such psychiatric diagnostic thinking is to medicalise ordinary human experiences. After all, 'anxiety' and 'depression' for example, are no more than just fundamental human states of being; they are not in themselves pathological conditions. Psychiatrists of course will reassure us that these words are only used to describe conditions that are relatively severe and which significantly impair functioning. But a shorthand tends to develop in the public mind so that distinctions are less clear. This situation is not helped by the fact that the psychiatric diagnoses as they stand simply do not capture the complex variety of difficulties that most children and adolescents present. The ever-abiding problem of 'co-morbidity' confounds the tidiness of diagnostic categorisations. Within each diagnostic category, there is such heterogeneity as to defy any kind of coherent understanding. Within the rubric of depression, for example, there is such a wide spectrum of disturbances, ranging from mild forms of reactive depressed feelings to undeniably chronic clinical conditions. Similarly, 'anxiety' manifests itself in many ways, not least because of the many reasons that lie beneath it.

The medical model: treatment and research

A major complicating effect of the establishment of psychiatric diagnoses relates to ideas about treatment. Because of their lack of clarity and precision, most diagnoses throw a confusing light on the paths of treatment that should be followed. To quote Timimi (Timimi 2013) again, 'there is no evidence to show that using psychiatric diagnostic categories as a guide for treatment significantly impacts on outcomes'. Despite this, a great deal of effort has been spent on conducting trials and tests to assess the most appropriate treatments for different conditions.

Various forms of scrutiny of psychotherapeutic practice can be applied but the one that has been taken as the most objective and fair is the RCTs – a clearly rational approach whereby individuals from identical backgrounds are allocated at random to one group which receives an intervention and another which does not. In this way, the idea is that a particular therapeutic ingredient can be isolated and identified. Once this is achieved, so the argument goes, a treatment can be directed. On the face of it, this makes sense and in relation to many of the medical physical therapies such as drug therapies, a great deal has been learnt for the good. However, can such a procedure be the right one to test a psychological therapy and most particularly a psychodynamic psychotherapy?

As supreme as RCTs are regarded and as influential as they may be in indicating the most effective psychotherapies, there exists a host of concerns about the way their researchers go about their business. These are thoroughly discussed in a paper published by the UK Council of Psychotherapy, 'NICE under scrutiny' (Guy et al. 2011). The National Institute for Health and Care Excellence was established in 1999 to provide guidance to health, public health and social care providers based on available evidence (NICE 2004, 2009). According to NICE's Guidelines manual in 2009, 'although there are a number of difficulties with the use of RCTs in the evaluation of interventions in mental health, the RCT remains the most important method for establishing treatment efficacy'.

The UK Council of Psychotherapy paper basically objects to NICE's methodology which it believes 'has been inappropriately applied to psychotherapy'. It is seen as adhering to an overly medicalised perspective on emotional distress and 'treats psychotherapy as if it were a drug for research purposes when a more appropriate metaphor might be therapy as a dialogue'. 'It uses an inflexible hierarchy of evidence which its own Chairman has criticised'. The Chairman at the time of this paper was Sir Michael Rawlins who said that 'to regard the randomized controlled trial as the gold standard is unsustainable' (Rawlins 2008).

The fundamental objection to the rule of the RCT is that so many of its trials have been conducted in laboratory conditions, not in real life clinical settings. This has been largely because of the need to control for research purposes the various variables involved in psychotherapeutic treatment. This is all very well in the tradition of experimental science and no doubt appropriate in investigating many of the physical treatments, such as drug therapy. In its application to psychological therapies, however, there is much to be desired.

For example, in most of these studies, in the researchers' desire to control the patient variable, they have been extraordinarily selective in deciding eligibility in the trials. In general, children selected for these trials have been recruited through personal or professional contacts or through advertisements, rather than in response to clinic referrals. Similarly, the therapists employed in these trials have been usually drawn from University departments with no specific or adequate training in the therapy under investigation. As a consequence of such rigid research discipline, many key factors that arise in everyday clinical practice are simply controlled out. The variable motivation of children is not taken into account, nor that of families with varying kinds of worries about their mental health, their job security, their economic status or the environmental conditions in which they live. The training and particular beliefs of therapists as well as the pressures of working in contemporary community-based clinics are also not adequately considered.

Despite these serious reservations about the conduct of RCTs, the prevailing scientific view that permeates the research review literature and the booklet rests heavily on the evidence obtained from them. The fact that so many are laboratory based does not seem to disturb the confidence of those who hold this view. However, in a remarkably honest recent review (Weisz 2014, 2015), it emerged that out of 461 Youth RCTs that had been conducted during the last 50 years, only 2% were carried out in actual clinical service settings by practitioners treating children who were clinically referred and seeking treatment. This review was carried out by John Weisz who himself has been actively involved with many of the RCTs that he reviewed. He could see, however, that laboratory-based trials did not take into account a range of highly relevant variable factors, and as such, their findings could not be successfully generalised into real-world clinical practice.

My practice as a psychodynamic psychotherapist

As a psychodynamic psychotherapist, I am left unimpressed, even incredulous, that the RCT findings and recommendations that favour manualised cognitive behaviour type treatments should hold such currency. Cognitive Behavioural Therapy (CBT) may have 'its place' (as they say) with some children such as those suffering from significant obsessionality and with others with moderate emotional difficulties. But to suggest as the booklet does that children suffering from anxiety, particularly at a severe level, are more likely to respond to CBT than the psychodynamic psychotherapy that I and others like me are doing is simply unconvincing. And am I really to believe, as indicated in the booklet, that meeting 'a few times' in systemic family therapy with a child suffering deliberate self-harm is really 'likely to help'?

What takes place in my consulting room reflects predominately who I am as a person and as a therapist. I come to my work with a set of beliefs and values that derive from my psychoanalytic training, my reading, my age, my gender, my emotional and social experience, my culture and above all what is engendered in me by my patients. Sometimes I am engaged. Sometimes I am confused. Sometimes I am scared. Sometimes I am angry. My therapeutic responses are not determined by some form of manualised diktat, but rather by the way I process what I feel and think in my direct relationship with the patient, primarily through as much self-awareness as I can muster. Psychodynamic psychotherapy rests uniquely upon whatever kind of relationship might develop between therapist and patient. It is in effect a form of conversation arranged in such a way as to facilitate reflection and joint understanding. It does not comprise a set of techniques, pre-set and formulaic. I do not attempt to corral patients into some kind of conformist compliance. I do not tell patients what to do; rather I attempt to enable them to feel, think and find their own solutions.

This psychodynamic psychotherapy moreover is not determined by any kind of psychiatric diagnosis as such. Of course, I seek to make sense of the problems that are presented to me in terms of patients current and past living circumstances. But I need to keep open what might proceed in therapeutic work to ensure that I do not foreclose on what may emerge later of crucial importance. If for example I see a child who is miserable, failing to concentrate in class and finicky in her eating habits, I do not attempt to rush her into a diagnostic category that is so broad as to be meaningless. I am more concerned to find a way of getting alongside her and gaining as far as possible her trust so that she can begin to share some of the feelings and thoughts that underlay her sense of disturbance. Similarly, in the event of my being asked to see a teenager who is underachieving at school and getting into trouble with the law, I do not hurry to categorise him as a conduct disorder but rather look for ways in which he and I can explore some of the preoccupations that may be getting in his way. And again, a teenage girl whose complaints of fatigue, inability to sleep and preoccupation with violent fantasies might in the first instance alert me to the possibility of an incipient psychotic process may nevertheless encourage me to listen and find a way in which she can feel safe enough to share with me her fears and desires.

Whatever commonalities may exist, there are significant differences between different psychotherapeutic approaches – but only some are favoured by the prevailing current scientific establishment. Throughout, the booklet trumpets the authority of the 'scientists' as if they carried some kind of divine oracle being so 'sure' of their assertions – for example, in the booklet, for a three-star type of help, the scientists 'are very sure about this way of helping'. Can anyone really be that sure of anything in the tangled and complicated life of psychotherapy?

So smug and lofty are these blithe statements that I find myself wondering, for the sake of comparison, what kind of a booklet might emerge if it were to be produced under the banner of something quite different, let's say that of 'the Artist'. The chances are that it would give us an alternative perspective and would draw its stimulus from a much broader range of evidences, lower down (but neverthe-less, important) in the revered hierarchy of evidence, such as case-control studies, expert opinion and personal experience. It would in short include much that can be gained from practice-based evidence, from casework discussions, supervisions, published clinical papers and even from philosophy and literature. The chances are that it would take into account other reviews such as Kennedy's and Midgley's thematic review of child, adolescent and parent–infant therapy (Midgley and Ken-nedy 2011).

Why does any of this matter?

On the basis of the prevailing scientific research findings, much of which is incom-plete, inconclusive and methodologically faulty, major decisions are being made in public services to seriously and destructively diminish the quality of CAMHS and reduce patient choice. The recently arrived new programme, 'Improving Access to Psychological Therapies', IAPT (IAPT 2010; YoungMinds 2015), is being imposed on the provision of CAMHS in many areas of the country. It is geared in the pre-dominant direction of CBT and related manualised psychotherapies with the result that the posts of senior experienced child psychotherapists and others such as the creative psychotherapists are being 'deleted' and young inexperienced novices are being recruited in their place to conduct basic CBT work. This development which is very dubiously called a 'transformation' in service development, is now forcefully under way. However, despite the assertions and protestations made on its behalf, it is facing questionable results. Timimi, for example, questions whether it is proving any better than what existed before (Timimi 2015). Increasingly reports are being made of inadequate therapeutic capacity to deal with the more severely disturbed young people – many of the new band of inexperienced recruits finding themselves fre-quently out of their depth, much to the cost of those they are supposed to be helping.

Conclusion

My intention in this chapter is not to complain about the demand for evidence but rather to protest against the overly influential dominance of just one type of evidence. My plea is that we need to open our eyes to the idea that different kinds of evidence suit different kinds of psychotherapies. I may well be accused, as a psychodynamic psychotherapist, of being arrogant, precious, self-congratulatory and resistant to any external enquiry. But equally those who fire these attacks are themselves not immune to similar criticism. Scientific neutrality in the field of psychotherapy is a myth. Luborsky et al. (1999) highlighted several years ago the 'research allegiance effect' whereby researchers show a marked tendency to find evidence that supports their therapeutic orientation (mostly cognitive and behavioural). From my own experi-ence, I am aware of a striking antipathy in many of the scientists I have known to the sheer emotionality and irrationality of psychodynamic psychotherapy – an antipathy which unsurprisingly is in itself highly emotional and irrational.

My deepest concern is that the majority of children and adolescents who are presenting the greatest difficulties (and there are many, certainly more than current CAMHS can cope with) are being ill served by a kind of scientific prejudice that is threatening the very survival of psychodynamic therapeutic approaches in public services and the much-needed help that they provide.

At the risk of being overly simplistic and reductionist, I think that it may well be the case that there are just two types of people who engage in scientific enquiry in the broad sense – those who learn at a distance through collecting and analysing data and those who learn 'close up' through direct emotional therapeutic involvement. The former may be frightened by the intensity of emotion in therapeutic work and take refuge in their relatively objective study. They may aspire to the greater precision and predictability of hard science (consumed with what has been called physics envy). The latter may be overly excited in their therapeutic involvement and may simply be unable to emerge sufficiently from their subjectivity. They may seek something quite different, more imaginative and speculative maybe, which we might call, by comparison, poetry envy. Both types have their place in making sense of the mysteries of the psychotherapies. In the end, they look for different kinds of evidence to help them understand and improve their practice. What evidence works for whom?

References

American Psychiatric Association.(1952–2022). *Diagnostic and Statistical Manual of Mental Health Disorders (DSM)*, Washington, DC.

CAMHS Evidence –Based Practice Unit, University College, London. (2006) *Drawing on The Evidence; Advice for Mental Health Professionals Working with Children and Adolescents.*

CAMHS Evidence-Based Practice Unit, University College & Anna Freud Centre, London (2007) London.*Choosing What's Best For You; What Scientists Have Found Helps Children and Young People Who are Sad, Worried or Troubled.*

Fonagy, P., Target, M., Cottrell, D., Phillips, J. and Kurtz, Z. (2002) *What Works for Whom? A Critical Review of Treatments for Children and Adolescents,* London: Guilford Press.

Guy, A., Thomas, R., Stephenson, S. and Loewanthal, D. (2011) *NICE under Scrutiny; The Impact of the National Institute for Health and Clinical Excellence Guidelines on the Provision of Psychotherapy in the UK.* London: UK Council for Psychotherapy.

IAPT. (2010) *The IAPT Data Handbook and Appendices: Guidance on Recording and Monitoring Outcome to Support Local Evidence-Based Practice, IAPT National Program Team* [Online], Available: http/www.iapt.nhs.uk/services/measuring- outcomes (viewed 20th December 2010): Appendices: https://www.iapt.nhs.uk/wp-content/uploads/iapt-data-handbook-appendices-v10.pdf.

Loewenthal, D. and Samuels, A. (2014) *Relational Psychotherapy, Psychoanalysis and Counselling: Appraisal and Reappraisal,* London: Routledge.

Loewenthal, D. (ed). (2015) *Critical Psychotherapy, Psychoanalysis and Counselling: Implications for Practice*, London: Palgrave MacMillan.

Luborsky, L., Diguer, L., Seligman, D., Rosenthal, R., Krause, E. D., Johnson, S...... Schweizer, E. (1999) 'The researcher's own therapy allegiances: a "wild card" in comparisons of treatment efficacy', *Clinical Psychology: Science and Practice* 6: 95–106.

Midgley, N. and Kennedy, E. (2011) 'Psychodynamic psychotherapy for children and adolescents: a critical review of the evidence base', *Journal of Child Psychotherapy* 37(3): 1–29.

NICE. (2004) *NHS Evidence – Defining Mental Health* [Online], Available: https://www.library.nhs.uk/mental health/viewresource.aspx?resid =105867 (Viewed 9th June 2010).

NICE. (2009) *Guideline Development Manual* [Online], Available: https://www.nice.org.uk (viewed 6th October 2010).

Rawlins, M. D. (2008) *De Testimonio. On the Evidence for Decisions about the Use of Therapeutic Interventions*, The Harveian Oration of 2008. Delivered for the Jack Tizard Memorial Lecture before the Fellows of The Royal College of Physicians of London on Thursday 16th October 2008, London: Royal College of Physicians. Slide notes, Available at https://rcplondon.emea.acrobat.com/p37057603/ (Viewed on 15th December 2010).

Shedler, J. (2010) 'The efficacy of psychodynamic psychotherapy', *American Psychologist* 65(2): 98–109.

Timimi, S. (2002) *Pathological Child Psychiatry and the Medicalisation of Childhood*, Hove: Brunner-Routledge.

Timimi, S. (2007) *Critical Voices in Child and Adolescent Mental Health*, London: Free Associations.

Timimi, S. (2013) 'No more psychiatric labels: Campaign to Abolish psychiatric diagnostic systems such as ICD and DSM (CAPSID)', *Self and Society* 40(4): 6–14.

Timimi, S. (2015) 'Children and young people's improving access to psychological therapies: inspiring innovation or more of the same?' *BJP Bulletin* 39: 57–60.

Weisz, J. R. (2014) 'Building robust psychotherapies for children and adolescents', *Perspectives on Psychological Science* 9(1): 81–84.

Weisz, J.R. (2015) *MOD Squad for Youth Psychotherapy in Everyday Clinical Care: Transdiagnostic Treatment for Anxiety, Depression, and Conduct Problems*. Unpublished paper delivered for the Jack Tizard Memorial Lecture before the Association for Child and Adolescent Mental Health, London June 2015.

World Health Organisation. (1948–2022) *International Classification of Diseases*, Geneva: WHO. On p17 central paragraph – ICD (World Health Organisation).

YoungMinds. (2015) *The Children's and Young People's Improving Access to Psychological Therapies Programme (CYP IAPT)*, London: YoungMinds.

Chapter 2

Latency and certainty

Previously published in Journal of Child
Psychotherapy 15 (1989).

Introduction

The latency child presents the psychotherapist with a peculiar doubled-edged challenge: to overcome seemingly unmoving, even obtuse resistance, and to unravel and understand rich and imaginative fantasy material. There is, in a sense, no ambiguity – little between emphatic closed defence and definite open expression. In effect, there is a quality of certainty in both positions – and it is this feature, both defensive and adaptive in the context of experiential uncertainty and the developmental precariousness of this period of life, which is the focus of this chapter.

The overriding popular view of latency is that it is a time of quiescence – a time of relative order and composure, in many ways unexceptional and quick to pass over. For example, Dare and Pincus offer the following concise, if cursory, description of latency.

> The next stage in the life cycle for children between six and ten is relatively quiet in terms of emotional development and appropriately called the latency period. If care and prevailing love are reasonably good, the child of six is comfortable enough in his relationships with the family to be quiet inside himself. He can turn some of his energies to the outside world which at this stage is represented chiefly by school with its friendships and by the sharing of interests with his peers. This is probably the reason why most contemporary studies of this age group tend to concentrate on primary education... So, in our exploration of the family life cycle, we shall move on to children in the age group between eleven and fourteen...
>
> (Dare and Pincus 1978: 90)

There is much, however, from clinical experience and psychological studies (Bornstein 1951; Shapiro and Perry 1976) to suggest that latency is anything but such a docile or peaceful time. Sexuality may be in abeyance or suspended, but in terms of cognitive and intellectual growth, latency is a time of considerable expansion. By virtue of his increased capacity to comprehend, the latency child is encountering new levels of awareness. He is also for the first time entering new realms of

DOI: 10.4324/9781003680437-3

activity outside the family, at school and elsewhere. Within the family, in which he sits, wide-eyed, observant, often overlooked, he is taking in, in a new way, all kinds of goings-on that are difficult to make sense of.

For the latency child there is much that is new to experience and to understand. In a sense, there is almost too much – at a time when, despite maturational and developmental advances, cognitive capacities are still relatively immature and concrete, and indeed when family permission for all to be understood is frequently withheld. It is in this developmental context that the need for certainty, however false or partial, is most pronounced – essentially to defend against the anxiety associated with the uncertainty of new experience. It is also needed to guard against the revival of the raw infantile life that has only so very recently been left behind and repressed. 'Certainty' is essentially about sureness, an absence of doubt. The word itself derives from Latin and Greek sources, referring to processes of discriminating, separating and deciding. In the absence of any actual sureness in the child's life, and drawing upon the child's cognitive capacities which are organised around the very same processes, the need for certainty – together, indeed, with the accomplishment of the sense of it – is a salient characteristic of the latency child.

This characteristic features powerfully in psychotherapy in the latency child's defensive rigidity and obduracy. It also manifests itself in the vivid, sharp clarity and exactness of many of his fantasy elaborations and imagery. The following illustration is taken from a sequence of material in the analysis of an eight-year-old boy whose mother at the time was pregnant. The play material was meticulously developed over a period of five sessions, interrupted only by periodic stretches of comic-reading, in which the child seemed totally disconnected from what he was otherwise doing.

He began by taking out a lump of plasticine, explaining that this was to be his island. He used a compass point to bore a hole into the plasticine. This he said was his secret tunnel. He set me up as the enemy on another island and constructed a powerful motorboat which he harboured at the entrance to his secret tunnel. He told me that my island was too big and had to be reduced in size, in proportion to his. For much of the time, he built his defences, fortified his armour and placed a flap over the entrance to his tunnel. He described what he had as "small". However, he soon began to mobilise his motorboat and in no time invaded and conquered a third "outer" island, situated between his and mine. This "outer" island served as a further protection for his motorboat.

As his play began to build in intensity, so he gradually moved aggressively towards my island and eventually conquered it. With this accomplished, he began to worry that I still had "Africa" on my side; and with a strip of plasticine, he moulded the shoreline of Africa and laid it out on my side of the table. He took a great deal of time on this and what was striking was the similarity and shape of this shoreline with that of a pregnant woman. He was about to invade Africa when the session ended.

Towards the end of the next session, following a lengthy period of comic-reading, he continued his invasion. He introduced aircraft to his forces, strengthened his motorboat and peremptorily destroyed my boat. There then followed a sequence in which he pretended to attack his own island, thereby misleading me to believe that his aircraft were not really my enemy. He ended the session by inserting his motorboat inside the harbour of my Africa and establishing a radio link from there to his island. Again, after further delay and hesitation (in which at one point he idly and apparently unthinkingly sang the words of a pop song — "Baby, baby, I can see you, I don't need you"), he became absorbed in the "outer" island lying between my Africa and his own. He explained that this island appeared to be unpopulated and sufficiently inactive on the surface for the enemy not to be attracted by it. "It's secret — you don't know about it and suspect anything," He constructed a cave in its interior, the purpose of which was to provide premises for the manufacture of "chemicals", to which he associated the word "Bio" — "to do with cells, germs and all that... under a microscope". Looking at my Africa, he suggested that the constructions on it were towers for "peeping" at his chemical island. He built an underwater tunnel from his cave to another underwater cave, which was situated closer to my Africa; from this second cave, it was possible "to listen to secrets" in my African continent.

He played at being a friendly "trading" boat and proceeded to go freely in and out of my Africa harbour. His next move was to buy five thousand million onions, which he took back to his hidden cave; he inserted into each onion an explosive and delivered them all back into my African harbour. He then proceeded to destroy my boats by zooming his overwhelmingly powerful planes up and down until they finally crashed on the boats. In the end, the whole African continent was demolished and pushed off the table. In the final session, the onions inside Africa exploded and the whole continent was again destroyed and flooded.

This remarkable segment of play material highlights the extraordinary vividness of imagery and clarity of preoccupation which this child was able to create alongside his unease, puzzlement and hazy perception of his mother's pregnancy. It is all the more noteworthy coming as it did from this particular child, who in his day-to-day life was described as vague and languid and lacking in spontaneity and purpose. In this play he was quite the opposite. His sessions proceeded in an aura of certainty. He had no doubts about what was happening or what was about to happen. In a sense the whole experience had a kind of sublime safety to it all. And yet, of course, in its midst was an array of wishes, desires, fears and defences that fully reflected his response and attitude towards the baby in his mother's 'Africa'. Powerful, unconscious conflicts were involved, close in form and intensity to those of early childhood. Oedipal wishes to penetrate, to see and destroy what is inside, to conquer and overcome rivalries and to avoid and defend against castration anxiety and fears of reprisal were all close to the surface, almost transparent in their clarity.

What was striking was that they were all available in the therapy for expression and working through. But at the same time, they were set in a mould of fantasy certainty, fixed and bound as it were at a level of displacement that made them manageable for this boy. What was constructed in the fantasy play was a story that, in its conviction and definition, forestalled the expression of uncertainty related to the imminence of childhood feelings or the mystery and apprehension of the mother's pregnancy.

Latency

Traditionally, from a psychoanalytic point of view (Freud 1905), latency is seen as a time of pause between the storms of infancy and puberty, fundamentally related to the biological temporary cessation of the growth of the genitals. In oedipal terms, partly because biological immaturity precludes consummation, the 'small lover' has to turn away from his hopeless longings. A temporary end is called to the desires, frustrations and anxieties of the Oedipus complex. A period of relative peace ensues in which sexual pressures are reduced, reaction formations and identifications are established and sublimations are developed. Latency follows the dissolution of the Oedipus complex (Freud 1924); it is, in effect, a period of life in which repressions predominate, feelings of shame, disgust and moral ideals are formed, and capacities for self-regulation and censure are developed.

It is also a period of life in which significant maturational advances occur, not least in the realm of cognitive development. In the development of concrete operational thought (Piaget 1954), logic and objectivity progressively characterise the child's thinking; children become interested and able in reasoning things out, in naming things and mastering classes and relationships. In terms of neuro-muscular development (Bremner Kaplan 1965), children also make considerable strides, with more refined abilities in laterality and directionality.

Children in effect are better equipped to handle themselves with more independence and meet society's requirement to take a greater part in life outside the family. There is much to suggest that, if all goes well in terms of development, maturation and environmental facilitation, children can enter into a short period of life in which they can enjoy a degree of order and structure. The achievement of such a state is developmentally important. It represents a time of consolidation and accumulation of skills and capacities. Erikson (1950) gives a clear description of this state, emphasising the emergence from infancy, the gradually acquired ego capacities and the progressive development towards the capacity to be industrious.

> The child must forget past hopes and wishes, while his exuberant imagination is tamed and harnessed to the laws of impersonal things — even the three Rs. For before the child, psychologically already a rudimentary parent, can become a biological parent, he must begin to be a worker and a potential provider. With the oncoming latency period, the normally advanced child forgets, or rather sublimates, the necessity to "make" people by direct attack or to become papa or mama in a hurry; he now learns to win recognition by producing things. He has mastered the ambulatory field and the organ modes. He has experienced a sense of finality regarding the fact that there is no workable future within the womb

of his family and thus becomes ready to apply himself to given skills and tasks, which go far beyond the mere playful expression of his organ modes or the pleasure in the function of his limbs. He develops a sense of industry — i.e. to adjust himself to the inorganic laws of the tool world. He can become an eager and absorbed unit in a productive situation.

(Erikson 1950: 258–259)

Central in Erikson's concept of latency is the process of sublimation – that is, the diversion of 'pre-genital libido', 'from sexual to non-sexual aims'. He gives as good account as any of what this means.

Thus, a measure of infantile curiosity concerning the "doings" in the mother's body may reinforce man's eagerness to understand the workings of machines and test tubes; or he may eagerly absorb the "milk of wisdom" when he once desired more tangible fluids from more sensuous containers; or he may collect all kinds of things in all kinds of boxes instead of overloading his colon

(Erikson 1950: 62)

Erikson sees nothing dull or boring about latency at all. Latency is essentially a time of growth and learning – altogether exhilarating, but essentially held and protected within a sense of structure, both internally and externally. A 'good' latency, in effect, refers to a few years of peace and quiet, freed from the turmoil of infantile or adolescent passions and anxieties in which there is access to learning and to new experiences beyond the family, without disruption from within or intrusion from without. What is of essence in this notion of latency is a kind of psychic truce. Winnicott writes 'Sanity is essential in the latency phase and the child who in this phase cannot maintain sanity is clinically very ill' (Winnicott 1958: 121–122).

He goes on to say that 'when the child is relatively well then it is not lightly that anyone will put his or her latency child in analysis' (Winnicott 1958: 123). There is, of course, here the suggestion that, in effect, psychotherapists rarely see a true well-functioning latency child in their clinical practice. They may well see many children of latency age, but they are children who have not achieved the state of latency that we are referring to. In Winnicott's understanding, this state is equated with sanity and the fundamental task is the maintenance of this sanity. In Erikson's formulation this state is equated with ego-mastery and a sense of industry and the fundamental task is the achievement of both. What is implicit is that latency is an achievement that has to be maintained. It is not something ordained or inevitable, despite maturation. Rather, it is a state that has to be earned and looked after, given adequate environmental facilitations. Despite its virtue of composure and orderly growth, it nevertheless sits perilously at the mercy of numerous disruptive forces. For, in essence, latency exists but a few years away from those two periods of instinctual force and major change, early childhood and adolescence. The meaning of latency, in fact, is not one of calmness and peace – but of things laying hidden, present but not apparent or active. It can never be forgotten – however much the latency amnesia prevails – that the surge and complexities of early childhood are still, as it were, well within living memory. Freud makes clear that early infantile feelings have not disappeared—it is simply that they have gone underground and have been dealt with in other ways. 'The phantasies of the pubertal period have as their starting point, the infantile sexual researches that were abandoned in childhood. No doubt too they are also present before the end of the latency period' (Freud 1905: 216).

The state of latency, however well achieved and consolidated, sits almost by definition in a precarious position – not far removed from the memories and experiences of early childhood and in uneasy anticipation of puberty. Latency is, in effect, laden with anxieties associated with semi-dormant pressures lurking below the surface, waiting for puberty and the awesome activity of adolescence. In these terms, the phase of latency is under constant siege – and it may be of no surprise that in a study in 1952, of 4,587 children of latency age, 62% bit their nails between the age of six and eight years (Malone and Massler 1952).

It is also not surprising that the establishment of a 'good' structured experience of latency can so easily be hindered or interfered with by environmental influences. The disintegrating effects of early trauma and deprivation can be such as to preclude ego development in latency. Children who are over-indulged, seduced or sexually abused in childhood and during latency frequently fail to establish adequate repressions and reaction formations. Children whose parents have been unavailable or absent, for one reason or another, often show poorly developed inner controls and sanctions, having lacked the experience of external authority and the opportunity for identification. Children whose parents are violent are frequently so frightened that they have little opportunity within themselves to create an orderly world. And finally, latency can be effectively cut short by precocious sexual and early pubertal development.

Many children whose latency has been encroached upon in these various ways, lead lives that internally continue to be as fragmented, random and as highly charged instinctually, as those of younger children. They do not have the chance to rest, as it were, in the half time of latency: to draw together their capacities and put some distance between themselves and their powerful feelings. At worst, they have poor impulse control, little sense of effective social or moral restraint. They live in a state of over-stimulation and excitement which impinges on their relationships and interferes with the development of their cognitive and intellectual capacities. Much of their behaviour is anxiety driven. They live, as it were, too close, undefended, to their childhood fears. As Winnicott has indicated, such children 'who cannot maintain sanity in the latency phase are clinically very ill' – their disrupted latencies constituting a poor prognostic sign for the future.

Case illustration

In the following illustration, an account is given of how a nine-year-old boy, Brian, struggled to make sense of feelings and uncertainties that related fundamentally to a secret in the family. Brian was supposed not to know about this secret, and it is not clear what 'knowledge' he had. Clearly he had observed various family events and in particular witnessed and experienced his mother's unhappiness. But it is unlikely that he comprehended the family story. He grew up in a family in confusion and distress, and as much as his mother provided adequate care, he suffered the effects of this and lived in a state of apprehension and uncertainty.

The salient aspects of the family background were as follows. At the time of Brian's birth, his parents were married and living together. They already had a younger daughter and son. Shortly following Brian's birth, his father had an affair with his (Brian's) maternal grandmother. As a result, Brian's mother, in great distress, left the family home with three young children and lived in various temporary accommodations for a year or more. The affair between Brian's father and his maternal grandmother continued over time and his mother was totally cut off, doubly rejected and excluded herself. She eventually remarried when Brian was five and shortly afterwards had another child, a physically handicapped boy. When Brian was six, he was allowed regularly to see his father and grandmother again – but he thought that his father was his uncle. Brian's mother was deeply ashamed of her circumstances and did not think it right to inform the children of the truth until their adolescence.

Brian was referred because of nightmares, enuresis and general moodiness. He was described as sadistic towards his brother. At school he had few friends and was under-functioning.

There was much in his initial presentation that was typical of a latency child. Physically, he was slim, slightly scruffy, hair uncombed and clothes half fitting. There was little that was exceptional about him. He seemed cautious, tentative and ready to be compliant. Of particular note, however, was his watchfulness; he sat silently, quizzically looking for signs and clues.

In his early sessions, Brian was particularly intrigued by puzzles. He brought these to his sessions and expected me to find the 'missing piece'. In his reverie, he would often sing repetitively, 'Who's got the answer?' It was as if, without doubt from the beginning of therapy, he was setting the scene to find out and know more about something. Curiously, however, despite this set purpose and the vigour with which he initially approached the puzzles, he rarely finished them. He stopped the jigsaw puzzles at the point when it looked as if we might complete them. I commented on a mystery; it looked as if he both wanted to find the missing answer and not to find it. He immediately replied, with remarkable clarity, 'sometimes things stay a mystery. It's better that way'. When I said he seemed at least sure about that, he said, 'I think I am going to get something out of coming here'. This was an odd exchange, but what was so striking was the vivid mixture of his unsureness and hesitancy and the broad finality of his statement.

Following this initial introduction, Brian moved his interest to the theme of families. He began by drawing his family tree. Straight away he categorised everyone according to whether they were good or bad. Most were good, but there were two exceptions – an uncle/grandfather and himself. He giggled. But then, with sudden sureness and seriousness, said he was the naughty one of the family. He did not like this but did not know what to do about it.

After this, sessions suddenly lost their liveliness. He brought with him books of the animal world and either read silently or drew some of the animals in slow detail. Whereas we were still interested in (animal) families, the tone of the sessions became factual and concrete. It was as if he had set an emphatic and impenetrable block – in retreat from his serious personal acknowledgement and in defence against his growing dependence on me. This period of book reading was inevitable. There was no way in which it could be hurried. Its air of concrete certainty had to be waited with – until he felt safe, or sure, enough with me to proceed.

After about three months, Brian brought with him to his sessions two of his favourite dolls. One was called Charlie the snake; the other, Harry the bear. Without much ado, he began to conduct vigorous fights between the two. The intensity was extraordinary and he made it quite clear that Charlie and Harry hated each other. These fights continued through several sessions. He clearly enjoyed them and easily became very excited by them. I was able to make the link between the rivalry between the two dolls and of Brian and his brother. He acknowledged that he hated his brother, that his mother got upset by this and he therefore felt bad. This was an important reflection to which we were able to return from time to time but the fights between Charlie and Harry continued unabated for some time.

Eventually the fights subsided – incidentally at a time when mother reported much improvement in the relationship between the two brothers – and Brian's play and preoccupation moved, as it were, to a more fundamental level. He began to make use of plasticine and increasingly shaped a series of monsters, all of which were either mother monsters or baby monsters. As he worked with them and positioned them on the table, so he gradually articulated a number of important statements, for example: mothers have to be strong and look after their weak and helpless children; babies are completely dependent on their mothers (one baby monster was blind for its first two years of life); mothers are vulnerable to attack from wicked stronger monsters; sometimes mothers survive these attacks and grow extra eggs so that more children survive; sometimes mothers are damaged by these attacks and her eggs are damaged too so some babies are born blind, and finally, babies try to grow up faster and faster so that they can protect and make their mothers better.

These statements emerged whilst Brian and I were engaged in moulding the plasticine monsters with great care and precision. They were made with much emphasis and deliberation, not to be challenged or questioned. For Brian, they were facts and it was at this level that I responded to them – keeping my focus on the predicaments of the mother and baby monsters there before us with periodic references to the plight of mothers and babies in general. I also made occasional direct references to his own mother and to himself and his physically disabled brother but I did not press these.

This absorbing period lasted about four months. Brian continued to work with the plasticine but his interest gradually shifted from the mothers and babies to a new scenario. This concerned a whole family, at first frightened by snakes under the floorboards and then threatened by the devious menacing designs of a wicked grandfather from outside. The wicked grandfather once lived with the family but he became greedy and was evicted. Ever since, he had been breeding monsters ready to attack and destroy the family. His ultimate aim was to take the family treasure. The family were terrified, especially the women and the animals. At first they hid indoors, but gradually, they were supported by a good grandfather and his sons who bred an army of super-good monsters. The situation built up to a point where, over a lengthy period of time, a battle ensued between the forces of good and evil. These battles were viciously conducted and involved all manner of destructive deeds – stabbings, mutilations, shootings and so on. There reigned a high level of suspense – the family constantly on the threshold of being demolished, tied up and bound, their swords taken and their power immobilised by powerful rays. Gradually, however, over time, the family grew in strength and triumphed over the wicked grandfather and his monsters. The women and the animals of the family were able to come out of their hiding places and the wicked grandfather was almost destroyed (left suspended over a volcano of hot lava).

Discussion

This boy lived in an atmosphere of secrecy and high tension. Perhaps more than most, it was difficult for him to be clear what was going on. He sensed mysteries and puzzles. He was confused. He was also troubled by his own feelings, his behaviour and especially his violence, which made him feel bad.

There was a lot he could not be sure of. And yet, in differing ways, his psychotherapy proceeded with extraordinary clarity. From the outset, he seemed sure of his purpose, despite apprehension, to find missing pieces. In his play, in the true spirit of latency, he was, at first, moralistic and factual, and then precise and exact in his use of the tangible: the dolls and plasticine. In his statements, he was unequivocal and unwavering. And in his inventiveness he was lucid – absorbing himself in almost trance-like certitude.

As in the first example in this chapter, this child's therapy proceeded in an aura of certainty. Within this, the child was able to go about his business of drawing closer to what he felt and to what he didn't know. Within the definition and structure of his play, with its own language and touchable symbols, he could experience the impact of his sibling rivalry, his anxiety about his mother's vulnerability and his guilt about his own destructiveness. He could also explore the mystery that lay behind it all and construct his own explanation. His representation of the wicked grandfather was an intriguing condensation of grandmother and father. His depiction of the wicked grandfather as greedy, deceitful and capable of destroying his mother was an uncanny understanding of the essence of what had occurred. His elaboration of the unending fights was his attempt to master his outrage and deal with revenge and reparation.

There was much in all this that alluded to actual reality. The child's rivalry with his brother could be clearly acknowledged; so too his worries and torments about his mother and himself, as well as his 'damaged' physically handicapped baby brother.

There was, however, a taboo, set by his mother, on any explicit direct reference to the situation concerning the father and grandmother. The psychotherapy had to take place within this constraint. Whereas in absolute terms this was unsatisfactory, in effect it was not crucial. For what mattered above all else was that this boy had the opportunity to build his own certainty about that which, for the time being, was to remain unspoken. The family itself was in an odd state of latency – things lay concealed and indeed his father was often present but not apparent or known as his father. Uncertainty was everywhere, leaving the child to make as much sense of it as he could in his own certain ways. Psychotherapy consisted in helping him with this, all the time attentive to the concrete imagery and predominating themes, but with fundamental respect for the spirit of allusion and displacement and with care not to dispel or intrude, through over-articulation or forced and unsanctioned explanations.

Conclusion

There is no doubt that there is much at stake in the phase of latency. The developmental and maturational progression from the childhood state and the achievement of a relative inner sense of order and composure are of crucial importance. They are important as foundations for a new phase of learning and as a preparation for the next turbulent stage of development in adolescence. Such advances, however, take place in the context of much anxiety and uncertainty. Latency itself exists precariously between the internal pressures of infancy and puberty – and is subject to so many disruptive impingements in family life. Parents and adults are baffling at best: terrifying at worst. The situation is made no easier for many children: overly exposed as they are without adequate guidance or protection, to the increasingly fragmented, often highly confusing and disturbing imagery of the media, not least television.

In view of this state of developmental siege, there is a premium in latency on preserving a sense of order: a kind of compensatory process in which certainty is emphasised as an adaptation to and defence against the prevailing and surrounding uncertainty and anxiety. Clearly, this is facilitated by the child's new cognitive capacities and by the standards and ideals set within him as a result of super-ego development. It is in the nature of his mode of thinking and of the relative directness of his immature super-ego that he tends towards the more definite. Nevertheless, the fundamental dynamic behind the quest for certainty is a fear of its opposite – of being rendered unsure and helpless under the sway of unrepressed emotions: overly aroused, confused and terrified by parents and adult activities.

The child in latency needs a few years to be left alone, as it were, unimpinged, in which to look up at the world and learn about it and in which to put his head down to detail and carve out his own certainty about it. This is his industry and sanity.

References

Bornstein, B. (1951) 'On Latency', *Psychoanalytic Study of the Child* 6: 279–285.
Bremner Kaplan, E. (1965) 'Reflections regarding psychomotor activities during the latency period', *Psychoanalytic Study of Child* 20: 220–238.

Dare, C. and Pincus, L. (1978) *Secrets in the Family*, London: Faber & Faber.

Erikson, E. H. (1950) *Childhood and Society*, New York: Norton.

Freud, S. (1905) 'Three Essays on the Theory of Sexuality', *Standard Edition* 7: 123–246.

Freud, S. (1924) 'The Dissolution of the Oedipus Complex', Standard Edition 19:171–180.

Malone, A. and Massler, A. (1952) 'Index of nailbiting in children', *Journal of Abnormal Social Psychology* 47: 193.

Piaget, J. (1954) *The Construction of Reality in the Child*, New York: Basic Books.

Shapiro, T. and Perry, R. (1976) 'Latency revisited: The age 7+ or -1', *Psychoanalytic Study of the Child* 31: 79–106.

Winnicott, D. (1958) 'Child analysis in the latency period'. In D. W. Winnicott (eds) *The Maturational Process and the Facilitating Environment*, New York: International Universities Press. p. 1965.

Chapter 3

'I don't know'

Previously published in Psychotherapy with Adolescents: Special Section, Journal of the British Association of Psychotherapists 39 (2) (2001).

The stimulus for this chapter is an expression often used by adolescents, not untypically in psychotherapy. The expression 'I don't know' is both endearing and infuriating to psychotherapists whose benign intention is to know, to explore and understand. This chapter seeks to make sense of the developmental significance of this expression. Fundamentally, it is seen as a necessary form of communication that allows for the internal acknowledgement of the adolescent's 'knowledge'. It is seen as an assertion of the need for privacy, in which to register the complexity and newness of experience. It is taken as a plea for time for contemplation. Issues of identity and integrity are seen as being contained and processed through this expression, the adolescent finding space to discover the nature of his knowing and not knowing. In the psychotherapy of adolescents, an approach of 'negative capability' is proposed, appreciating the particular meaning of the adolescent's 'I don't know' rather than seeking to interpret it as a resistance.

A 14-year-old boy has recently been expelled from school. He has been involved in a series of fights for several weeks and the schoolteachers have had enough. They feel they cannot contain him, and he is referred for psychological assessment and alternative placement. It turns out that his parents have recently separated, having endured a long, acrimonious and violent marriage. His younger sister has been sent away to live with relatives. He now lives alone with his depressed and bitter mother.

Amongst other things, he is eventually ushered into psychotherapy. He and I sit in guarded anticipation of each other – he, reluctant, confused and angry; I, interested, unsure and wondering what difference I can make. He tells me the gist of his story well enough – a flat, factual account of his family life and a complaint of injustice at school. He doodles a bit, mostly cartoon figures holding balloons (but with no captions). As the initial weeks go by, we catch up on latest events and although not much is said, we more or less agree to meet until the following summer (a three-month stretch, on trial as it were). Our weekly life together is for the most part rather awkward, ungiving and unforgiving, and it is as much as I can do (or he) to keep sufficiently engaged to carry on. In fits and starts, wherever I see an opening, I make some comment or suggestion about how he might be feeling – to establish some form of contact, to touch on what might be beneath the gloom. Sooner or later, I ask him

DOI: 10.4324/9781003680437-4

about the different aspects of his life that he has told me about – his fights, his expulsion, his parents' divorce, their violence, the loss of his home, his unhappy mother. What does he think? How does he feel? His answer: 'I don't know'. I carry on with similar questions or thoughts as best modulated and unintrusive as I can; again, I meet the same response, 'I don't know'. At suitable distances, I try to take it further. I say, for example, 'I should think you are getting worried about what is going to happen next at school, whether you are going to go back or what'. 'Dunno'. I say something else in a similar vein, but drawing more on what might be his anticipation or experience of seeing me. 'Maybe it's not easy for you to trust me – maybe, in view of what's happened, you can't imagine that I might care'. 'I don't know'. Whatever variant is used – 'Suppose so', 'Whatever' – we are pretty well left in the dark – he uncommitted; me baffled.

To those who have entered into this kind of psychotherapeutic tangle with an adolescent, the challenge cannot be unfamiliar. It is one that consists of many imponderables, seemingly impenetrable. The sound of 'I don't know' has a ring of finality, an end of sentence; yet, too, of possibility, a sentence poised for the next (whomsoever's sentence it may be that takes the conversation further). The 'I don't know' may be momentary, a passing, a necessary pause, quietly reflective. Or it may be pervasive, more entrenched, characteristic, a dominant feature of communication, for weeks or months.

'I don't know'. Three little words – innocent enough, a phrase more or less familiar to most of us. We know, or think we know, what it is that we know. We know too our sense of not knowing. We are simply ignorant of some things and curiously unknowing about others – experiences that, at a pre- or unconscious level, may be known but not yet revealed or thought. The complexity of our experience resides in the many layers of acknowledgement of our knowledge. Bollas (1996: 6) has drawn our attention to tacit assumptions, built in the course of mother–child intimacy, that become part of what is known. These he refers to as 'unthought knowns' and he sees 'the evolution of life, in part, as gradually realising the bases of one's unthought knowledge'. Of central significance is the process of realisation or recognition of what is 'known'. Ballas writes, '… the primary repressed unconscious is full of unthought known forms of knowledge waiting for developed forms of thinking to evolve, so that part of what is known is eventually available for representation in speech, imagination, affect or enactment'. Such 'unknowing' becoming known over time is clearly in the nature of the growth of human awareness. It is a thoroughly perplexing yet intriguing process, even more so, perhaps, at certain transitional periods of life. The capacity to say, 'I don't know' and to bear waiting to know may be of crucial developmental significance, serving the purpose of integration – the integrating of what has been, and has yet to be, discovered.

In adolescence, young people are engaged in a very critical transition. They are in the midst of a kind of internal migration, leaving behind their childhood bodies, familiar dependencies, earlier trusts and certainties of latency. So much 'disappears' that many lament that 'nothing will ever be the same again'. At the same time, in transit, they are moving forward – 'passing over, or across or through' – reaching, changing, making their own way. Their passage into uncharted territory is fraught with 'unknowables'. They have no way of knowing the way and can do no more than keep curious and hang on to find out. Their discovery of each new experience, moreover, is precious: something fresh being found that is personal, unique in its meaning for their emerging selves. Each experience consists of aspects of the unthought known, together with those of the unanticipated – unexpected sensations and capabilities. The adolescent needs to safeguard for a while what he or she knows, and hold his or her distance from those who might impinge or take away. With all this in mind, the adolescent rightly and frequently says in his everyday life and inevitably in psychotherapy, 'I don't know'. It is his or her marker of identity, as well as a plea for time to contemplate. It is something to be respected – not berated, disbelieved or tackled as a resistance to be overcome. Adults and psychotherapists have to allow for the indeterminacy inherent in the adolescent experience.

In many respects, these observations and comments sit oddly in the throes of a contemporary youth culture in which assertive upfrontedness shouts through teenage minds and confronts the adult kingdom in bewilderment. In one lyric after another, in magazine upon magazine, in one video beyond the next, loud certainties proclaim themselves, underpinned by the sharp edge of technology's increasing potency. 'The knowledge' about sex, life and death is all up there in your face; teenagers seem now to know more than past generations ever dreamed. For many, in the way they appear to know, they seem to know it all. And it is the adult who, caught off balance, says, 'I don't know' (what to make of my child).

And yet, in the ordinary daily business of emotional living, it is likely that not too much has changed. Within adolescents, pubertal bodies still startle in all of their mysterious ways; some begin earlier, others become bigger than others. But at the heart of the matter, fears of the sheer physical power of these changes, of losing control of new internal pressures, and the dread of growing onwards without limit into some sort of monster or freak remain. There is of course excitement, empowerment, exhilaration – but uncertainties persist, and the shadowy underside continues to torment. Compelling commercial images of monumental and desirable men and women may fill teenagers' screens, preen their fantasies, and shape their imitations. But beyond all this, in the aloneness of the bedroom, the shape of the nose, the size of the breasts, the hardness of the penis, the flow of the menses, the countless other encounters with the phenomena of the body remind them of the vivid, unprecedented newness of growing up, and too often of the inadequacy of words to account for it all. In the fumbling and wandering forays into early conversations, there remains, for most, an inarticulateness in catching hold of the things that are novel, fascinating, but essentially unknown and yet to be discovered.

Much of this discovery cannot be readily shared. It is private, bodily private; intimate in the solitary bedroom, filled with ruminations about normalities, adequacies, differences. Whatever the teenager aspires to be or is supposed to look like, there is invariably an anguish, a kind of despair in never, ever being quite perfect or even good enough perfect. The teenager ultimately has to settle for the genetic and hormonal truth of his or her own puberty – and to accept it as his or her own. His or her body is for sure no longer 'theirs' – those parents, who have assumed naturally enough over the years due care and control. 'This body is mine', says the teenager, 'to do and play with as I see fit. Keep off'. Independence has its roots in this bodily ownership – well fortified by well-known adolescent defences against the regressive lure of incestuous ties (Freud 1958: 268). And yet of course such insistence on privacy carries with it its own fears – of loneliness, loss of dependency, of self-exposure. The teenager is faced with a profound prospect of growing into an adult: separate, distinctive, filled with unnerving questions about who and what he or she is to become. These and many others abound – and despite the supreme confidence of the stars and heroes of our times, seemingly unfettered by any hint of equivocation, the teenager in his or her own private domain is left with few clear answers. There is much that he or she does not know, yet.

The predicament of adolescence is thus not a certain one – growing up 'alone', in transition between the relative order of latency and the limitless breadth of adulthood, frightened by the intensity of incomprehensible feelings and excited yet dismayed by the prospect of 'becoming'. Adolescence in more ways than one is caught in its disconnections and contradictions. The teenger feels curiously detached from all that held him or her together in the past, yet loosely connected with any sense of a future or adult identity. He or she seeks refuge in narcissistic fantasy and sits in wonder about his or her place in the world, waiting to discover something about himself or herself that has yet to happen – something 'that is born or awakened in adolescence that was not generated in childhood' (Frankel 1998: 49).

In the midst of such complexity, it is simply too difficult for adolescents to know for sure about themselves or their intentions, and certainly out of the question for most of the time to answer other people's queries about such matters. Lewis Carroll (Carroll 1965: 49–50) captures sharply the quandary. In 'Advice from a Caterpillar' in *Alice's Adventures in Wonderland*, he lights up a conversation that in essence is not untypical of the discourse of the adolescent and psychotherapist. Alice and the Caterpillar are talking to each other. Both carry the characteristics of each other and both are bewildered and frustrated by each other.

> The Caterpillar and Alice looked at each other for some time in silence: at last, the Caterpillar took the hookah out of his mouth and addressed her in a languid, sleepy voice.
> 'Who are you?' said the Caterpillar.
> This was not an encouraging opening for a conversation. Alice replied, rather shyly, 'I -l hardly know, Sir, just at present – at least I know who I was when I got up this morning, but I think I must have changed several times since then.'
> 'What do you mean by that?' said the Caterpillar, sternly. 'Explain yourself!'
> 'I can't explain myself, I'm afraid, Sir,' said Alice, 'because I'm not myself, you see.'
> 'I don't see,' said the Caterpillar.

'I'm afraid I can't put it more clearly,' Alice replied, very politely, 'for I can't understand it myself, to begin with; and being so many different sizes in a day is very confusing.'

'It isn't,' said the Caterpillar.

'Well, perhaps you haven't found it so yet,' said Alice: 'but when you have to turn into a chrysalis – you will some day, you know – and then after that into a butterfly, I should think you'll feel a little queer, won't you?'

'Not a bit,' said the Caterpillar.

'Well, perhaps your feelings may be different,' said Alice: 'all I know is, it would feel very queer to me.'

'You!' said the Caterpillar contemptuously, 'Who are you?'

Which brought them back again to the beginning of the conversation. Alice felt a little irritated at the Caterpillar's making such very short remarks, and she drew herself up and said, very gravely,

'I think you ought to tell me who *you* are, first.'

'Why?' said the Caterpillar.

In this encounter, Alice, perhaps with the greater precision, 'hardly knows'. The diversity of who she is, the unpredictability and changeableness of it all, are all too much for her – and indeed for the Caterpillar. Her (and his) puzzlement about who she is, her inability to give a clear fixed answer to a question, pervades and overwhelms the conversation. Both her identity and integrity are at stake. Whatever it is that makes up Alice is not settled yet, not ready to be decided upon, what with 'so many sizes in a day'. There is still much left unaccounted for, and no amount of 'explaining yourself' is going to compromise Alice's truthfulness to herself. Saying 'I hardly know' is a hard thing to say – because her knowledge about herself is so elusive, so difficult to grasp. She might as well say to the Caterpillar, 'If I did (hardly) know, there wouldn't be anything left to know about'; or to transpose what she might say to the psychotherapist (Caterpillar), 'If I did know what the problem was, I wouldn't be here to "explain" myself to you in the first place'.

It would of course be misleading to suggest that adolescents 'know nothing'. There is, in fact, much that is going on during adolescence that is forever expanding a body of knowledge of all kinds. Beyond the broader understanding, through education, of the external world, there develops a greater conscious intimacy with the body and a more perceptive awareness of the nuances of family life and friendship. There is a greater cognitive capacity. The attainment of formal operational thought (Piaget 1954) in early adolescence enables the adolescent 'to encompass the awareness of the discrepancy between "the actual and the possible" and to discover that "the actual is wanting"' (Elkind 1968). Within the adolescent's family, the eyes of the adolescent are invariably the most discerning, much to the discomfort of those under observation.

With so much going on, the adolescent's 'I don't know' has an essential purpose – to make clear the state of complexity and to demand not to be rushed. In its simplicity, it says many things. 'I am confused, there is too much to know, so I don't know'. 'I may know but I'm scared to tell what I know'. 'I am not supposed to know so I don't know'. 'If you knew what I know, you wouldn't want to know, so I don't know'. 'I know what I feel, but that's mine – it's not for you to know'. As one adolescent put it most succinctly: 'If I were to share some of my thoughts with someone else, it would be like losing something private... like my thoughts would not be mine anymore'.

Throughout, there is an inherent demand to be given time and freedom from commitment. In this, there is ultimately a fierce insistence, a defiance of those who might trespass on private property and extract premature answers. 'Who are you?' asks Alice, to demand an explanation of the richness of what I am. In the assertion of 'I don't know' is the affirmation and preservation of the nature of the adolescent's own identity, or in Winnicottian terms, of the true self. To say anything otherwise would be a betrayal of what one is, or of what one was at the last count, or of what one might be at the next.

Psychotherapists working with adolescents, however much under external pressures or driven by time imperatives, have to respect the dignity of the adolescent's 'I don't know'. If the adolescent is to be assisted to know enough about him or herself to make more sense to gain greater mastery – rather than to be cajoled or manipulated into rectifying certain pieces of his or her behaviour – then the adolescent and the therapist have to wait. They have to bear the not knowing. In a seminal paper, drawing upon an essay by Camus entitled 'Between Yes and No', E. James Anthony (1975) emphasised the importance of 'an immersion for a short period in an environment of ambiguity and reticence [that] could well facilitate the healing process'. In this paper, he saw the value of an experience 'of suspension of activity, decision or committed views' as therapeutic, essentially guarding against false solutions and defensive acting out. He argued, in particular, for the therapist to exercise 'a negative capability' that Keats (1817/1945) had earlier defined as the capacity to endure ambiguity, doubt and mystery 'without an irritable reaching after fact and reason'. He sought to find an in-between area between the dictates of definite 'yes' and 'no' positions to allow for the adolescent to pursue his own 'maybe' line of enquiry. Other writers, sensitive to this process, have stressed the importance of ensuring space and privacy – careful always not to get caught up in the intensity of the moment or the panic of the crisis. Frankel (1998: 170), for example, describes movingly his approach to helping an adolescent deal with his anger, through giving 'form to the anger, finding out how it is shaped, discovering its rhythm, and sense of timing, and most importantly what it is seeking. This approach fosters the adolescent's ability to bear the tension between repressing anger and discharging it'. The focus here is not so much on 'explanation' as on facilitating through different senses the adolescent's awareness of his knowing.

Anthony commented at one point that 'this method of ambiguity has a valuable corrective function for certain types of therapists who suffer from a morbid condition of wrapping up a case before it has been started and who cannot wait to impart their certainties to the patient'. It is undoubtedly a method or approach that

may help many psychotherapists who, though possibly not so pressing or omniscient as 'the certain types of therapists' that he refers to nevertheless experience, at
times, impatience in the face of the persistence of the adolescent's 'I don't know'.
However talkative and often insightful an adolescent at times may be, his or her
expression of not knowing (however momentary or sustained it may be) may well
at times confound us. It counteracts all of our best legitimate intentions as psychotherapists to explore, open up and understand. It sits there in all of its recalcitrance
to be confronted and interpreted. It may well look like a repression resistance,
or a culmination of obdurate transference to be interpreted and worked through.
Clearly, in all young people there is much that is being kept back and much that is
being transferred (through the transferences) – and all of this needs to be borne in
mind. However, in the psychotherapy of adolescents, it is essential to take heed of
the peculiar nature and purpose of the adolescent 'I don't know'. It is of a different
order and quality to the adult's not knowing. It is something other than a defensive
clinical manifestation. It is much more a developmental assertion of integrity (that
contains its own requirement for privacy). Not knowing in the adolescent is a form
of a necessary being, an essential mode of communication that, for the time being,
can be taken in no other way.

In the following case, an illustration is given of a psychotherapy in 'negative
capability' _ in the midst of a whirlwind of frenetic acting out of an adolescent
who was unable to say, 'I don't know'. The process of psychotherapy essentially
was one that facilitated her to say, 'I don't know', enabling her in turn to think a bit
more about what she had known.

Case illustration

Sarah, a 16-year-old girl, lived a life that was in perpetual chaotic motion, interspersed by times of morose inertia. Her mother was on tenterhooks, wondering
what would happen next. Her brother was furious with her irresponsibility and
her closest friend described her as 'desperate'. Sarah, meanwhile, seemed not to
care. She danced, she raved, she stayed out late at night, she drank, she took drugs.
She flung herself into reckless, wild situations. Her schoolwork deteriorated and
her health became precarious, often undernourished by erratic feeding or overstimulated by drugs unknown. She was in many respects beside herself – and at
times collapsed exhausted in her room, tearful, angry, scratchy – receptive to her
mother's comfort.

Her early childhood had been enjoyable in a secure, intact family. She had
always been an active, lively, tomboyish kind of girl, and though at times tiresome,
she had been much loved. Two major events, however, unsettled her life. When she
was eight her mother contracted cancer, and for two or three years was worryingly
ill, under constant medical supervision. When Sarah was 12, her father died unexpectedly of a heart attack. She is reported to have 'adored' her father, and his death
truly came as a blow. Following his death, she became for a while more subdued

than usual and especially close, at times clinging, to her mother. However, at the age of 13, something 'came over her', almost overnight. She 'snapped' and before anybody could do anything about it she was tearing about everywhere, flinging herself into abandoned and self-destructive behaviour.

She was referred for psychotherapy at a point when her mother felt that she could no longer carry on – and when, indeed, she became ill again. I saw Sarah for a year on a weekly basis. I had regular contact with the mother on the telephone during this time, and was also in contact with the school.

The therapy in the beginning was for the most part a race. Sarah sort of hurtled her way through sessions, full of accounts of new clubs that she had been to, endless boyfriends that she had met and hair-raising incidents that she had put herself through. Unusually, she seemed unconcerned about recounting all of these activities; it was all very much in the open, 'a blast', a boast. For many weeks, I found it impossible to establish any real contact with her, to acknowledge with her what indeed might be a problem. Everyone, including her and me, was at sea and the question grew: where were we all going? Sarah seemed to be in full flight in a world of defiance, in masterly denial. In such illusory command, she 'knew' that she was all right – that the dangers that she underwent were harmless, that the people that she met were trustworthy, that her mother and brother were 'fine'. There was no problem. Her enduring refrain was, 'I know (what I'm doing)'.

It took about four months to reach any kind of point of meeting with her. This happened, by chance, following a break. Her close friend, who had described Sarah as so desperate, wrote me a letter – a brief letter, but one with some urgency, wanting me to know that Sarah had spent the last week at her home crying all the time. Sarah had been unable to say why she was crying and the friend was very frightened that Sarah might kill herself.

With the friend's permission, I shared the letter with Sarah. Although Sarah had told the friend that she hadn't minded her writing to me, when she read the letter with me, she was initially furious, feeling betrayed and misunderstood. She said she didn't know what the friend was on about. She didn't know anything – why she was coming to therapy, what she felt, what she understood. She resented my interest because in effect, like the Caterpillar, she felt that I was asking her to explain herself. Suddenly, she and I entered an unexpected and critical phase in the therapy. Quite unlike before, she presented me with an emphatic volley of 'I don't know's: they greeted me at every turn. My thoughts, my enquiries, my raising of possibilities – it was as if she were drawing a blank or a blanket over everything. After a few weeks, something of the manic pressure of her earlier anecdotes subsided – but what predominated was an apparent refusal to know (what she knew). The therapy entered a state of suspension, a necessary impasse. Sarah did know the fact of her crying, but it was as if she could not bear to know too much about it, to know the depths of what lay behind it. In many respects, her 'I don't know' had all the hallmarks of a repression resistance. However, beyond that, what seemed most largely at stake in her 16th year was her need to keep to herself her knowledge, to both protect her 'ignorance' and to retain a kind of loyalty to her father and to her childhood in her own privacy.

By way of therapeutic duty, I had to pursue what lay beneath this complicated adolescence – and yet, I knew for somewhile that I had to expect little, I had to play with time, I had to wait. It would be no good to chivvy her along and untimely to interpret. Whatever the alarms ringing in the outside world, still Sarah 'hardly' knew. Eventually, however, a passing remark touched a chord. In what was a slightly dismal session in which Sarah complained of nothing ever happening, of her friends no longer caring about her and of them increasingly leaving her, I quietly commented, 'But I am still here. I am not leaving'. Suddenly she was in tears, gasping, unlike ever before in a session – and very much like how her friend had described her in her letter. She couldn't find the words, she felt awful, she didn't know… and yet, as if talking aloud out of a dream, she uttered 'But my dad did'.

In this moment, we seemed at the centre of her grief, beneath the realm of 'I don't know', close to her knowledge that had found its time, as it were, to be known, to be spoken. She recalled wretchedly and in detail her memory of her father's death, her bewilderment and rage, and the gamut of guilt that was confused in it. The session ended as if in a gush – a release of emotion that had been there all along, known yet unknown, that had broken through the preserve of 'I don't know'.

She regained her composure in subsequent sessions. Enough had been made known; there was no need to make things 'more public'. Her thoughts remained her own and she hated to think that I now 'knew all about her' or that what 'I said then, I believe now'. She held on to her own experience and I once more was to be kept at arm's length. She was again in a position of 'I don't know' and this I respected. It was a protection of the privacy of what she knew; she needed time for reflection, uncomplicated by any consideration of transference. Gradually, she allowed herself to share more of her sense of loss, of her playful childhood memories with her mother, father and brother, of her terror of her mother dying and her dread of the future. It was she herself in the end who made the connection between the feverish, blind desperation of her manic behaviour and her thinking that she knew it all. She could see that she had 'found more of myself' through her greater uncertainty and acknowledgement of what 'I didn't know'. As she and I decided to end therapy ('for the time being' as she put it), much of her reckless behaviour diminished, much to her relief as well as her mother's.

Conclusion

Winnicott (1961) introduced the image of the 'doldrums' to describe the state of adolescence. He wrote of:

> a few years in which the individual has no way out except to wait and to do this without awareness of what is going on. In this phase, the child does not know whether he or she is homosexual, heterosexual or narcissistic. There is no established identity and no certain way of life that shapes the future and makes sense of graduating exams. There is not yet the capacity to identify with parent figures without loss of personal identity.

It is in the nature of the adolescent experience that the expression 'I don't know' prevails as an essential communication. However much it may threaten to stultify therapeutic exploration, it is a necessary expression of the complexity of knowing and not knowing and an assertion of the adolescent's integrity and privacy. However mindless, blank and obtuse adolescents may seem when saying once again that they don't know, they are communicating in fact how mindful they are – keeping in mind their profusion of feeling, their identity in flux, their opportunities yet to be explored. It can well be said that the capacity to not know is a crucial ingredient in the culture of adolescent mental health. The converse is a false knowing and, through distorted integration, a greater possibility of acting out.

The case example illustrates a course of psychotherapy that went through different qualities and layers of knowing. It moved from an initial omnipotent 'I know (what I'm doing)', associated with destructive behaviour, to the emergence of a chorus of 'I don't know's, seeking to hide painful memories, yet containing and permitting over time their personal acknowledgement. It was through a process of not knowing that Sarah could hold in mind, in her own time and with dignity, what she felt. Psychotherapy was made possible largely through the therapist's recognition of the nature of knowing and not knowing in the adolescent and through a degree of forbearance and 'negative capability' that allowed room for the next steps to follow. Psychotherapy in this sense is a waiting game – always interesting in anticipation but not always without its boredom. Adam Phillips captures best the spirit of this experience in his essay 'On being bored'. He describes boredom as:

> that state of suspended anticipation in which things are started and nothing begins, the mood of profuse restlessness which contains the most absurd and paradoxical wish, the wish for desire... So, the paradox of the waiting that goes on in boredom is that the individual does not know what he is waiting for until he finds it, and that often he does not know that he is waiting. One could in this sense speak of the analytic attitude as an attentive boredom.
>
> (Phillips 1993: 71)

This is no more so the case than in the psychotherapeutic attitude in work with adolescents. In adolescents, it is in the boredom that the transition of adolescence takes place. It is in the 'I don't know' that the knowing proceeds.

References

Anthony E. J. (1975) 'Between yes and no: the potentially neutral area where the adolescent and his therapist can meet'. In S. C. Feinstein and P. Giovacchini (eds) *Adolescent Psychiatry*, New York: Jason Aronson.

Bollas, C. (1999) *Hysteria*, London: Routledge.

Carroll, L. (1865/1965) *Alice's Adventures in Wonderland*, New York: Random House.

Elkind, D. (1968) 'Cognitive development in adolescents'. In J. F Adams (ed) *Understanding Adolescents*, Boston, MA: Allyn and Bacon.

Frankel, R. (1998) *The Adolescent Psyche*, London: Routledge.

Freud, A. (1958) 'Adolescence'. *The Psychoanalytic Study of the Child* Vol. XIII, New York: International Universities Press. pp. 268–233.

Piaget, J. (1954) *The Construction of Reality in the Child*, New York: Basic Books.

Phillips, A. (ed) (1993) 'On being bored'. In *On Kissing, Tickling and Being Bored*, London:Faber and Faber. pp. 71–82.

Winnicott D. W. (ed.) (1961) 'Adolescence: struggling through the doldrums'. In *The Family and Individual Development*, London: Tavistock Publications. 1965.

Chapter 4

Psychotherapy with adolescents

Previously published in J. Holmes(ed) A Textbook
of Psychotherapy in Psychiatric Practice. London:
Churchill Livingstone (1991).

Introduction

Adolescence is well known as a time of major growth and change. It is by definition transitional: it is 'The Age Between' (Miller 1983) – an unsettled position both
Beyond and yet Not Yet. It is neither one thing nor the other. Childhood has passed;
adulthood, yet to happen. Past certainty, however false, has faded; adult sureness,
however illusory, has yet to be acquired. The adolescent wants to be cared for as a
child and respected as an adult. It is a very indeterminate and contradictory state of
affairs. The adolescent is confused, the adult perplexed. So too the psychotherapist.

Winnicott, in inimitable form, summed up the problem. He introduced the image
of the 'doldrums' to describe the state of adolescence:

> A few years in which the individual has no way out except to wait and to do this
> without awareness of what is going on. In this phase the child does not know
> whether he or she is homosexual, heterosexual or narcissistic. There is no estab-
> lished identity and no certain way of life that shapes the future and makes sense
> of graduating exams. There is not yet a capacity to identify with parent figures
> without loss of personal identity.

> (Winnicott 1961)

Much of the essence of adolescence is captured in this statement – not least its
unclear identity, its curious state of awareness and fear of submission. What is
conveyed is a time of waiting, an inevitable ennui, in which things might or might
not happen. But the notion of the doldrums, oceanic, equatorial, 'where calm and
baffling winds prevail', is apposite. Adolescence is a time of unpredictability. It is
not surprising that Winnicott concludes:

> There is only one cure for adolescence and this is the passage of time and the
> passing on of the adolescent into the adult state.... We hold on, playing for time,
> instead of offering distractions and cures'.

> (Winnicott 1961)

DOI: 10.4324/9781003680437-5

Faced with the weight of this sigh, it is tempting to conclude that adolescents are inherently untreatable, best kept out of sight until adult and recognisable. There is, indeed, little doubt that many psychotherapists steer a wide berth, or at best keep a tight ration of adolescent patients on their caseloads – preferring the greater stability and conformity of the motivated and self-observant adult, or the relatively greater compliance and charm of the younger child. In brief, neither the child nor the adult, regardless of individual idiosyncrasy, presents such ambiguity or ambivalence as does the adolescent.

It is, nevertheless, clear that adolescence is a critical phase of development, in which fundamental solutions are found and decisions made affecting the future life of the individual. It is a unique period of life, in which childhood experience is reawakened in an especially powerful way by the impact of puberty. 'The individual recapitulates and expands in the second decennium of life, the development he passed through during the first five years' (Jones 1922). The possibility arises in adolescence of reviewing and rearranging past experience in the light of present and future requirements. By virtue of being a time of change and reformulation, adolescence is a potentially optimal time for intervention.

It is also a time of considerable energy and remarkable cognitive development. This may not necessarily lead to clarity of understanding or vision, but it nevertheless augments the adolescent's inherent curiosity and fascination in himself and others. Most adolescents spend hours in private preoccupation – about their bodies, families, friendships, achievements and fantasies. All of this is new and intense, frequently bewildering and potentially overwhelming. Most cope well enough by themselves with their friends. Others, however warily and uncertainly, need and seek adult help.

Thus, despite forebodings and undoubted difficulties, there is much in the maturing adolescent – in terms of capacity and motivation – that can be brought into the service of making good use of psychotherapy.

Adolescent development and disturbance

Adolescent development

Adolescence is fundamentally concerned with the negotiation of two specific developmental tasks. The first has to do with adjusting to the impact of puberty and the changing body (Laufer 1968). This is primary, and involves the adolescent's preoccupation with questions of control, adequacy, mutuality in relationships and sexual orientation. The second concerns the problem of separation and individuation (Blos 1967) – the adolescent struggling to differentiate himself from those upon whom he has implicitly depended as a child, and to establish a degree of autonomy and self-resource, sufficient to accept the dependence of others as an adult. The two tasks are interrelated, each essentially referring to the growing capacity and readiness of the individual to take responsibility for his body and self.

There is undoubted excitement in this development. And yet always there is the prospect of failure, the fear of the unknown, the peril of disintegration and loss of control. Throughout, there is an essential narcissistic concern with coherence, identity and value. Much depends on the extent to which the adolescent can keep hold of a realistic and positive sense of himself, and achieve a degree of self-assurance and integration of the disparate parts of his personality.

The fears of adolescence and the confusions that surround them cannot be minimised. There is, above all, a brooding sense of increasing unbridled power and of limitless destructive possibility. There is also increasing disquiet in the shifting relationships within the family. Childhood assumptions of care and protection no longer stand so firm. The adolescent perceives his parents in new and more critical ways and becomes more acutely aware that he is on his own. The internal and external demand for self-reliance, though exhilarating, is daunting. Friends and groups clearly play a crucial part – but again there is here no certain comfort or panacea. Issues of identity, of sexuality and intimacy and of belonging become highlighted in this group context. The adolescent may well be part of the group, but frequently, he feels very different, oddly exceptional and uncomfortably isolated. The adolescent thus lives in an internal world of considerable apprehension, with major questions about whether he will ever 'make it' in the broadest sense of the term. There can be no immediate solutions, and the adolescent is left in limbo, as it were, awaiting adulthood for the answers. Adolescence is, in more ways than one, the 'meantime'.

It can be of little surprise that, in response to so much anxiety and uncertainty, there should be a significant force within the adolescent to retreat in behaviour and fantasy to the actual or illusory comforts of childhood. There are few adolescents who do not yearn at times to be Peter Pan. Indeed, it is this regressive pull back, counterpointing so dramatically with its opposite, that accounts for much of the exasperating inconsistency and variable maturity of so many adolescents.

The capacity and freedom to regress is clearly an essential part of growth – to replenish and draw on past experience in order to move forward. At the same time, regression can also draw the adolescent towards the sheer rawness of childhood experience, and effectively undermine his striving for control and coherence. However benign or favourable childhood once was, the revival of intense infantile feelings – of greed, rage, possessiveness, fears of annihilation, of loss of love and approval – can be very disturbing. This regressive force, though necessary in the process of integration, also threatens the capacity to integrate. The more vulnerable adolescent is caught in a quite desperate tangle – both wanting to escape from the demands of growing up, and yet terrified, excited and confused by the return of childhood experience.

Clearly, these internal developmental issues take place in the context of the 'adolescent family' (Berkowitz 1979; Shapiro 1978). Current and past parental attitudes and family dynamics are crucial to the facilitation of the adolescent's development. Adolescents carry within them, from childhood, parental values and expectations and, in addition, face ongoing parental responses to their growing autonomy. The ease with which the adolescent can achieve separation and individuation depends on the parents' ability to relinquish their implicit parental control and revise their assumptions and requirements of their child as a growing adult. As the adolescent increasingly differentiates himself, so the parents have to face difficult feelings of loss, disappointment and envy. They also have to confront their own sexuality and marriage, as their children develop adult bodies and enter into sexual relationships.

The 'adolescent family' is notoriously in a state of turbulence, and it is not surprising that, in many families, tolerance of the adolescent's curious and variable state, with its inevitable secrecy, rebellion and ingratitude, is severely strained. In the more vulnerable family, the adolescent may well find his moves towards independence restricted and opposed or construed as proof of his badness with convenient grounds for scapegoating. Optimally, an adolescent needs relative stability around him in order to find his own bearings; families and parents who are immersed in their own disturbance do little to foster healthy adolescent development.

Adolescent disturbance

Given that there is inevitable anxiety and inherent vulnerability in the state of adolescence itself, the question is often raised as to what can be considered 'normal' and 'disturbed' development. Most adolescents, after all, are likely to act at various times in impulsive, shocking, even dangerous ways. There can be no conventional pathway to adulthood. In appreciation of this, Anna Freud wrote:

> In general, the adolescent upset and its manifestations are not predictable... Adolescence by definition is an interruption of peaceful growth. The adolescent manifestations come close to symptom formation of the neurotic, the psychotic or dissocial order and verge almost imperceptibly into borderline states and initial, frustrated or fully fledged forms of almost all mental illness.
>
> (Freud 1958)

There is an undoubted difficulty in gauging what is within the range of normality and what falls within the category of established disturbance. At what point, for example, does adolescent risk-taking and recklessness (for example, staying out late, in dubious company, where delinquent activity and drug-taking are prevalent) become a significant manifestation of pathological self-destructiveness?

There are no precise guidelines. Perhaps the most distinguishing mark of adolescent disturbance, however, is the element of compulsivity – that is, where adolescents are engaged persistently and repeatedly, as if driven from within, in extreme forms of self-destructive behaviour, often against their better judgement. These are adolescents who have fundamentally failed adequately to negotiate the developmental tasks. They are unable to draw stimulus from the tensions of their life, and cannot find ways of mastering anxiety in the service of creativity. Their development is essentially restricted by internal preoccupations and conflict, and by lack of family support and encouragement. They are overwhelmed by demands made upon them, both internally and externally. They are especially frightened of being alone, and have limited capacity to tolerate depression. Equally, in relationships,

they are frightened of losing their precarious sense of identity or of being dominated, humiliated or rendered useless. They find relationships confusing and have
difficulty in tolerating their disappointments and the frustration of their need for
closeness. The power of their emotions, of their aggressive and sexual feelings and
desires is particularly terrifying to them.

These young people have invariably experienced various extreme forms of
trauma and deprivation in their childhood. They have not grown up in an atmosphere of order and cohesion, and have frequently been overlooked or abused. It is
not surprising that they lack any sure internal sense of structure or of organisation.
By virtue of their past environmental circumstances, they have not been equipped
with the means of controlling impulse, testing reality or developing any sense of
value in themselves or in others. They are especially vulnerable to the anxiety
engendered in adolescence by the revival of past disturbing childhood experiences.

The disturbance in these adolescents can be understood in terms of *unmanage-
able anxiety, poor ego capacity* and *inadequate defensive responses*. Much of their
behaviour and symptomatology can be seen as a kind of panic reaction, a blind
defensive flinch to avoid feeling left, forgotten or attacked. Their delinquency is
often an attempt to avoid the experience of loss or emptiness by grabbing supplies
felt to have been withheld. It can also represent an attempt to avert fears of submission or helplessness by exerting false dominance over others. Their self-harming
is frequently a desperate measure to avoid mental anguish by substituting physical
pain. Their promiscuity is not uncommonly a way of pre-empting abandonment,
through seductive control and active leaving.

Other adolescents, with less severe but nevertheless disturbing experiences in
their background, may respond to the complexities of relationships and emerging
independence by retreating into social isolation (often retaining firm but ambivalent
links to their parents), in an insulated dream world or in obsessive bodily preoccupation. The anorexic girl is clearly in hiding from the sensations and implications of
her growing sexual body. The under-achieving, drug-abusing boy is often in retreat
from the power of his destructive and sexual fantasies and the feared consequences
of his triumphs or successes. In many of these cases, the picture is not so much of
limited ego capacity to control impulse, as of excessive conscience and omnipotent
ideals. These necessarily derive from severe standards, prohibitions and pressures
to achieve, internalised in childhood. They continue to exert impossible demands
in adolescence, leaving the young person unable to tolerate imperfection of any
sort and thus unable to play, make mistakes or enjoy ordinary relationships.

Psychoanalytic psychotherapy with adolescents

Whether or not psychoanalysis is to be recommended for adolescents is a debat-
able issue. Certainly, there is much in the nature and complexity of adolescent disturbance that requires firm containment and detailed attention and understanding.
There are many psychoanalysts who believe that only through the re-experiencing

of earlier trauma in the transference can there be any true possibility of enabling the adolescent to achieve a satisfactory degree of integration. The Laufers (1989), for example, forcefully argue for the necessity of psychoanalysis as a treatment of choice for certain severely disturbed adolescents who have undergone an adolescent breakdown: 'Not to undertake psychoanalytic treatment of such vulnerable adolescents is a chance lost and... would leave them open to more severe and crippling pathology in early adulthood'.

Such intensive psychoanalytic treatment, however, should not be undertaken without very careful consideration of the capacities of adolescents to make use of it and the abilities of psychoanalysts to conduct it. For such treatment to be effective, it requires above all the commitment and experience of trained psychoanalysts. These, of course, are in short supply and, in the ordinary course of events in ordinary psychiatric settings, psychoanalysis is not practicable and should not be attempted. There is also the question of whether or not psychoanalysis is in any case, suitable. Many adolescents are unready to make such a major commitment, and are frightened by the intensity of the psychoanalytic relationship. The psychoanalytic re-awakening of the past fits, as it were, too closely to the adolescent's internal processes of recapitulation of the past. The adolescent is wary of his precarious controls and bids for independence being undermined. The very containment and continuity that psychoanalysis fundamentally provides may in fact be counterproductive – its embrace only serving to consolidate and prolong dependency, in substitution for the parental relationship, at a time when progressive processes of detachment need to be under way.

There is undoubtedly considerable tension inherent in the relationship between the psychoanalytic pursuit and the spirit of adolescence and its disturbance. The challenge of psychotherapy with adolescents is to find ways, at any given time, of resolving this tension (Wilson 1986).

Of critical issue in the psychoanalytic psychotherapy of adolescents is the interest and preparedness of the psychotherapist to adapt technique and expectations to the particular developmental state of affairs that characterises this period of life. At a practical level, this invariably means offering a less intensive psychotherapeutic experience – usually once or twice weekly. It also involves a certain realism on the part of the psychotherapist with regard to the aims of psychotherapy. Young people seek help because they are unable to work, study or form or sustain satisfying relationships. Others are troubled because they are caught in some obsessive-compulsive preoccupation or activity. They are fundamentally seeking symptomatic relief, and it is important in the psychotherapy of adolescents to hold this as a legitimate aim – not simply to relieve immediate difficulties and distress, but more substantially to enable young people to get back onto the path of normal development, so that, for example, they can actually begin to enjoy study or find that they can hold a job down or that they have found the courage to join a group. At a more urgent level, the aim of therapy may be to help and support a young person through a crisis, and prevent or forestall extreme behaviour that could disrupt family life or endanger their own lives.

In approaching the adolescent, the psychotherapist has to be prepared to encounter certain resistances that are specific to adolescence and derive essentially from the adolescent's immaturity and conflict in relation to his dependency. Clearly there are differences according to the age and developmental level of individual adolescents (Wilson and Hersov 1985). Older adolescents, by virtue of their greater independence and more developed capacity for self-observation, tend to show a greater readiness to make use of psychotherapy than do young adolescents. The characteristics that apply in early adolescence, however, pervade most of the adolescent period in varying degrees. What is at issue is a developmental, rather than an individual or pathological, problem. This concerns both the adolescent's attitude to, and capacity to make use of, psychotherapy.

Anna Freud (1958) has succinctly clarified the nature of the adolescent's resistance to psychotherapy, in terms of characteristic defences against dependency on his parents. In his struggle to detach and separate from his parents, the adolescent turns his investment and energy towards activities and people outside the home. He withdraws within himself, away from his parents; additionally, he reverses affect, turning loving childhood passive feelings into their opposites – the essence of rebellion. In psychotherapy, the psychotherapist is experienced in one way or another as a parent, and the same defences are redeployed. The adolescent, in order to avoid being dominated by the therapist/parent averts his gaze and keeps on guard against the psychotherapist's concern and potential control.

The adolescent, in short, is mistrustful of adults – he is suspicious that they will take over or control or misunderstand. He has a need to keep himself to himself. Privacy is essential, and the keeping of secrets often vital. Telling the truth is not always possible. The adolescent needs his own time to experience and find out things – and he has to do things which adults and parents would ordain not good for him.

It is crucial that the psychotherapist appreciates this state of affairs – and does not punish or fight against it. It is essential, too, that the psychotherapist gives the adolescent time and space to encounter and secure his own impressions and experience before being expected to give an account of them publicly. Many of these experiences and feelings are baffling to the adolescent, difficult to articulate and in many respects embarrassing and frightening. Some concern sexual and bodily preoccupations, and are couched in shame, guilt and uncertainty. Some involve ideas and fantasies that are unexpectedly intense, frightening and best not mentioned. Others concern observations and impressions of family and parental life which the adolescent may feel unable, out of loyalty, to disclose outside the family.

The psychotherapist thus needs to be sensitive to and respectful of the adolescent's caution in approaching psychotherapy. He needs, too, to be tolerant of the adolescent's difficulty in making use of help. The adolescent's capacity for self-observation is relatively limited, still in the process of formation. Young adolescents in particular have difficulty in containing anxiety, and are more prone to relieve tension through action rather than thought. Their excitement is in the doing of things in the here and now, rather than in reflection. Moreover, their typical defences tend to be more rigid and concrete than in the older adolescent. They are inclined to dissociate themselves from their mental distress, and project and put responsibility elsewhere. And, of course, often they simply do not have the words to formulate or express what is on their minds.

Therapeutic setting

The primary task of a psychotherapist is to ensure conditions of work that facilitate communication, and enable both psychotherapist and patient to observe and think about what is happening within and between them.

The concept of a therapeutic setting refers to everything that forms the background in which psychotherapy takes place. At a basic level, it refers to the actual place and physical surroundings. In terms of procedure, it is built on an agreed set of ground rules. Particularly with children and adolescents, it exists in the context of the family. Ultimately, it is determined by the presence of the psychotherapist – his orientation and personal style and, in relation to the adolescent, his specific countertransference and general attitude.

Place

The importance of providing a place which is pleasant and comfortable, and which ensures privacy and safety cannot be emphasised enough. Such a provision serves as a fundamental communication – far better than any words can convey – to the adolescent that he is worthwhile and to be respected. This is frequently overlooked, especially in services for adolescents, who are mistakenly seen as bejeaned and dishevelled and not warranting such attention to detail. It is important, too, that the waiting room is welcoming and not bare and that receptionists are friendly, without being intrusive. Care should also be given to the size and arrangement of the therapy rooms. They should not be too large or imposing, nor too small and enclosing, and where possible, they should not be cluttered with desk top paraphernalia or diverting pictures (such as of the psychotherapist's family). Where psychotherapy takes place in institutions or in hospital wards, care should be taken to locate psychotherapy rooms separate from the everyday hurly-burly and sufficiently distant not to excite curiosity or envy from other patients.

Ground rules

The ground rules laid down by the psychotherapist in the beginning sessions set the tone and define the boundaries of the therapeutic setting. Adolescents, at first, are often not at all sure what they are doing with a psychotherapist, and even less clear what is expected of them. Hill puts this quite directly: 'It is only too easy to assume that the adolescent understands the ground rules... that he is supposed to volunteer suitable information, refrain from prying into the psychotherapist's private life and recognise this sort of confidential conversation as treatment' (Hill 1989).

It is important, therefore, that the psychotherapist is as straightforward as possible about what he understands of the adolescent's problem, and how he thinks psychotherapy can be of help. This, of course, is not always possible to convey nor easy for the adolescent to hear in the inevitable tension and confusion of early meetings. Nevertheless, the psychotherapist should endeavour to make a statement, at some point during the course of the first session or so, that registers something of his or her position and understanding.

Case study: Jim, a 17-year-old boy – the chance to talk

The following statement includes some of the major points that need to be covered. This was made towards the end of the first session with a 17-year-old boy who had been urged by his mother to see someone in an outpatient setting. For illustration purposes, this statement is written as if given without interruption. This, of course, was not the case in actuality.

What I understand so far is that you have been feeling miserable for some time. You are bored at school and, although you say that exams don't matter, you think you are a failure and you're feeling hopeless about the future. You tell me you feel bad about your mother – because you have let her down. In fact, you are here because of her. She wanted you to get some help and she fixed it here with me. I wonder what you think about that. Not much, maybe. I think you think it is all a bit pointless and you cannot see what on earth I can do for you.

Well, right now, nor do I. I hardly know you. My guess is that you are feeling that you are not worth much and that you are frightened of what is going to happen to you. I also think you're very dissatisfied and angry about something. If I am to be of any help, I am going to need some more time to get to know you. And you are going to have to decide whether you think it's worth coming here.

I would like to help you – but you have to know now that I have no magic.

I have no tricks or quick cures. The best I can do is to offer you the chance to talk over what's on your mind; about what is happening and has happened in your life. It would be good too, to find out what you want to do. At the moment it's all a bit of a mystery. We may be able to make some sense of it and you may begin to feel you can do things differently or do some things that you want to do that you think you cannot do. A lot is up to you – whether you really want to change anything. You cannot possibly know right now how talking can help – you will just have to give it a try.

I should also say that what we talk about here is private and confidential.

There is no reason why you should believe that – it's a matter of trust. All I can say is that I shall not talk or communicate with anybody about you without your consent. Similarly, if I hear about you from other people, I shall do my best to let you know what I know. This is the only way we can work.

Having said that, I have to tell you that your mother did in fact telephone me before the session. She wanted me to know that you are taking a lot of drugs. She also said you are not getting up until the middle of the afternoon. You are miss-ing a lot of school and you treat her like a doormat. She said she cannot make you out anymore and you are throwing your life away. It sounded as if you are driving her crazy.

You haven't said much about all that so far today. I suppose you'd prefer not to think about it. The only reason I've raised it is because it was what your mother told me – you need to know what I know. She has quite a lot to say, doesn't she? It sounds as if she could do with some help – but my job is not to be her right-hand man. I am here for you. But let me say just one thing about what I think, before we go any further. It may be that your mother has got it all wrong about the drugs – but if there is any truth to what she says, then I have just four words 'Drugs are Bad News'. I cannot stop you taking them. I won't be your nanny but I can tell you straight to cut them out. They are not going to help you or me to help you.

I suggest that we meet for another six sessions until Easter – each week for an hour each time. We can see at the end of that time where we have got to. It may be that you will think enough has been done by that time. Or it may be that you will want to carry on and find out more about yourself – in which case we can arrange that. So, see you next week.'

A statement such as this contains a number of important messages. It puts into words what the psychotherapist understands of the adolescent's problem and of the anxiety that lies behind it. It clarifies the reason for meeting, the concern of the mother and the role of the psychotherapist. It emphasises the importance of talking and of trust, and pays respect to the adolescent's independence. The statement also indicates a readiness to help but not a promise of cure; it conveys a sense of authority and expectation but not of excessive omnipotence. Finally, it conveys with some force the psychotherapist's concern (hence the unequivocal statement on drugs) – but also leaves open whether or not the adolescent chooses to commit himself to change and to psychotherapy.

One aspect that is not included in this statement concerns the behaviour of the adolescent in therapy sessions. Clearly, standards of acceptable behaviour will vary from one psychotherapist to another and in different settings. An adolescent unit or a therapeutic community may be prepared to allow more aggressive behaviour than can an individual psychotherapist in an outpatient setting. In individual psychotherapy, it is essential that the psychotherapist is clear within himself what he can and cannot tolerate. In one way or another, it is important to convey to the adolescent that there are limits to what is permissible – for example, that the patient is not to damage property or to attack the psychotherapist. Laying down these ground rules is often difficult in initial meetings without arousing unnecessary alarm or seeming overly combative. With the majority of adolescents, this is not necessary. However, there are some adolescents whom the psychotherapist may believe to have poor impulse control or be unclear about boundaries, in which case, it is important that he be explicit from the outset.

Finally, it is important that the psychotherapist expects the adolescent to attend sessions punctually and regularly. The psychotherapist, paradoxically, may well anticipate that the adolescent will forget or miss sessions or be late – but he should never expect it. He should let the adolescent know that he cares about this boundary of time as much as any other, and be as clear and unequivocal about the time of ending sessions as of beginning them.

The family

Psychotherapy with adolescents always takes place in the context of the adolescent's relationship to his parents or caretakers. It is important that consideration is given to how and where the parents are placed in relationship to the adolescent's psychotherapy. With older adolescents, this is generally not a major issue since, by and large, they seek and receive psychotherapy in their own right. With younger patients, however, who are more dependent on their parents, the position is quite different. In most cases, parental consent to and sanction of psychotherapy for their children is necessary. Without this, there is little hope of success – the parents effectively sabotaging the adolescent's attendance and the adolescent feeling unable to make a commitment out of loyalty to his parents.

In principle, where there are parents who feel responsible or concerned, they should be seen by the psychotherapist at some point in the initial stages of psychotherapy. This may include parents of older adolescents if they have been influential in one way or another in persuading the adolescent to seek help. Some adolescents, of course, are suspicious of the psychotherapist's contact with their parents, and feel that their own space and privacy are being invaded. Older adolescents may not agree to any such contact, and this simply has to be respected. Others, however, particularly younger adolescents, often feel reassured that their parents and psychotherapist are in contact with each other – relieved that the psychotherapist has bothered to see their parents and that there is a sense of shared concern around them. Whereas there is some danger of the parents exerting pressure on the psychotherapist to exact compliance from the adolescent to meet their requirements, there is general overall advantage in having the opportunity to assess the adolescent in the context of his family and, indeed, to have actual sight of the parents and vice versa.

In general, with young adolescents, it is most useful in the first instance to see them together with their parents or families, and then, if need be, to move onto individual psychotherapy. The parents may subsequently be seen periodically for review or in the event of crisis. If they have significant problems in their own right, they should be referred for help elsewhere. With older adolescents, it is more advisable to insist on offering the adolescent individual interviews in the first instance, to be followed, if necessary, with interviews with the parents – either together with or separately from the adolescent, according to the adolescent's preference.

The older adolescent is more concerned to establish his own separateness and individuality, and it is generally inadvisable for the psychotherapist to have ongoing contact with the parents. Clearly, again, if the parents are very concerned about developments, or in the event of a crisis, it should be agreed that they have some right of access to the psychotherapist.

Confidentiality is inevitably a major issue in these various arrangements with parents and family. Clearly, the basic principle of confidentiality should be upheld, and parents encouraged to respect their adolescent's privacy in psychotherapy. Where confidentiality is likely to be threatened – for example, arising out of parental discussions, telephone calls – the psychotherapist can do no more than try to be as open as possible with the adolescent about what has been said. It is often helpful, where the psychotherapist has arranged to meet the parents during the course of the therapy, to ask the adolescent what he would like and not like to have discussed. The adolescent ultimately has to trust that the psychotherapist will honour the agreement that has been made.

There may arise situations in which the psychotherapist judges it necessary to inform parents and others who are responsible for the adolescent, of the adolescent's intentions, for example, to commit suicide. The therapist may have to act in this way without the adolescent's consent – but always with his or her knowledge (Wilson 1986).

The psychotherapist

Ultimately, the general tone and atmosphere of the therapeutic setting will be determined by the personality and style of the psychotherapist – for it is he who provides the place, lays out the ground rules and makes the arrangements with the parents. The question of who the psychotherapist is and what he or she brings to the situation is crucial.

In general, it is to be hoped that the psychotherapist is someone who carries within him or her a level of personal authority and integrity that enables him to deal with anxiety and confusion without losing control or the ability to listen. Similarly, it is to be hoped that the psychotherapist brings to the therapeutic situation a high degree of self-awareness and a reasonably coherent conceptual framework that can serve to regulate and structure his or her feelings, perceptions and thoughts – in the interest of offering some clarity to the patient.

These general characteristics are essential to all psychotherapists, but perhaps more so in relationship to adolescents who, above all else, need to have a sense of being contained within clear boundaries and who are quick to sense weakness, prevarication and dishonesty in others.

A very basic requirement of any psychotherapist is the capacity and readiness to be receptive. In practical terms, this simply means that the psychotherapist ensures that he has time and space to see and hear his patients – that he can ensure regular times of meeting and that he can be present in the session without undue preoccupation elsewhere or intrusions of telephones or bleeps. In emotional terms, it means a relative freedom from intrusive irrational feelings and prejudices. In relation to the adolescent, it is important that the psychotherapist is alert to the influence of his countertransference, as well as positive in his attitude towards young people in general.

Countertransference

Countertransference refers to the wide range of irrational feelings and thoughts, expectations and attitudes that are evoked, largely unconsciously, in the psychotherapist in response to the presence of the patient (Moehler 1977; Money-Kyrle

1956). Continuous situations arise in psychotherapy in which the psychotherapist feels at different times helpless, stupid, powerful, persecuted, humiliated, rejected, desired, seduced, punitive and so on. These feelings may well mirror the way in which the patient has felt as a child and/or how he has experienced his parents.

The psychotherapist is thus forced back into areas of his own personal vulnerability. The danger arises of the psychotherapist, by force of the patient's transference, being drawn into ways of reacting that are excessive and unhelpful to the therapeutic needs of the patient. Thus, the past can all too easily repeat itself in the therapeutic situation, to no avail and without understanding. The therapist finds himself reacting, in effect, in the same way as the parents – and the possibility of reflection and of change is lost. All that happens, in accordance with the dictates of transference, is further repetition.

Countertransference can present more of a major problem in the psychotherapy of adolescents than in that of children or adults. Adolescents' emotions are often very powerful and poorly defended against. Moreover, they bring into the therapeutic situation experiences and attitudes revived and re-enacted both from the past and from current family relationships. If the therapist is to be open to the disturbance within the adolescent, it is inevitable that he will feel the pressure of many of these confusing feelings. What is crucial is that this is monitored and not blindly acted upon. In so many subtle and indirect ways, countertransference reactions can disturb the sense of stability and of continuity that is the foundation of the therapeutic setting, which is so important to the adolescent patient. Interpretations can easily be made, for example, not so much to improve understanding as to control or excite or punish the adolescent patient.

It is essential that adequate supervision and/or consultation is provided as part of the overall therapeutic setting – to help the psychotherapist clarify, amongst other things, what feelings belong to the adolescent and what belong to him as an individual.

Attitude to adolescents

Beyond the specific feelings of the psychotherapist's countertransference to an individual adolescent, there reside in all psychotherapists certain fundamental attitudes towards the state of adolescence itself. These relate to the psychotherapist's own experiences of adolescence and to his current predicament as an adult.

Psychotherapists have all, of course, been through their own adolescence. Some have been rebellious, others compliant. Some have experienced breakdown; others have enjoyed success. Some remember their adolescence with anguish and hostility towards their parents and authority, whilst others look back with affection and a sense of fun and achievement. As a result, some psychotherapists are excited by the lives of their adolescent patients, and tend to be permissive in their judgements. Others look upon their adolescent patients with alarm and envy, and are inclined to control or even rebuke them in their quest for independence. These feelings are additionally compounded by others related to the psychotherapist's current life as an adult; for example, they may be burdened with family responsibilities, and so resent the adolescent's greater freedom and irresponsibility.

These diverse elements shape the psychotherapist's attitude towards young people in general, and influence his approach to the uniquely transitional and tentative state of the adolescent patient. If left unacknowledged and uncontained, they can easily impede the psychotherapist's capacity to tolerate the adolescent's unpredictability with patience, sympathy and forbearing. Above all, the psychotherapist has to be sensitive enough to appreciate the adolescent's equivocal relationship to dependency, and to hold the balance between respecting the adult and caring for the child in the adolescent. The psychotherapist has, on the one hand, to trust the adolescent's pursuit of independence, allowing space for the adolescent to find his own way and make his own mistakes; on the other hand, the psychotherapist has to be alert to adolescent's self-destructive and impulsive tendencies, and be ready to intervene, keep on asking questions and to set boundaries when needed.

The psychotherapist's task is difficult and fundamentally relies upon his enjoyment and respect of the adolescent state. Without this, he will be unable to be sufficiently flexible or adaptive to make sense of the inherent contradictions in his adolescent patient.

The working alliance

The most difficult task of all in the psychotherapy of adolescents is to establish a working alliance. Much of the art and skill of the psychotherapist resides in the process of forging, often against the odds, a relationship in which the adolescent becomes interested both in understanding his or her difficulties and in the possibility of change, and in which a spirit of cooperation and enquiry prevails. Many adolescents, despite the potential to be helped, are lost through a failure on the part of the psychotherapist to establish such an alliance – whether it be because of the psychotherapist's inept introductions, inappropriate expectations or sheer inability to understand and respect the adolescent's inherent equivocation. The adolescent usually enters into therapy in a confused and ambivalent state. He is mistrustful, frightened and frequently in resistance to those who have suggested he come to therapy in the first place. There is much that he wants to keep to himself. He knows that he is troubled and that there is something wrong, but he prefers to disown his problem and put blame elsewhere. At the same time, he is curious about himself and about the possibility of help. There is often an overwhelming wish to be understood and to find someone who can magically offer salvation or certitude. There is in most adolescents a readiness for new experience and possibility.

The overriding initial therapeutic task is for the psychotherapist to appreciate this ambivalence, and to find ways of exciting the young person's curiosity about himself and of engaging with that part of the adolescent that is worried about his normality or adequacy. The extent to which this can be achieved depends as much on the attitude of the psychotherapist as on any particular technique or procedure. There is usually a certain element of urgency in the beginning sessions of psychotherapy with an adolescent, for the adolescent is half ready to leave unless reassured by the psychotherapist's manner and level of understanding. The adolescent needs to feel that the psychotherapist is taking him seriously and can grasp the gist of what is worrying him, without knowing too much about him or trying to take him over.

The psychotherapist has to adopt an essentially paradoxical position – conveying, as it were, both interest and disinterest. On the one hand, the psychotherapist needs to be active and positive in expressing concern about the adolescent – inviting dialogue and conversation, and generally trying to capture the adolescent's imagination. On the other hand, he has to be careful not to be too forceful – he must hold back, keep things open and not press the adolescent for commitment. Miller (1983) has argued that, with certain adolescents, it is sometimes necessary to take on a certain larger-than-life, omnipotent manner – answering their request for somebody to take command and prevent them from engaging in further self-destructive behaviour, such as suicide or different forms of delinquency, that could preclude any further help. It is clear, however, that the adolescent also needs to be reminded that the psychotherapist is not omnipotent and cannot bring about magical change, for such an approach inevitably brings its own disenchantments and arouses intolerable anxieties of domination. The opposite position is well described by Anthony (1975) who suggests a 'preparatory course of inaction' in the early phases of treatment, in which the psychotherapist exercises a 'negative capability' to allow for the adolescent's ambiguities before any therapeutic commitment is decided.

The psychotherapist has to live with the paradox that the adolescent wants and does not want to be treated as a child; that he wants and does not want to have his problems taken care of. The psychotherapist in turn finds himself having to be both active and omnipotent, and laid back and laissez faire. The unifying factor has to reside in the psychotherapist's tolerance of the essentially contradictory nature of the adolescent. The psychotherapist holds the opposites, and thereby prevents psychotherapy ending prematurely, either because the adolescent is unimpressed or bored, or because he is overwhelmed and frightened.

In the example that follows, an account is given of the fifth session with the 17-year-old adolescent introduced earlier. In this session, the adolescent and therapist were still occupied in forming some kind of working alliance. It was all very much at a delicate and uncertain stage. He was clearly drawn by the prospect of the therapist's interest and attention, and yet he was frightened and resistant. Much of how he behaved in the session was typical of adolescent resistance, but clearly, it also reflected significant transference currents to do with his fear of humiliation and rejection. The account gives some indication of the therapist's attempt to play both lightly and seriously with the adolescent's assertion of independence, whilst at the same time engaging with the part of him that was lost and very troubled by the intensity and confusion of his feelings. The therapist was all the time trying – both explicitly and through his attitude and behaviour – to convey what psychotherapy was and could be about.

Case study: Jim, age 17 (continued): 'I don't talk about problems to anyone'

In this session, the main question was whether or not Jim could be bothered with psychotherapy. After all, he maintained, there was little wrong with him. There was nothing unusual in being miserable – everyone was. As for school, well, exams were irrelevant. There was no point in learning all that stuff – the teachers could not teach and what they did was boring. He could learn better by himself. He had better things to do.

The therapist said he was glad about that. What were they? At first, Jim said he had not come here to talk about 'pleasure'. The therapist said they could talk about anything that mattered to him. He then talked at length about his fascination with radio, hi-fi and TV. He spent hours working on them. He reckoned that within a year or so, he would have built a completely new and unique system. He would then market this and become rich.

The therapist listened, showed interest and asked questions. For a while Jim was animated. He enjoyed impressing me. The therapist said he had an image of a kind of super DJ – Jim at the top, super controls and flashing lights, turning the world in and on. He was amazed. How did I know? That was exactly it. He already did a few gigs. It was great. He felt like a king; they would get better and better.

Suddenly, he said that the therapist was taking the piss. 'You probably like Mozart and opera and all that junk. You're a phoney – just egging me on. You don't care at all – you just say all this because you're paid'. The therapist said, 'Pow – what's all that about? One minute we're talking about what interests you, the next minute you are more or less kicking me out'. For a while he went on about how all 'you psychiatrists' are all alike – clever, devious, just in it for themselves. And anyway, talking was a waste of time. 'I don't talk about problems to anybody – I'm not giving my secrets away. I have all the understanding I need, thank you very much'.

The therapist said that right now he felt at the end or a very strong radio transmission that was saying loud and clear 'Keep Off', to put it mildly. If that is what he really meant, then of course he would. He was not there to frog march him into anything. If what he was telling him was that he really believed that he had no particular problem, that he was fully occupied and that he understood enough of what he needed to know then clearly there was no point in being there at all. Jim said the only reason he was there was to keep his mother quiet. The therapist asked whether she was quiet, and he said he did not know, he did not care. 'If you don't care, why are you bothering to keep her quiet?' He laughed and said: 'Because I can't stop her nagging – she's always putting her big nose in my business. She's always barging into my room. Why doesn't she keep out? She doesn't care anyway. Whatever I do she puts it down. And anyway, she's out half the time with her bloke. I hate her – she's a whore'.

He was suddenly close to tears and for a moment looked furious at the therapist. They sat in silence. The therapist said he knew there was a bit of Jim that would rather not be there. But at the same time, he knew things were not right and he was telling him. He was not upset for nothing – clearly there was a lot that was difficult in his relationship with his mother and no doubt he had a lot of feeling about her bloke – not to mention his father. The gist of it all, the therapist said, seems to be that Jim felt badly let down – by his parents, by adults, by psychiatrists. Nobody can be depended on. No wonder, he said, he was giving him the business earlier on – no way would he trust him yet.

Jim listened but appeared not to be immediately receptive. He reasserted that he knew the therapist didn't care. 'Nobody does'. There was no point in talking about it: 'There is nothing to talk about'. He insisted that he was quite able to take care of himself. The therapist said that no doubt he was right – at 17 he was going to have to take more care of himself. Maybe he didn't like that – it could leave him feeling very alone. He immediately assured the therapist that he liked his own company best; he didn't need anyone else – anyway he had his radios and hi-fi. He was quick then to warn the therapist off 'analysing' anything about his radio. The therapist said once again that Jim was on the alert – wary that the therapist would put him down or dismiss what was important to him.

The therapist made ii quite clear that, however Jim saw him; he was not there to diminish him. Nor was he there to deceive him, or to extract his secrets. He was there to help him sort out something that was clearly troubling his mind, and that was getting in the way of what he wanted to do. The therapist added, rather forcibly, that he was not too convinced that Jim could take care of himself yet, and told him that he had not forgotten about the drugs, even though he had not mentioned it. The therapist also disagreed that Jim 'had nothing to talk about'.

As the session ended, Jim grumbled about how difficult it was to travel there. The therapist simply said, 'I hope to see you next week'. He said, 'Do you want to see me?' The therapist said, 'Yes'. His response was 'Perfectly understandable – it's your job'. The therapist said something like 'It ain't going to be easy to convince you otherwise. How about you – do you want to see me?' He smiled and reminded the therapist about 'my mother's nose'. The therapist said, 'Let's talk about it'. He said, 'OK – have a good weekend'.

Therapeutic process

Once a working alliance is more or less established – it can never be taken for granted – psychotherapy can take on a life of its own. A therapeutic process is set in motion in which all the various elements of a therapeutic interaction become active in one way or another. In psychotherapy with adults, the predominant activity revolves around the patient verbally bringing experiences and memories to the therapist for thought and understanding. This generally proceeds in an orderly fashion, in which the psychotherapist can retain a degree of distance and objectivity and focus his interest primarily on interpreting the unconscious meaning of what is being said in relation to the transference.

With some adolescents, particularly late adolescents, this model of practice is also possible, and if it is not, it remains a reference point to which to aspire or return. With many adolescents, however, it is rare that psychotherapy can take place in such a straightforward or settled fashion. Most cannot be relied on to talk freely or honestly in a sustained spirit of introspection. Many have difficulty in expressing themselves in words. Their mood and sense of themselves is often extremely variable, they have difficulty just sitting and they remain typically resistant, as adolescents, to the scrutiny and dependency implicit in psychotherapy.

Throughout treatment, as in establishing a working alliance, the psychotherapist has to maintain a flexible attitude (Steinberg 1986). Much more so than with the adult, the psychotherapist has to take responsibility for attracting and holding the adolescent in therapy, especially at times of resistance and disillusionment. He has to be more prepared to be adaptable. Winnicott's (1971) simple definition of psychotherapy – 'Psychotherapy has to do with two people playing together' – rings especially true in work with adolescents. The psychotherapist has to be ready to be playful in response to the changeable nature of the adolescent – and to do so seriously and with humour.

Evans (1982) has addressed the significance of play in adolescent life and in psychotherapy. He sees many aspects of adolescent behaviour as a form of play, in which the adolescent enacts various roles that actively express different aspects of himself and of his relationship to others. This role-playing is only partly under the adolescent's conscious control, and is essentially a transitional phenomenon as the adolescent 'works out a new identity'. In psychotherapy sessions, for example, the adolescent may present himself at times as a defiant, insolent layabout who does not care about anything; or as a helpless, hopeless, ingenue who does not know what to do next; or as a sharp, smooth operator who knows all the answers; and so on. These are not simply superficial postures, but substantial modes of communication – dramatised no doubt in order to feel the more real and to see the more clearly. The psychotherapist must be ready to receive them as such and to react accordingly.

Similarly, Eissler (1958) has recognised how variably adolescents can present themselves and how, in effect, each presentation requires different responses from the psychotherapist. His view is that in adolescence, psychopathology is in a state of flux, and the adolescent manifests many different clinical conditions and levels of ego capacity. Because of this:

we encounter technical problems specific to puberty. In many instances, psychopathology switches from one form to another, sometimes in the course of weeks or months but also from one day to another and even within the same psychoanalytic hour. The symptoms manifested by such patients may be neurotic at one time and almost psychotic at another. Then sudden acts of delinquency may occur only to be followed by a phase of perverted sexually activity... the frequency of symptomatic changes manifested by many adolescent patients makes it evident that no one technique can fulfil the requirements for the treatment of adolescents.

(Eissler 1958)

It is clear that, faced with such a variable picture, the psychotherapist cannot sustain the classical analytic position of neutrality. In Eissler's terms, the psychotherapist needs to be in a constant state of alertness and adaptation, seeking always the correct timing of a change in technique to meet the adolescent's varying clinical manifestations. He gives a hypothetical illustration in which at times the psychotherapist is predominantly: interpretive in relation to the neurotic aspect of the adolescent; limit setting and authoritative in relationship to the delinquent; gratifying and reassuring in relation to the acute schizophrenic; and actively anxiety-arousing and conflict-generating in relation to the perverse.

Evans (1982) sees the role of the psychotherapist as 'a transitional object, a substitute authority who is only partially real and with whom the adolescent can "play" through the assumption of temporary roles in relationship to the therapist'. Implicit in his view is the psychotherapist's preparedness to participate in this play – both standing, as it were, for reality and boundary, and also reacting to the adolescent's role-play, by adopting corresponding roles. This is a complex process, which borders closely and dangerously on the psychotherapist becoming embroiled in and lost in the adolescent's transference re-enactments. Evans makes it clear that the therapist must 'simultaneously' be 'able to stand back and observe what is happening'.

Important in this emphasis on the psychotherapist's conduct and manner is the idea that the psychotherapist conveys meaning not only through his words, but through the way he behaves. Osorio (1977) has recognised how adolescents 'express themselves through a language of action', and suggests that the psychotherapist needs to respond in a corresponding way to the symbolic meaning of the adolescent's behaviour. He refers to the concept of 'behavioural interpretation' – the psychotherapist communicating to the adolescent through posture, gesture or manner. Such behaviour is based on and fashioned by the psychotherapist's understanding; it serves to highlight this understanding in action, in counter-response to that of the adolescent. For many adolescents, this can carry far greater weight than words alone. If, for example, an adolescent is dismissive of the psychotherapist, and provocative in his sessions, what he may be primarily expressing is his fear of humiliation and yet need for some boundary and care. If the psychotherapist is able to remain calm, be firm and show humour, he is in effect conveying an awareness of this adolescent's concern. The psychotherapist is not trying to make the adolescent feel 'better' through some form of corrective emotional experience; what he is doing is 'answering', through his way of being, the adolescent's call for understanding.

It would be misleading, however, to suggest that verbal communications are of no significance, for clearly, within the context of the therapeutic relationship, there is ample opportunity and much need for thoughts and ideas to be shared and understood. Much of the work with adolescents is spent in helping the adolescent find words for his feelings and ways of thinking that help him make sense of his relationship and difficulties. Often, the psychotherapist has to be quite active, asking questions if need be to keep things going, offering ideas and perspectives to stimulate and clarify thinking, and at times, where necessary, putting quite openly and honestly his views of the adolescent's behaviour (for example, with regard to drug or alcohol abuse, or attempted suicide). In many respects, this level of

activity, which is often quite concrete and down-to-earth, has an educational function, appealing to the adolescent's developing cognitive capacities and growing
interest in himself (McAdam 1986).

The focus of this kind of work is close to the adolescent's conscious awareness.
It is more about clarifying reality than interpreting what the adolescent is unaware
of. Interpretation, in the sense of elucidating unconscious processes particularly
in relationship to the transference, refers to a different level of psychotherapeutic activity. This, clearly, is at the heart of all psychodynamic psychotherapy, and
undoubtedly plays an important part in psychotherapy with adolescents. It must
be remembered, however, that such interpretations are often experienced by adolescents as invasive and controlling. They are strenuously resisted and frequently
misconstrued. The danger is that they can so easily be merely complied with or
defied, rather than received and assimilated with interest. It is important for the
psychotherapist not to be carried away with interpretative zeal nor, indeed, with
the belief that verbal understanding alone is effective (Wilson and Hersov 1985).
Interpretations need to be given clearly, in the language of the adolescent, and with
good evidence. The adolescent must understand how the psychotherapist arrives at
his perceptions and must always be allowed room for disagreement and manoeu-
vre. The effectiveness of interpretations depends as much on their timing as on their
accuracy and the way the psychotherapist conveys them. Interpretations can so easily be used by the psychotherapist, out of his negative countertransference, as tools
of control and censure, rather than as levers for self-discovery, and may awaken the
adolescent's dread of passive surrender (Balint 1959; Khan 1974; Stewart 1989).

For transference to be an effective therapeutic tool, it is essential that the patient
has the capacity to sustain a split between what Greenson (1978) has called 'the
experiencing, subjective, irrational ego' and the 'reasonable, observing, analysing
ego'. This is fundamental; the patient has to be able to experience the psychotherapist both as a transference object and as an actual psychotherapist. Intense feelings,
revived from the past, need to be allowed to emerge whilst contact with the reality
of the therapeutic situation is securely held. Without this capacity, transference can
be an overwhelming and confusing experience. Many disturbed adolescents do
not possess this capacity, nor do they have adequate impulse control, capacity for
reality testing or the ability to differentiate between self and object. Their hold over
themselves is precarious, and they frequently fail to appreciate the metaphorical
nature of transference. They see the psychotherapist as more or less real, and cannot make sense of transference interpretations. They frequently become frustrated
and angry that the psychotherapist does not directly fulfil their needs and desires.
For some adolescents, the therapeutic relationship and the transference that evolves
can be an excruciating tease.

Case study: Jim, age 17 (continued): understood and withstood

The following account gives some impression of the process of once weekly psychotherapy over a period of a year with the 17-year-old boy mentioned earlier. This

continued to carry much of the tension present from the beginning, and there was similarly little sense of reliability or predictability. A working alliance was, however, achieved so that, despite his various attacks on the therapist and on understanding, Jim did hold on to an agreement to meet regularly and persist with the concerns that he initially brought.

During the initial six months of psychotherapy, he showed much of the defensiveness and arrogance that had characterised his earlier sessions. His moods were variable. At times he could be light-hearted and ready to share feelings with the therapist. At other times, without any apparent reason, he could be extremely cross, fraught and critical.

In his better moods, he enjoyed talking about his achievements and his cleverness in the world of radio and hi-fi. It was clear that he felt at ease, safe within this knowledge. His purpose in talking about it to the therapist – apart from diverting him from more troubling matters – was to capture his interest and admiration. He demanded the therapist's audience – who for the most part played along, implicitly acknowledging Jim's need for control and time in which to preserve distance from him. The therapist was particularly struck at such times by Jim's narcissistic vulnerability, his fear of humiliation and denigration. The therapist was concerned not to prematurely challenge this for fear of producing some form of forced compliance or, indeed, outright rejection of psychotherapy. His going along with the role assigned to him was not so much a collusive giving in to Jim's imperious demands as a form of behavioural communication of acceptance and respect for his vulnerability. Occasionally, when feeling less threatened, Jim was able to extend his interest beyond his own self-preoccupation and show interest in the therapist as somebody separate from him and with whom he could learn rather than impress. At such times, they shared interest in the connection between Jim's technology and the therapist's music, and moved on to some reflection on various songs and their lyrics that bordered on his own feelings.

There were sessions, however, in which Jim seemed full of fury and malice. He was blatantly contemptuous and quick to contradict and denigrate anything the therapist might say. In all this, his overriding complaint was that the therapist didn't listen, that he was prejudiced and only interested in himself, and disdainful of anything Jim might think important. He was at times almost beside himself with rage, tearful with clenched fists. The therapist was filled with a kind of impotent fury. In so many ways, Jim seemed hell-bent on provoking a powerful explosion or the therapist's rejection of him.

What mattered above all else for the therapist in this situation was to hold on to some understanding for himself of what was happening, based on Jim's evident feelings and those engendered within the therapist himself. In brief, what made sense to him was that Jim was reliving some earlier painful fight, intensified in puberty, with his mother, whom he perceived as both overwhelmingly controlling and seductive. This transference situation needed to be managed, held within bounds and not further complicated with words. As far as possible, the therapist drew from his understanding some sense of Jim's fear of abandonment and explosive denigration, and managed to behave in a relatively calm, firm and unprovoked manner. Of course, at times Jim caught the therapist's exasperation and anger, and almost seemed relieved that he had touched him in this way, as well as remorseful that he had hurt him. But for the most part, the therapist tried to meet Jim's anxiety with a behaviour that reflected and conveyed appreciation of this anxiety. At a fundamental level, the therapist survived his attacks. Jim felt both understood and withstood.

During the first six months of psychotherapy, there was a great deal of variability both in Jim's moods and, indeed, in the therapist's responses.

As is so often the case in work with adolescents, a turning point was reached when he felt reassured, out of his testing, of the therapist's implicit understanding of him and capacity to hold some limit. The last six months settled, with periodic eruptions, to a level of psychotherapeutic work that was more orderly and reflective. He became more ready to acknowledge his sense of failure and futility in ever being able to 'get somewhere'. He could also see his loneliness as a reflection of his inability to 'get on with anybody' – he quickly felt sensitive to any possibility of being stood up or criticised. His acceptance of such vulnerability within himself contrasted with the way he had dominated in earlier sessions. He and the therapist were able to draw on some of their memories of how it had been between them and began to make some sense of what mattered to him in his family life. It became increasingly clear how very divided he was in his feelings towards his mother – both very attached, almost obsessively jealous of her boyfriends, and very angry both at her betrayal and the way in which she had ridiculed and frightened him as a child.

The therapist was able to make sense of his moods, his drug-taking and failure at school, in terms of this anger which found so many ways of effectively thwarting and punishing his mother. His life, it seemed, was set to refuse to comply with her wishes – or indeed those of anybody with power. It has been seen how this had found expression in his attitude towards the therapist – he too had felt frustrated and ridiculed, as both Jim and, no doubt, his mother had in various ways. Putting this into words in the form of an interpretation had meaning, and was of use to Jim because of the inescapable evidence provided by what had happened between them in the therapeutic relationship.

Psychotherapy ended after a year, when he moved away to start working. Clearly, there was much that was left incomplete. The understanding that he had gained needed consolidation and there were many other areas, not least his sexuality, and feelings for his father, that had not been adequately covered. Enough, however, had been done to enable Jim to become unstuck, less held back in his revenge against his mother. He was less miserable and less reliant on drugs. He was planning to study again. He found himself better able to tolerate other people without fear of humiliation or of disappointment. He was beginning to allow himself to join the mainstream of normal development, albeit with much idiosyncrasy left intact.

Summary

Throughout this chapter, the main question has been about the possibility, or otherwise, of creating a relationship out of very different interests: on the one side, psychoanalytic therapy with its essential scrutiny and call for reflection; on the other, adolescence, with its essential privacy and preference for action. Both tug away or against each other, and for the two to come together each has to be prepared for at least some partial inversion of what they stand for. The adolescent, by dint of his disturbance, agrees to come to therapy and thereby compromises his independence. The psychotherapist in turn agrees to be flexible and foregoes something of his 'adult' discipline.

Effective psychotherapy with adolescents is a question not so much of specific technique or accurate interpretation as of the development and maintenance of a therapeutic attitude which is sensitive to and respectful of the adolescent state. The psychotherapist has to understand and contend with a mass of contradictions that exist at the centre of the adolescent predicament – sometimes an adult, sometimes a child and always neither. The adolescent needs to find his own way and not be called too much to account; yet, he needs attention, guidance and someone to care about him. He does not want to be understood, and yet, he does. He wants licence, and yet, he needs boundaries.

In response, the psychotherapist's position has to be inevitably and likewise con-tradictory. At one and the same time, the psychotherapist needs to be ready to be flexible, to play roles and change posture – and yet remain essentially a firm and reliable presence. He has to retain faith in the usefulness of words and yet remind himself that much of what he does non-verbally is crucial. He has at times to be active and involved, sometimes even larger than life and directorial – and yet never lose his fundamental capacity to listen and observe, and tolerate the adolescent's confusion, failure to respond and, at times, sheer silence. Winnicott (1961) sug-gested that adolescents 'eschew psychoanalytic treatment, though they are inter-ested in psychoanalytic theories' because their 'preservation of personal isolation is part of the search for identity'. Of importance here is Winnicott's concern with the development of the core of true self, uncompromised or intruded upon by the external world. In adolescence, this core self is in a state of delicate and partial for-mation, and requires both protection and leaving be. Phillips (1988), in his account of Winnicott's work, summarises succinctly the contradiction that characterises so much of the psychotherapy of adolescents: 'The paradox that he [Winnicott] had begun to formulate was that the infant – like the adolescent... – was an isolate who needed the object, above all, to protect the privacy of his isolation'.

References

Anthony, E. J. (1975) 'Between yes and no: the potentially neutral area where the adolescent and his therapist can meet'. In S. C. Feinstein and P. L. Giovacchini (eds) *Adolescent Psychiatry: Developmental Clinical Studies*, Vol. 4, New York: Jason Aronson.

Balint, M. (ed) (1959) 'Regression in the analytic situation'. Chapter 11 In *Thrills and Regression*, London: Hogarth Press.

Berkowitz, D. A.(1979) 'The disturbed adolescent and his family: problems of individuation', *Journal of Adolescence* 11: 27–39.

Blos, P. (1967) 'The second individuation process of adolescence'. *Psychoanalytic Study of the Child* 22 (1): 162–186.

Eissler, K. R. (1958) 'Notes on problems of technique in the psychoanalytic treatment of adolescents: with some remarks on perversions', *Psychoanalytic Study of the Child* 13: 223–254. New York: International Universities Press.

Evans, J. (1982) *Adolescent and Pre-Adolescent Psychiatry*, London: Academic Press.

Freud, A. (1958) 'Adolescence', *Psychoanalytic Study of the Child* 13: 255–278. New York: International Universities Press, Inc. pp. 268–233.

Greenson, R. R. (1978) *The Technique and Practice of Psychoanalysis*, Vol 1, London:Hogarth Press.

Hill, P. (1989) *Adolescent Psychiatry*, London: Churchill Livingstone.

Jones, E. (1922) 'Some problems of adolescence'. In *Papers on Psychoanalysis*, London:Bailliere, Tindal & Cox. 1948. Reprinted London: Karnac Books, 1977. pp. 384–406.

Khan, M. M. R. (1974) *The Privacy of the Self*, London: Hogarth Press.

Laufer, M (1968) 'The body image, the function of masturbation, and adolescence: problems of the ownership of the body', *Psychoanalytic Study of the Child* 23: 114–137.

Laufer, M. and Laufer, M. E. (1989) *Developmental Breakdown and Psychoanalytic Treatment in Adolescence*, New Haven and London, CT: Yale University Press.

McAdam, E. K. (1986) 'Cognitive behaviour therapy and its application with adolescents', *Journal of Adolescence* 9: 1–15.

Miller, D. (1983) *The Age between: Adolescence and Therapy*, London: Faber & Faber.

Moehler, M. L. (1977) 'Self and object in countertransference', *International Journal of Psychoanalysis* 58: 365–374.

Money-Kyrle, R. E. (1956) 'Normal counter transference and some of its deviations', *International Journal of Psychoanalysis* 37: 360–366.

Osorio, L. C. (1977) 'The psychoanalysis of communication in adolescents'. In S. C. Feinstein and P. L. Giovacchini (eds) *Adolescent Psychiatry: Developmental and Clinical Studies*, Vol. 5, New York: Aronson. pp. 442–448.

Phillips, A. (1988) *Winnicott*, London: Fontana.

Shapiro, R. L. (1978) 'The adolescent, the therapist and the family; the management of external resistances of psychoanalytic therapy of adolescents', *Journal of Adolescence* 1: 3–10.

Steinberg, D. (1986) *The Adolescent Unit: Work and Teamwork in Adolescent Psychiatry*, Chichester: John Wiley.

Stewart, H. (1989) 'Technique at the basic fault/regression', *International Journal of Psychoanalysis* 70: 21–230.

Wilson, P. (1986) 'Individual psychotherapy in a residential setting'. In D. Steinberg (ed) *The Adolescent Unit: Work and Teamwork in Adolescent Psychiatry*, Chichester: John Wiley.

Wilson, P. (1986) 'Psychoanalytic therapy and the young adolescent', *Bulletin of the Anna Freud Centre* 110: 51–59.

Wilson, P. and Hersov, L. (1985) 'Individual and group therapy'. In M. Rutter and L. Hersov (eds) *Child and Adolescent Psychiatry* 2nd edn. Oxford: Blackwell.

Winnicott, D. W. (ed) (1961) 'Adolescence: struggling through the doldrums'. In *The Family and Individual Development* London: Tavistock Publications. 1965.

Winnicott, D. W. (1971) *Playing and Reality*, London: Tavistock Publications.

Chapter 5

Delinquency

Previously published in M. Lanyado & A. Horne (eds) The Handbook of Child and Adolescent Psychotherapy: Psychoanalytic Approaches. London & New York: Routledge (1999).

Introduction

Delinquency is a term that has different meanings and usages. Most commonly, a juvenile delinquent is defined as someone who has transgressed the law: 'a young person who has been prosecuted and found guilty of an offence that would be classified as a crime if committed by an adult' (Graham 1991). This definition has the virtue of precision. Its limitation, however, is that it does not take into account the full extent of behaviour or attitude. In psychodynamic terms, delinquency carries a much broader meaning: it relates to a more fundamental concern about responsibility and honesty, both in relation to oneself and to others. The essence of delinquency lies in its failure of duty to meet both the legal and moral requirements of the prevailing social order. The word itself draws its source from the Latin *linquere* – to leave, forsake or abandon. The delinquent is unable or unwilling to do that which is owed to the group, community or society. Delinquency is thus not an activity confined to a criminal minority, but refers to a tendency that is integral to the development of all social relationships.

There can be a few children for example who do not break rules, who do not tell an untruth, who do not take what is not theirs, who do not defy those around them. All children, from time to time, do what they are not supposed to; they try the forbidden and test the limits. In the interests of their growth and curiosity, they break new ground, often ruthlessly and regardless of constraints and consequences. There is in the very process of becoming social an anti-social necessity. Delinquency in this sense is part of being a child and adolescent.

The nature of delinquency and child and adolescent development

Delinquency expresses itself in three major ways: through stealing, deception and physical or verbal violence. All constitute an attack on or an abandonment of the other; all, as it were, 'leave' the other. The spectrum of delinquent activity is wide. Stealing covers many activities: 'borrowing', shoplifting, taking and driving away, robbery and burglary. Deception includes a broad repertoire of

DOI: 10.4324/9781003680437-6

lies from the periodic white lie to systematic deviousness, duplicity and fraud. Violence consists of fighting, bullying, intimidating, physical and sexual abuse, assault, torture or murder. Many of these activities are not criminal (and thus not delinquent in the legal sense); they are, however, in one way or another, dishonest and offensive (and thus delinquent in the psychodynamic sense). The degree to which these activities become problematic is in part determined by the requirements of the law, but also by the sanctions and prohibitions of the social group – whether this be the family, the peer group, the community or society at large. Some groups turn a blind eye to certain forms of theft; others collude with different kinds of deception or condone various forms of violence. Delinquency is thus relative to the tolerance of the group.

To a large extent, delinquency, as a failure in social adaptation, is a mental health issue. Mental health refers essentially to the capacity to function effectively and creatively in the social group. It consists of the ability to initiate and sustain mutually satisfying relationships. Crucial to children's development is their ability and readiness to develop sufficient self-control and conscience to guide their behaviour within the rules of the group. Mental health problems and more severe mental disorders and illnesses reflect, in varying degrees, impairments of these abilities. Delinquency is one particular form of such impairment. Some delinquents behave in a disruptive and aggressive way which is excessive and impervious to modification by the normal range of social sanctions; their behaviour gives rise to disapproval and is associated with significant suffering and disturbance in personal functioning. In psychiatric terms, these young people are classified as having a conduct disorder, an indication of the extent and problematic nature of their delinquency.

The conditions that are likely to determine the development of mental health or of delinquency are now well documented in the literature on risk and protective factors (Farrington 1996, 1997, Utting et al. 1993; Wadsworth 1979). These can be grouped broadly into those pertaining to the inborn characteristics and personal resources of children, and those relating to familial and societal circumstances. In the first group, a number of genetic and early physical pre- and perinatal factors (e.g. physical abnormalities, premature birth) can be identified that produce vulnerabilities in infants. Inherent temperamental differences are of key importance pointing to whether or not children are overly sensitive, cranky or regressive/ progressive in their basic tendencies. The personal resources of children – their intelligence, ego resilience, social skills development – determine whether they are able to comprehend and adapt to what is happening in their lives and thus gain a sense of self-efficacy and control over events.

Familial and societal factors cover a broad range of circumstances. Major risk factors in the family include parental psychopathology and criminality, discordant family relationships and divorce, inconsistent parental supervision, harsh and erratic punishment, physical abuse and neglect and lack of emotional warmth. Set against these are a range of protective factors, most notably the establishment of secure infant attachment and bonding, the provision of authoritative and consistent parenting, a basic belief in the family in the value of education and residential stability. The degree to which mothers can cope with adversity is critical; this in turn is dependent on the stability of their marriages or partnerships and the presence of significant care networks in their families or neighbourhoods.

Psychoanalytic thinking (e.g. Bion 1962; Bowlby 1951; Freud 1965; Winnicott 1960) emphasises the significance of infant and early childhood experience and attachment. The role of the family in ensuring sufficient emotional containment of children is crucial to the provision of a sense of inner safety and coherence. This lays the foundation of basic trust and positive expectancy. Children feel essentially nourished, understood and affirmed; they are enabled to think and to learn, with a readiness to enter into relationships and to accept the constraints necessary for socialisation. Later experiences of feeling held and valued within a reliable family environment that establishes clear expectations and boundaries are necessary for the development of self-control and the establishment of ideals and of a moral sense. Children's capacity to benefit from school and community opportunities is greatly influenced by these primary family experiences. In contrast, where such favourable conditions do not prevail, children are less likely to be equipped to process adequately and make sense of their experience. The impact of maltreatment – whether it be physical, sexual or emotional neglect or abuse – is essentially traumatic, overwhelming children with sensations, tensions and feelings they cannot assimilate and exposing them to primitive anxieties over which they cannot achieve mastery – fears of annihilation, loss of control, disapproval and rejection. Children feel betrayed by parental failure to safeguard their safety and integrity. In response, they become resentful and on guard, without faith in those around them and disinclined to comply with their social requirements.

Delinquency represents an attempt to defend against these anxieties and give expression to this resentment. Delinquents find ways of ridding themselves of tension, through various projective mechanisms, and rendering others prey to the very feelings of anger, fear and confusion that they themselves find so intolerable. Campbell (1996) emphasises that 'it is the reliance upon action to project painful thoughts and feelings outside of himself and into the environment that is a fundamental characteristic of the delinquent's psychological defences'. He also draws attention to the delinquent's tendency to master traumatic experiences through sexual fantasy. This contains elements of excitement and risk (Stoller 1975) that both serve a defensive purpose and give expression to sadistic and revengeful wishes. Galway (1991) refers to deficiencies in the internal capacity to contain anxiety, and in more disturbed young people, a lack of an 'internal container altogether'; they are unable to make use of fantasy or the development of the capacity to think in order to process experience. As a result, their behaviour is more determined by the impulse to act and by a need to seek containment externally through provocation and manipulation.

It is clear that mental health or delinquent outcome is dependent on the interplay of multiple factors within the child, family and environment and in relation to the severity of the child's circumstances. The extent to which children are resilient, and thus able to rise above negative circumstances or manage to mitigate the effect of these circumstances, is a major variable. Horowitz (1987), for example, refers to the complex interrelationship between children's inherent vulnerability and the 'facilitativeness' of their environment: resilient children in adverse environments may make remarkable progress whilst vulnerable children in more facilitating ones may not.

Adolescence and the circumstances that surround it have a further determining effect on the development of delinquency. The peak age for all offending in England and Wales is 18 for males and 15 for females (Home Office 1995). There are numerous environmental risk factors that can lead to delinquent activity, including disadvantaged neighbourhoods, community disorganisation and neglect and availability of drugs. Poverty, poor schooling and unemployment also play their part. Young people's internal experience of adolescence, however, is of key significance in determining how able they are to cope with these adversities. Ordinarily, adolescence is an exciting, if at times alarming, time of growth and discovery. For those adolescents, however, whose early experiences have been unfavourable, the process of adolescence can be very unsettling. They are less able to negotiate adequately the developmental tasks of adjusting to the impact of puberty and negotiating separation and individuation (Laufer and Laufer 1984); their adolescent state does not excite them; they are fearful of their physical growth and sexuality and of taking responsibility by themselves for their actions. A great deal of delinquent behaviour in adolescence can be seen as a breakdown in the capacity to deal with these anxieties and to fill a developmental void (Greenberg 1975) inherent in the process of the separation. Some adolescents become extremely overwhelmed and disorganised, breaking down severely in suicidal and psychotic type behaviour. Others are more able to 'manage', drawing on the adolescent tendency to find expression through 'a language of action' (Osorio 1979) and veering towards a delinquent outcome.

According to the severity of negative childhood experiences and adolescent turbulence, the degree of delinquency becomes more marked and problematic. Most young people whose delinquent behaviour is persistent and extreme experience the world as fundamentally uncaring, withholding and untrustworthy. They harbour within them a sense of injustice and outrage and an abiding resentment chat leads to a contempt and disregard for others. The delinquent act is intended to attack and confound those perceived to be responsible for their difficulties. In effect, it carries its own sense of justice – the delinquent feels emboldened to take what he perceives to be his, and to deceive and violate those whom he believes have betrayed and abused him. There is in all of this an exhilarating and powerful mixture of despair and hope – the delinquent determined both to 'leave' the ungiving or hostile other and yet engage and register protest. Winnicott (1965) emphasised the essential purpose of the delinquent act as a positive, self-affirming protest. He viewed 'the anti-social tendency' as a consequence of and response to 'environmental failure'; it represents a testing of the environment and a way of 'staking a claim' on what has been hitherto being withheld. He expressed his position most clearly in the following passage:

First I must try to define the word psychopathy. I am using the term here (and I believe I am justified in doing so) to describe an adult condition which is uncured delinquency. A delinquent is an uncured anti-social boy or girl. An anti-social boy or girl is a deprived child. A deprived child is one who had something good enough, and then no longer had this, whatever it was, and there was sufficient growth and organisation of the individual *at the time of the deprivation* for the deprivation to be perceived as traumatic. In other words, in the psychopath and the delinquent and the anti-social child there is logic in the implied attitude' the environment owes me something.

(Winnicott 1965)

Child psychotherapy and delinquency

Child psychotherapists face major problems in working with delinquents. Many of the factors that give rise to delinquency fall beyond the reach of psychotherapy: little can be done through psychotherapy to change inherent personal characteristics or environmental factors. In relation to inner experience, many delinquents are unable or unwilling to acknowledge their suffering or learn through self-exploration in a therapeutic relationship. They are mistrustful and defiant and unable to hold in mind ideas and thoughts without defensive recourse to action. In adolescence, their need to preserve privacy and defend against dependency additionally works against therapeutic enquiry. In view of these difficulties, the issue of motivation is complicated. Some delinquents for example feel little remorse or concern about their behaviour and thus see no reason to change. As Eissler (1958) puts it:

> the technical difficulty in treating a delinquent arises from his total lack of desire to change. His symptoms are painful not to him but to others in his environment. He has no need or motive to reveal to his analyst what is going on in him. Furthermore, he sees the analyst as representative of that society against which his aggressions are directed and therefore meets him with distrust and fear.

On the other hand, beneath their antagonism or indifference, many delinquents feel anxious, confused and ashamed of their destructiveness. They are sometimes painfully conscious of their failings in their social, family and vocational lives, and yet they feel helpless in their predicament and unable to stop or comprehend their delinquency. Such acknowledgement of vulnerability is a potential source of motivation; it is, however, difficult for them to bear and invariably defended against through attacking those who offer care and interest.

Child psychotherapists need to take into account these various factors that complicate motivation for change and improvement. They need also to be realistic about the extent of their contribution, set alongside other initiatives in the field, tackling the problem of delinquency (Sheldrick 1985). These include vocational and educational training, diversionary programmes in the Youth Justice System (Jones 1987; NACRO 1988) and a range of psychosocial treatments, such as problem-solving skills training, parent management training, family therapy. Many of these have a behavioural and cognitive focus and have been positively evaluated (Kazdin 1997). Psychodynamic child psychotherapy has been less well evaluated and needs more outcome research, despite methodological problems, to counter criticism (see, for example, Rutter 1985).

Despite these difficulties, however, child psychotherapy can be of considerable value to many delinquents in helping them to acknowledge and understand better their internal experience and thus gain a greater sense of self-control. In many respects, the practice of child psychotherapy with delinquents is no different from that with more neurotic or psychotic young people. Basic to the process is the establishment of a secure setting in which sufficient stability is ensured to enable young people to feel safe enough to explore and discuss their difficulties. The endeavour is to create an experience for them in which they can learn about themselves through the therapeutic relationship and from observations, clarifications and interpretations (Wilson and Hersov 1985). The fundamental purpose is to improve their understanding of the anxieties that interfere with their development and contribute to their delinquency.

The establishment of these basic conditions is especially important in working with delinquent young people, whose need for clear boundaries, reliability and predictability is central. Beyond this, however, there are three issues that need to be addressed in particular in order to deal with the mistrust and hostility of delinquents and their equivocal motivation to change. The first concerns the establishment of *a working alliance*, the second, *the management of transference*, and third, the *adaptation in approach* to different types of delinquency.

Establishment of a working alliance

Without the establishment of a working alliance (Meeks 1971), there can be no prospect of collaborative or explorative work. In view of the many resistances inherent in delinquency, it is incumbent on child psychotherapists to reach out to convey in some way an appreciation of the delinquent's behaviour and underlying difficulties and to engender a sense of direction and hope in the possibility of change. This requires their willingness to take a more proactive and supportive approach than is customary. Some writers (Miller 1983), drawing on the work of Aichhom (1965), suggest that psychotherapists adopt a relatively forceful, almost omnipotent position, in order to capture the imagination of otherwise indifferent and hostile delinquents who nevertheless seek leadership and guidance. Whilst this approach may be effective in certain circumstances with some adolescents, it carries with it considerable dangers, not least in compromising the stability of the therapeutic setting and building unnecessary expectations and inevitable disappointments. What is paramount, however, particularly in the early stages of therapy, is to find ways of engaging delinquents' curiosity about themselves and their circumstances.

The maintenance of a working alliance is of central importance throughout the course of therapy. It is dependent on mutual trust and as such is vulnerable to pressures within the therapeutic relationship. Delinquents may attack the alliance in many ways, and child psychotherapists may overly protect it at the cost of therapeutic progress. It is not uncommon during psychotherapy, for example, for young people to continue their delinquent and criminal activities both within and outside the therapy. They may conceal what they are doing or seek to manipulate child psychotherapists to accept and condone their delinquent behaviour. Child psychotherapists need to hold a difficult tension between alliance and non-compliance with these delinquents' manoeuvres; this corresponds with the delinquents' ambivalence about being caught and found out. Much depends on child psychotherapists' insight into their own relation to delinquency and to authority; it is through this that they can best hold the balance within themselves between moral censure of, and indulgent collusion with, delinquents' activities.

The management of the transference

Whereas transference (Freud 1914) is always a powerful phenomenon in therapy, its impact in the psychotherapy of delinquents is especially forceful. In the transference, young people re-enact childhood experiences intensified in their revival in adolescence. They convey through their behaviour that which is familiar to them. They bring into the therapeutic relationship aspects of how they themselves felt in the past and of how they perceived others who were involved with them. A teenage girl, for example, who has endured sexual abuse by her father as a child is likely to feel, in the reliving in the transference, her own childhood sensations of terror and excitement as well as the fears of a domineering and invasive father. In psychotherapy, she may find herself, in the growing dependency of the therapeutic relationship, having similar sensations as well as anticipating abuse from the psychotherapist. She may retreat from the therapy or, alternatively, re-immerse herself in the entanglement of her past in the therapeutic relationship. She may find ways to seduce or provoke the therapist into bullying her – both to repeat the past experience and to master anxiety, through turning a passive experience into its active counterpart. She may reverse the past experience and attempt to dominate the psychotherapist, rendering him or her both harmless and as abused as she had felt. It is likely, too, that she may act out outside the therapy through violent behaviour, prostitution or theft in order to relieve this intolerable tension and to be apprehended and punished.

The value of such transference experience is that it opens up possibilities for the understanding and working through of central anxieties that underlie the delinquency. The above picture, however, gives some indication of the volatile and potentially disruptive nature of this experience. Unless the transference can be properly managed, it can become anti-therapeutic. Much depends on child psychotherapists' capacities to withstand the impact of these powerful and conflicting feelings and to provide some degree of containment so that they can be perceived and understood. The key therapeutic task is to resist the young person's implicit invitation to repeat the past – for example, for the psychotherapist to behave like a dominant or abusive father, or to become overwhelmed by feelings of helplessness. The child psychotherapist's ability to find ways of responding that are different from what the young people expect and which do not meet the dictates of the transference is essential. Ultimately, it is through the child psychotherapists' behaviour that they convey their understanding of the meaning of the young person's delinquency and provide the safety and boundary that the delinquent needs. Such behaviour, sustained by the child psychotherapists' own insights, constitutes interpretation and serves as a stimulus and basis for further verbal forms of communication and understanding.

Adaptation in approach

There are many individual differences between delinquents, and psychotherapeutic work clearly needs to be adapted to address these differences, taking into account historical and personal circumstances and based on careful assessment and diagnosis. Various attempts at classification have been made of delinquent and criminal people (e.g. Galway 1991); for the most part these have attempted to identify the degree of persistence and extremity of the offending behaviour and the neurotic or psychotic basis underlying the delinquent personality. For purposes of clarification, delinquent young people can be broadly divided into three main groups: those that are impulsive, explosive and/or compulsive. These categories are not intended as diagnostic categories, but rather as guides to consider the predominate elements of the delinquent behaviour in question and make the most appropriate response. None, of course, is intended to be seen as exclusive of the others.

The impulsive delinquent

Impulsive delinquents are young people who are largely dominated by the sheer pressure of their wishes and desires. Their behaviour is demanding, insistent, grabbing in nature. They take things on impulse and steal without apparent remorse or concern. They lie frequently and are often aggressive, bullying if they can get away with it and at times violent if cornered or threatened. There is a sense in which their delinquency is 'mindless' – defensive, reactive, without thought or regard for others and with little comprehension of the consequences of their actions. Delinquency of this kind has many causes. In some young people, there may be genetic factors, as in hyperkinetic syndrome, as a result of which they have inherent difficulty in focusing their attention or controlling their impulsive behaviour. In others, early abusive or neglectful childhood experiences may have left them with inner feelings of chaos and terror and with limited resources to manage their anxiety. Anna Freud's (1965) developmental perspective on the nature of lying and stealing is of particular relevance. Some of these young people, because of their immaturity, are less able to distinguish between inner and outer reality or between ideas of what is 'mine' and 'not mine'. In terms of their functioning, they are more likely to react to intolerable realities through regression to infantile forms of behaviour and wishful thinking.

The therapeutic response to these delinquents needs to address their basic difficulties in controlling their impulses and tolerating frustration as well as the underlying anxieties that propel them into such trouble. Systematic behavioural and cognitive approaches are useful in enabling them to develop problem-solving skills, build social competencies and clarify their thinking in relation to the consequences of their actions. These approaches can be carried out either individually or in groups, in different settings in school, special educational establishments or in the community in various diversionary schemes. The involvement of the family in supporting these therapeutic interventions through family therapy or parent management training is important. Child psychotherapists have a significant contribution to make in working to understand the anxieties of these young people, particularly those who have some rudimentary capacity for self-reflection and a wish to change. Despite the apparent randomness and remorselessness of their behaviour, many feel fundamentally very frightened and confused and desperate that they cannot control themselves or indeed what happens to them. Child psychotherapists may have to adapt to their needs, through being relatively more structured, focused and supportive in their approach. In view of the need of these young people to feel held within a consistent and comprehensive system of care, it is important that child psychotherapists do not work in isolation but maintain regular liaison with other practitioners involved with the young person – for example, teachers, social workers, youth workers.

The explosive delinquent

By contrast, explosive delinquents function at a higher level of organisation; their personalities are more structured, less buffeted by impulse and more coherent in relation to others. For most of the time they appear to behave normally and get along well enough with others. The problematic area of their delinquency resides in their periodic outbursts of violence and revengeful preoccupations; the latter can lead to acts of theft, deception and intimidation with no apparent regard for their victims. At the core of this kind of delinquency is often a major narcissistic disturbance, in which the young people are highly sensitive to perceived rejection or humiliation. The causes of such disturbance are complex, but are frequently associated with what Greenberg (1975) has described as a 'symbiotically warped' mother–infant relationship. In this, vulnerable young people have experienced, as children, an accumulation of narcissistic injuries in response to their mother's extreme ambivalence: that is, they have been subjected both to the mother's often engulfing and sexualised overinvolvement and yet sudden and unpredictable withdrawals of affection, indifference and hostility. This perplexing intimacy can have a highly disturbing effect leaving them feeling as children and as adolescents helpless, valueless and confused. There is engendered from such experience a deep sense of hurt and anger that constitutes what Kohut (1972) refers to as 'narcissistic rage'. This vulnerability is intolerable and is for the most part defended against through compensatory grandiose or idealising fantasies. When these are challenged, whether through direct criticism or rebuke or through actual or perceived betrayal (e.g. in an idealised relationship), the rage may erupt and find expression in acts of violence.

The extent of the denial in this kind of delinquency is extensive, often fortified by a sense of righteous justification that allows for no recognition of wrongdoing. The violent outbursts are troubling, but experienced as episodic and 'forgettable'. Cognitive and behavioural therapeutic approaches that have a useful structuring and guiding effect for impulsive delinquents are largely irrelevant for these delinquents. Anger management techniques may be helpful, but they do not meet the depth of the underlying disturbance. Long-term psychodynamic therapy can, in some cases, be effective in reducing the extremity of behaviour and preoccupation. This psychotherapy needs to be based on an understanding of narcissistic psychopathology and to proceed on the basis of building an essentially supportive and affirming relationship. Once this is established, there exists the opportunity of re-experiencing and working through elements of the early narcissistic hurt and rage in the transference, and thus of greater integration and control. The work of Kohut (1972) in treating narcissistic personality disorders through mirror transferences is of particular relevance.

The compulsive delinquent

Compulsive delinquents are those whose behaviour is repetitive and chronically destructive both to themselves and others. It is behaviour that combines both impulsive and explosive elements but is relatively more controlled and sustained. Behind this behaviour is an attitude of contempt that derives from a basic fear of dependency and dread of humiliation. These delinquents are often clever, streetwise, well-resourced in terms of social skills and competence; they are adept at controlling others through seduction and manipulation and are callous and sadistic in their attacks on others. Their overriding purpose is to get what they want as quickly and immediately as possible, regardless of the rules or sensibilities of others. To this end, they are able and willing to defy and undermine others through concealment and duplicity.

At the source of this kind of delinquency is again a fundamental narcissistic disturbance drawn from comparable early infantile circumstances as described in relation to the explosive delinquent. There is additionally a complex overlay of more neurotic conflicts that give rise to a sense of guilt which, though denied, has a powerful unconscious influence on behaviour. It is this factor, together with a fear of omnipotence (a sense of limitlessness, of there being no bounds to what they might get away with), that gives rise to the self-destructive and compulsive nature of their delinquency. This takes the form not only of theft, deception or fraud, but also of activities that are self-punishing – for example: the burglar who repeatedly breaks into houses until he is caught or the boy who takes and drives away cars until eventually he crashes.

Delinquency of this kind is perhaps the most difficult to deal with in psychotherapy; it is habitual, a way of life that for many may be 'successful' enough. Nevertheless, despite this, many such young people experience a pervasive sense of unease that can lead to a desire for change. They are frightened of their destructiveness, of their potential loss of control, of their sense of being bad and unwanted. Many express a strong need for a relationship and to be understood.

In the following example, an account is given of the psychotherapy of a young person whose delinquency contained impulsive and explosive elements, but whose life was built upon deception and compulsive delinquent activity. The fundamental task of the psychotherapist was to establish and maintain a **working** alliance that could allow for moments of experience that were genuine and non-delinquent and that could be used for exploration and gradual integration.

Case illustration: Paul

- Paul was a 15-year-old boy, tall, well-built and always dressed stylishly. He was referred for psychotherapy by his mother who had decided she could no longer tolerate his behaviour. The school had complained to her for some time about his stealing from other pupils, his tendency to bully and sexually pester girls. In recent months he had got into trouble with the police. He had been questioned about a number of car thefts in the neighbourhood; matters had come to a head recently when he had been caught driving a stolen car. His mother felt she could never trust him.
- Paul lived alone with his mother. Paul's father had left the family home when he was aged six. There had been numerous violent marital arguments when Paul was a small child and he had at times been victim of his father's violence. His relationship with his mother had been very close and it was clear that in many ways she was very proud of him. However, she had also been preoccupied with her own design business and had had several relationships with other men. This, Paul had resented; he had, for example, stolen money from the wallets of his mother's boyfriends. His father had remained a constant presence in his life, though always elusive and unpredictable. Paul remained loyal to him and looked up to him, although he never could be sure where his father was or what he did. 'He comes and goes in big cars and flash suits'.
- Paul was seen in once-weekly psychotherapy for just over a year. His attendance was erratic although this improved towards the end. The therapy terminated because of his family moving to another area; this was premature and progress was by no means complete. Enough was accomplished, however, to help him understand his delinquent behaviour better and to begin to try to change his ways.
- Paul made it clear from the outset that he was happy to come to therapy. He said he knew he needed to sort himself out. His mother worried too much but

he could well understand her feelings. He loved his mother and he did not want to upset her. He also wanted to do well and 'go into the design business' with her. He intended to go to college and get down to studying. He understood that I knew the extent of his mother's concern and of his delinquency and police involvement. He acknowledged that he was 'in a bit of trouble' but he was quick to point out that he had learnt his lesson and was about to change.

- In all of this, his tone was assured, grown-up, conciliatory. He smiled a lot and it seemed that his overall purpose was to disarm and circumvent me as much as he could. To some extent, the early sessions moved along well enough as he began to talk about his feelings towards his parents, his memories of having felt frightened and confused as a child and his wish to know more about his father. He talked, too, at the beginning about his interest in cars and achievements in computer design. There remained, however, a lack of depth or connectedness. Despite his apparent sincerity, I felt as if he were play-acting, almost in mockery of the therapy. His attitude was flippant, he turned up late for sessions with poor excuses, he hinted at various criminal activities – but never explicit, always keeping me guessing. At one level, it seemed clear that he was attending therapy to be 'good' and to get out of trouble with the police. The degree of control and manipulation, however, in the way in which he maintained distance in the therapeutic relationship, indicated a more profound level of fear of dependency in the transference. His mockery seemed an effective way of rendering me powerless, feeling as foolish and duped as he did.

- Throughout, Paul's delinquency was a feature of the therapy. This was something I needed constantly to keep in mind whilst always remaining open to his underlying vulnerability and possible search for help. It was an achievement in itself that Paul attended therapy, albeit at times irregularly, and that he opened up the opportunity to talk about aspects of his life. Nevertheless, there was much in what he said that was false and in denial of his difficulties. This became particularly noticeable when he talked about his relationship with girls. On the one hand, he said he had a steady girlfriend whom he would never leave; on the other hand, he talked of other girls whom he had 'had' – seemingly oblivious of his effects on them or indeed on his girlfriend.

A turning point occurred in psychotherapy towards the end of the third month. Its impetus was a telephone call from Paul's mother informing me that he had been arrested with someone else for a burglary in a large house in the neighbourhood. Paul attended his subsequent session in his usual breezy manner without making any reference to this information. Eventually I informed Paul of what I knew. Paul's initial reaction was to smile, shrug it off; it wasn't really him who was involved, it was his friend. His mother, he said, fretted too much; she wasn't well. I stayed silent for a while, and then said simply, 'I am listening but I am wondering why I don't feel convinced about what you're saying'. Paul smiled again and picked up a pen on the desk. He mimed at smoking it like a cigarette and asked uncertainly what I was getting at. I repeated what I had said and added that I thought that Paul was kidding himself as well as his mother and me about what he was up to. Paul was at first quiet, but then, suddenly and violently, threw the pen across the room and got up to walk towards the door. He swore at me, accusing me of being a flash Harry, a twisting bastard, a bully who 'couldn't give a toss'. As he opened the door, I simply but firmly said, 'Stay – don't leave this'. Paul hung about but eventually walked over to the pen, picked it up, put it back in its proper place and slumped back into his chair. Suddenly he cried – at first in anger at me for not caring, and then at the police and at his mother for messing him about and his father for never being around. He sat in his chair for several minutes and said nothing. He then looked directly at me and said, 'I am well and truly messed up. I hate it, I don't know what to do'.

This was an extraordinary moment in therapy, quite uncharacteristic. It touched on something genuine in Paul that for the most part he sought to conceal. There were other comparable experiences later in the therapy, but this first moment served as a central reference point – to understand the desolation and vulnerability that underlay his delinquency. Following this, he became more open to exploration of his feelings, not least his sense of betrayal by his mother and father. He was able to gain some understanding of his excitement in invading the privacy of the house that he had burgled: it had belonged to a woman who was a friend of his mother. He also acknowledged that he had been relieved to be caught. He felt bad and he deserved it. Throughout he conveyed a sense of yearning for a relationship – wanting in the moment of burglary to be close to and inside his mother – and in his taking and driving away cars, seeking to be alongside his father. The reality of his impending court experience and sentencing together with his experience of therapy had a moderating effect on his delinquency.

Summary

This chapter has drawn upon a broad definition of delinquency, encompassing a wide range of activities, some of which are criminal, all of which are designed to attack and confound other people. Delinquency represents an inability or unwillingness to relate to others with respect and honesty. Although integral to development and to mental health, it becomes problematic according to its persistence and extremity and to the extent that it disturbs the social group. Numerous risk and protective factors exist to determine a delinquent outcome. Psychodynamic thinking emphasises the importance of early childhood experience, in particular the traumatic impact of childhood maltreatment. Delinquent behaviour is understood in relation to the failure of the environment to provide sufficient care and emotional containment for children to develop the capacity to process and master anxiety. It is seen as a necessary expression, defensive against anxiety and purposeful in evoking a compensatory response from the environment.

In the face of considerable complexity and perplexity, child psychotherapists are faced with considerable therapeutic difficulties, not least delinquents' antagonism, mistrust and equivocal motivation to change. Their responsibility is to find ways of engaging with young people to enable them to overcome their resistances to change and to make sense of the inner experience. This requires a capacity to develop an effective working alliance with young people, to manage the therapeutic potential of the transference and to adapt therapeutic approaches to meet the needs of the different kinds of delinquents. Child psychotherapists need to appreciate the depth of narcissistic disturbance that resides at the centre of much delinquent behaviour and to ensure a secure therapeutic setting in which delinquents can feel contained and facilitated to think. The main struggle in the psychotherapy of adolescents is about trust – to acknowledge and explore what is genuine and authentic. It is that which child psychotherapists search for, and delinquents avoid but need to find.

References

Aichhom, A. (1965) *Delinquency and Child Guidance: Selected Papers,* New York: International Universities Press.

Bion, W. R. (1962) *Learning from Experience,* London: Heinemann.

Bowlby, J. (1951) *Maternal Care and Mental Health,* Geneva: World Health Organization.

Campbell, D. (1996) 'From practice *to* psychodynamic theories of delinquency in adolescence'. In C. Cordess and M. Cox (eds) *Forensic Psychotherapy: Crime, Psychodynamics and the Offender Patient,* Vol. 1, London: Jessica Kingsley. pp. 213–225.

Eissler, K. R. (1958) 'Notes on problems of technique in the psychoanalytic treatment of adolescents: with some remarks on perversions', *Psychoanalytic Study of the Child* 13: 223–254. New York: International Universities Press.

Farrington, D. (1996) *Understanding and Preventing Youth Crime,* Joseph Rowntree Foundation York: York Publishing Services.

Farrington, D. (1997) 'A critical analysis of research and the development of antisocial behaviour from birth to adulthood'. In D. M. Stoff, J. Breiling and J. D. Maser (eds) *Handbook of Antisocial Behaviour,* New York: Wiley. pp. 234–240.

Freud, A. (1965) *Normality and Pathology in Childhood,* New York: International Universities Press.

Freud, S. (1914) *Remembering, Repeating and Working Through,* Standard Edition, Vol. 12, London: Hogarth. pp. 145–156.

Galway, P. (1991) 'Social maladjustment'. In Holmes (ed) *Textbook of Psychotherapy in Psychiatric Practice,* London: Churchill Livings-cone.

Graham, P. (1991) *Child Psychiatry: A Developmental Approach,* 2nd edn, London: Oxford University Press.

Greenberg, H. (1975) 'The widening gyre: transformation of the omnipotent quest during adolescence', *International Review of Psychoanalysis* 2: 231–244.

Home Office. (1995) *Aspects of Crime: Young Offenders 1993 Statistics* 1, London: Division of Home Office Research and Statistics Dept.

Horowitz, F. D. (1987) *Exploring Developmental Theories: Toward a Structural/ Behavioural Model of Development,* Hillside: N.I. Erlbaum.

Jones, D. W. (1987) 'Recent developments in work with young offenders'. In J. Coleman (ed) *Working with Troubled Adolescents,* London: Academic Press.

Kazdin, A. E. (1997) 'Practitioner Review: psychosocial treatment of conduct disorder in children', *Journal of Child Psychology and Psychiatry* 38(2): 161–178.

Kohut, H. (1972) 'Thoughts on narcissism and narcissistic rage', *Psychoanalytic Study of the Child* 27: 360–400.

Laufer, M. and Laufer, M. E. (1984) *Adolescence and Developmental Breakdown,* New Haven, CT: Yale University Press.

Meeks, E. (1971) *The Fragile Alliance: An Orientation to the Outpatient Psychotherapy of the Adolescent,* Baltimore, MD: Williams and Wilkins.

Miller, D. (1983) *The Age between: Adolescence and Therapy,* London: Jason Aronson.

NACRO. (1988) *Diverting Juveniles from Custody,* London: NACRO.

Osorio, L. C. (1979) 'The psychoanalysis of communication in adolescents'. In S. C. Feinstein and P. L. Giovacchini (eds) *Development and Clinical Studies,* Vol. 7, New York: Aronson.

Rutter, M. (1985) 'Psychosocial therapies in child psychiatry: issues and prospects'. In M. Rutter and L. Hersov (eds) *Child and Adolescent Psychiatry: Modern Approaches,* 2nd edn, Oxford: Blackwell.

Sheldrick, C. (1985) 'Treatment of delinquents'. In M. Rutter and L. Hersov (eds) *Child and Adolescent Psychiatry: Modern Approaches,* 2nd edn, Oxford: Blackwell.

Stoller, R. (1975) *Perversion: The Erotic Form of Hatred,* New York: Pantheon Books.

Utting, D., Bright, J. and Henricson, C. (1993) *Crime and the Family: Improving Child Rearing and Preventing Delinquency,* London: Family Policy Studies.

Wadsworth, M. (1979) *The Roots of Delinquency,* London: Martin Robertson.

Wilson, P. (1991) 'Psychotherapy with adolescents'. In J. Holmes (ed) *Textbook of Psychotherapy in Psychiatric Practice,* London: Churchill Livingstone.

Wilson, P. and Hersov, L. (1985) 'Individual and group psychotherapy'. In M. Rutter and L. Hersov (eds) *Child and Adolescent Psychiatry: Modern Approaches,* 2nd edn, London: Blackwell.

Winnicott, D. W (ed) (1960) 'The theory of the parent infant relationship'. In *The Maturational Processes and the Facilitating Environment*, London: Hogarth. p. 37–55, 1965.

Winnicott, D. W (1965) *The Maturational Processes and the Facilitating Environment,* London: Hogarth.

Chapter 6

Narcissism and adolescence

Previously published in J. Cooper & N. Maxwell
(eds) Narcissistic Wounds: Clinical Perspectives.
London: Whurr (1995).

It can be no surprise that adolescents are peculiarly bothered about themselves. There is a great deal going on. The fundamental pubertal changes, combined with expanding cognitive capacities, create an unprecedented state in the life of the individual. The adolescent lives in a state of new physical tension, with sharpened awareness and broader understanding. These changes occur in the context of shifting patterns and alliances within the family and in relation to a demand both from within and outside the family to achieve independence, find work and take on adult and parental responsibilities. In the midst of all this, preoccupations with self-value and self-coherence are inevitable.

There is, by definition, no stability in adolescence. The adolescent is in a constant process of adjustment and transition, contending with new unexpected sensations and fantasies and struggling to find a place in the outside world – with siblings and parents and with other people in the community beyond. The sheer pressure of the developmental and maturational advances of adolescence is such as to give rise to considerable anxiety. There is the fear of the loss of childhood dependency and familiarity: a growing uneasy sense of alienation and aloneness. There is the uncertainty about the challenge and demands that lay ahead and doubts about adequacy, success and the capacity to survive by oneself. There is anxiety too, given the increase of sexual and aggressive potential and the loss of earlier equilibrium and containment, that things will get out of hand – that there will be a failure to contain impulse or hold things together. There is above all in adolescence a particular terror of limitlessness – of there being no bound to possibility, no end to what might happen or be found out.

These anxieties constitute the core of adolescent experience; they give rise to a specific kind of developmental vulnerability that is characteristic of this period of life. It is of vital concern to adolescents to hold on to a measure of self-control and to gain a sense of themselves that encompasses the new diversity of experience and opportunity. The central focus in the fray of all the buffeting is to draw together the various aspects of this experience and achieve some kind of self-integration and definition. Adolescence is thus a time then when narcissistic preoccupations prevail. Perhaps more than in other any other period of life, the overriding and compelling concern is with the nature of the self and its continuity, and with the

DOI: 10.4324/9781003680437-7

search for integrity and worth. The questions that nag and persist, against a constant background of change and uncertainty, are familiar: 'Who am I?', 'What am I?', 'What am I for?' and 'Am I the same as I was yesterday?' These are private questions, integral to the process of individuation and separation and to adolescents' realisation that they must find and take responsibility for themselves (just as they must care for and take ownership of their own bodies). In achieving this, adolescents need to distance themselves from their parents and care takers; the emotional investment that they once placed in parents as children has to be withdrawn and directed more exclusively towards themselves (Blos 1962).

There is in fact a very distinctive insularity in the adolescent experience and a keen, almost overwhelming sense of its fragility. Adolescents exist in a disturbing vacuum, created by the growing detachment from their parents. They are aware, at different levels, of the loss of childhood protection and of the belief in parental omnipotence. They are living in a new phase of disillusionment – as Phillips (1994) puts it 'in the twilight of the Gods' – and yet they feel as if they lack any sense of effective power or influence over what is around them. They feel exposed, still helpless as children and unformed adults, and not at all sure of their capacity or value. Increasingly, they are becoming more aware of their limitations and ultimately their mortality and as yet unsure of what they can achieve.

Adolescents are, as such, in a peculiarly precarious and isolated position. They feel curiously disconnected from all that has held them together in the past and confronted with all that is new and unfamiliar and potentially threatening in the future. They are unavoidably driven back into themselves and, for the time being, as they struggle to keep their balance and find a way forward, they take refuge as it were in the realm of narcissistic defence. It is always part of the eddy of adolescence that progressive and regressive trends swirl about with such unpredictable and varying force. Alongside the curiosity about what is new and the readiness for new dimensions of experience, there are the opposites and the yearning for the way it was before.

It is very much within this dynamic of regression – this narcissistic retreat to earlier modes and defensive patterns – that adolescents veer towards grandiose or idealising solutions (Kohut 1972, 1977). Faced as they are with the vexing questions about self-coherence, value, potency, even existence – they resort unconsciously to the primitive defensive 'configurations' that Kohut has delineated so clearly. These underlie the adolescent experience and shape in one way or another what Greenberg has called 'the omnipotent quest during adolescence' (Greenberg 1975).

Greenberg has captured how adolescents make use of what he calls 'magical manoeuvres' to deal with the underlying sense of narcissistic vulnerability and loss of omnipotence and to fill the 'aching void created by the dethronement of his objects'. He describes how adolescents invest in different kinds of surrogate objects who are idealised and experienced as carrying the very qualities that adolescents feel themselves to lack. The 'Friend', the 'First heterosexual object choice', 'Adults and Older Adolescents', the 'Hero' and the peer group are all seen as restoring adolescents' sense of well-being – giving them a sense of narcissistic 'completion' and of effectiveness through identification and by proxy. Alternatively, the self is invested with omnipotent power. 'The teenager temporarily takes himself as his love object investing himself with the omnipotence of the parents'. There is much, in other words, in adolescents' imagination and perception of themselves and the external world that is larger than life. Adolescents are in a sense full of themselves – self-preoccupied and innocently arrogant; they know it all, they are invincible and can ride alone. There is much, too, in their inclination that is counter-phobic – taking risks, going to the brink, drawing close to the limits of their strengths and capacities. Equally, they are absorbed with strong infatuations and devotions to other people, known and not known, or to causes or activities that consume them and motivate them. Adolescents can identify with the purity and perfection of these others. It is out of these temporary self-creations that a real adult self can eventually be formed as adolescents gradually adjust and adapt to the demands of reality and their own realistic abilities.

This is all the extraordinary mental stuff of ordinary adolescents' lives. Adolescence is a time of heightened narcissism, a necessary transitional period of realisation about the nature of the self, of its limitations and its relation to the outside world. Adolescence is inevitably difficult, bewildering, disconcerting, but equally it is energising, exciting and above all potentially very creative. The majority of adolescents make the most of it, feeling free to risk defeat and frustration, able to tolerate their imperfections and those of others, and ready to enjoy the excitements of the unknown. They can learn and have fun and they know (just about) when to stop – they can keep within the limits of their abilities. Most adolescents get by – some more robustly than others, depending on the core of well-being and personal resource they have gained and built, largely from positive and affirmative parental love in childhood.

There are many adolescents, however, who do not seem to have secured within themselves such a holding, inner core of strength and of self-belief. Various experiences in their lives have rendered them especially vulnerable in adolescence; more terrified than others of separation and independence; more fearful of the demands made on their minds both from within their bodies and the outside world; and more exposed to feelings of inadequacy, significance and potential disintegration. Some may have experienced traumatic loss in early life due to parental death or separation or overwhelming abuse either directly or indirectly, through living in situations of domestic violence. Others may have undergone complicated and confusing early parent/child relationships, set by the ambivalence and inconsistency of their parents that only served to exacerbate and make more frightening the process of separation in childhood. Others too may have been born with particular temperamental dispositions that have rendered them unusually susceptible to both traumatic and less extreme stresses of family life.

Adolescents with these kind of histories and sensibilities feel especially helpless and fearful of what will happen to them next. They lack confidence and they anticipate anything that is new or different as potentially destructive. They feel deeply the loss of their childhood safety and belief in parental protectiveness (however illusory). They feel betrayed and let down by those they have idealised and affronted by the reality of their own imperfections and limitations. The narcissistic defensive processes that are already characteristic of the adolescent state become in these more vulnerable adolescents more prominent. In their attempts to contend with their fears of passivity and loss of control, they are especially inclined to retreat into a pretend world of grandeur. Either they duck the frustrations and complexities of their actual experience by retaining a fantasy of their own omnipotence, or they revere idols who symbolically represent clarity and inviolability. They are inclined to withdraw from social interaction, fortifying themselves in grandiose or idealising fantasies which in turn serve to isolate them further from others. They build in effect an inner world of certainty and perfection which they struggle to protect at all costs against any incursion.

The effects of such narcissistic retreat can be seen in a wide range of adolescent disturbance. Adolescents who engage in reckless delinquent behaviour, for example, are often excessively taken up with an inflated image of themselves, at the cost of losing touch with the realistic consequences of their actions. Other adolescents may take refuge in various compulsive activities, such as drug or alcohol abuse, or computer game addictions, or eating disorders, which are extremely self-absorbing and often contain a great deal of omnipotent reverie. The lives of many of these adolescents are necessarily restricted, although they are able to function more of less adequately in the everyday course of life, attending school and work and having some sort of social life.

There are some adolescents, however, who remove themselves more extensively from the outside world (Wilson 1988). Their withdrawal is not psychotic: their reality testing is intact and they have the capacity to relate appropriately with other people. It is rather that they have chosen to insulate themselves within an encapsulated inner world, immersed in private preoccupation and fantasy and occupied in solitary activities. Their position is one of massive retrenchment, an extreme form of narcissistic retreat. Many drop out of school or work. They give up their studies and literally disappear into their rooms, often staying in bed throughout the day, only occasionally making limited forays out of the house. Their lives become set, stuck and very lonely. They effectively hole themselves up in self-created fortresses and quite actively, often violently, fend off any threat of encroachment. Their self-imposed isolation of course does not exist in isolation. It occurs in the proximity of others who are inevitably concerned. It functions both to defy and torment those who are around – and paradoxically to call forth the very interference it seeks to resist.

Case illustration

Ronald, a 16-year-old boy, was referred to me by a distraught mother who felt she could no longer stand by watching her son 'do nothing'. He spent his time almost entirely at home; by day, watching television in the living room, and in the evening locking himself into his room. His mother thought that he read comics and played computer games. She knew that occasionally at night he went out – but she didn't know where he went. For the most part, Ronald made sure that he was not seen by the rest of his family. He completely ignored his father and became increasingly nasty and offensive to his mother and younger sister. The only sign of warmth or pleasure that he showed was in his relationship to his dog whom he fed and cared for tenderly.

Ronald's mother described him as a worrying child from the beginning. As a baby he cried and fretted a great deal. He was a restless toddler and slept poorly. He was especially clinging, attending nursery school and this worsened following the birth of his sister when he was aged four. In infant school he started well enough and had a very close friendship with another boy who lived next door. This unfortunately came to a sudden end when the friend's family moved away. He was very upset by this and seemed to 'lose heart and give up' at school. In secondary school, he was frequently absent, leaving school in the middle of the morning and returning home. When he was 13, he was caught shop lifting with a group of other boys on a number of occasions and for a while hung around with them on the streets. Eventually he gave this up and for most of the time he was a loner. His one claim to fame was that he was a good cross-country runner and he ran for a local club in his fourth and fifth years. For a while he had a relationship with a girlfriend, but that soon seemed to drift away. Towards the end of his school days, he was described as a sullen and withdrawn young man, rather awkward and gauche in his manner and just 'throwing away his chances'. He left school with poor GCSEs and did nothing for a year after leaving school.

There had apparently been no dramatic or disturbing events in his family history. The family had remained intact through his childhood with a supportive extended family nearby. Mother recalled how she had fallen ill when Ronald was eight and that he and his sister had been cared for by her sister. His father at that time had been away on business. It was at that time that Ronald lost his close friend who moved out of the area.

I saw Ronald in once weekly psychotherapy for 15 months. He initially complained about coming – 'I'm here on sufferance' – but in fact he did not miss a session during the entire length of the therapy. Ronald was a tall rather plumpish young man, slightly sleepy and vague in his manner with a wrought and wary expression. Initially he was silent and resistant. He waited for my questions and then dismissed them. There was no point, he said, in coming, he had no problems, he had 'no feelings'. All that mattered was that he should be left alone. He knew why his mother had wanted him to see me; but he dismissed her concern – 'she's always making a fuss'. In the first few weeks, I chose not to press on this issue, but instead looked for ways of finding some contact, however tenuous. Gradually, almost despite himself, he started to talk about his comics and his computer games. These were activities that clearly absorbed him and it soon became clear that he knew a great deal about both. His knowledge of the various heroes and villains in the comics was remarkably detailed and his understanding of computers seemed very impressive.

As the therapy became more established, so he became increasingly free and open in telling me more about all these interests. He was visibly *very* excited to have me as an audience. He boasted and bragged and looked for approval. For the most part, he seemed to assume that I knew the characters that he was referring to and the technicalities as well as he did. He enjoyed quizzing me and catching me out and thereby demonstrating his superiority. Occasionally he became angry with my ineptitude and failure to pay attention to the many details he told me. I was inevitably left floundering.

There was much in all of this that was quite boyish, almost delightfully so in its innocence and excitement. And yet there was another side, something more pressured and desperate. When for example he described the activities of the various comic characters, he became noticeably tense and harsh in his tone of voice. He clearly derived a great deal of sadistic pleasure from much of the violent behaviour that the comic heroes engaged in. In his insistence, too, on my going along with what he had to say, there was also something ominously intimidating. These early sessions proceeded nevertheless remarkably smoothly, considering his initial almost obdurate resistance. It was clear, however, that the overall agenda of the sessions was very much set by him. In response to my interest and effort to make a connection, he filled the sessions with his own private preoccupations, to the exclusion of all else that might be of concern to his mother or the reasons for him being in therapy. He implicitly required me to follow and admire what he was doing and talking about. He sought in effect to have me under his control, within the orbit of his fascinations – rather than as someone separate, who might take another line of interest. There was in fact something quite sealed off about these early sessions, as if an 'external world' did not exist.

The spell, however, had to be broken. About three months after the beginning of therapy, I had two frantic telephone calls from Ronald's mother saying that things were getting worse. Ronald had in fact had a very violent row with his father and had locked himself in his room for the whole weekend. He had not come out to eat and was silent and his mother had been worried he might have damaged himself. When I brought this information to Ronald in the next session, his manner changed abruptly. He looked grey and tense and he avoided any eye contact with me. He fell silent again. Eventually, he asked 'what do you want to know?' I simply wondered what had been going through his mind since we last met. 'None of your business' was all he had to say. The session passed uncomfortably with nothing more to add. Similarly, several sessions proceeded in this way – 'I have nothing to say, I feel nothing'.

Gradually however, in the following sessions, he did begin to talk about what was on his mind – and not least about his family and other people. He hated his father and sister and he despised his mother – they were all 'stupid' and 'hypocrites'. His father was weak and untrustworthy. His sister was a 'pathetic girl' and his mother just 'snivelled and whined'. He had no time for any of them. As far as he was concerned, they could 'suffer'. He wasn't prepared to explain this intensity of denigration and contempt, but from time to time, he gave hints of how he had loathed his parents for the way they had rowed with each other and had nearly separated in the past. He remembered how his mother had been ill when he was a little boy; he conveyed not so much concern about her as of anger that she had left him in the care of his aunt.

The extent and power of his hatred for his family was alarming. He continued for several sessions in this vein to express yet more and more invective against them. This inevitably spread to other people outside the family for whom he said he had 'no regard' – middle aged 'tarted up' women, children 'who pester', motorists who 'carve you up'. He condemned them all and vowed to have nothing more to do with anybody. And he added vehemently – 'if they mess with me, I'll kill 'em.'

After a month or so, this tirade subsided and he slowly returned to his interest in comics and computers – a world which he now called his 'comic zone'. It was as if he lived in two different worlds – a pleasurable world of his own making and under his own control and a hostile world beyond his ken and altogether persecutory. His retreat seemed in many respects quite straightforward – simply away from the latter into the refuge of the former. As far as he was concerned, he needed no one and he had no intention of 'budging'. 'They can put up with it – sod "em"'. This same sentiment existed in the transference. Either I complied with his implicit demand that I take part in the comic zone on his terms, or I was to be dismissed.

The therapy now proceeded along a difficult tortuous path. There was a continuous tension between his requirement for me to remain within his 'comic zone', and my concern to keep alive the feelings he had expressed and his difficulties in the outside world. To some extent, of course, I followed his preoccupations with his comic heroes, I listened to his stories, I remembered the characters and I took part in his quizzes. And, above all, I paid attention to the significance of these characters for him – their super-powers, their invincibility, their existence 'above us all'. But, especially against the background of mounting parental anxiety, he and I could not ignore his withdrawal and his avoidance at what was going on in his actual life. As time went on and the more I pressed, so his fury with his parents and so many others became more passionate. At the same time, he asserted ever more insistently his indifference for what happened and his own superiority. He had no need he said for education, for example, for he knew all there was to know about computers. He 'knew' too that he could always make a living 'writing comic books'. People simply didn't know what he knew – and he had no intention of letting them know anyway.

The more he continued like this, the more he sought to dismiss and belittle me. He often mocked me and accused me of wanting to get him 'down and hoodwink' him – just like his father had done over the years. He was flippant, and ridiculed me for being 'mad'. Periodically, however, something harder showed through, something more angry and menacing. This he just about managed to hold in check, though there were many times when he found my failure to remember all of the details of his 'comic zone' and my refusal to stop enquiring about his feelings and his activities outside the therapy room 'very annoying' – even as he put it 'deliberate and insulting'. He sustained his demand that I should 'shut up – and stop the smart talk', (i.e. my references to the difficulties he had told me about in his life and his attempts to not have to 'think about them too much' because 'They're uncomfortable'). Despite all of his protest and derision, however, he was able at times to listen and reflect, albeit that he quickly got back to his 'comic zone'. He was never late for sessions: he never totally stopped me from speaking and equally he never tired of drawing my attention to 'what's in there?' (comic zone).

After about seven months of therapy, his mother phoned again this time to tell me that, unless her son pulled himself together, she and her husband were going to throw him out of the house. She reported that there had been yet another violent row between Ronald and his father. Ronald had also frightened his sister, threatening her with a knife. I, as before, reported this telephone conversation to Ronald in the following session. He was furious. 'She's got no right to be calling up'. 'She doesn't care'. 'She's a bitch' and so forth. The more he ranted in this way, the more he lost his composure – so the more he sought to dominate and daunt me, 'It's none of your business', 'keep your nose out of it'. I dealt with this similarly as before, acknowledging his anger, dissatisfaction and pointing out how desperately he tried to hide all this in his 'comic zone'. I also added on this particular occasion a question that I had not put to him so simply before – 'What has hurt you so much in the past to make you so angry now?' This took him by surprise. He was silent for a moment and then spluttered 'Hurt, hurt; what do you mean, bloody hurt!' Suddenly he was beside himself, his lips quivered, he was close to tears. He got up from his chair and strode around the room glaring down at me and raising his fist as if to hit me – 'Hurt! What hurt! Who's hurt! I'm not hurt. I'll show you what hurt is'. For a few moments, he was incoherent. I didn't move and I said no more and he eventually sat back in his chair. In a cold and deliberate way, he informed me that I was stupid, I understood nothing, it was always a waste of time to come and see me, and if I said anything more, he would leave the room immediately. As far as he was concerned, nothing had got to him and what he did feel was his private business anyway. It was a tense, frightening, quite distraught moment – but eventually I was able to speak. I quietly said that I thought he had in fact felt hurt and frightened a great deal – by his parents threatening to evict him – and that in some way this had touched on other earlier experiences he had suffered in his life that had similarly made him feel useless and unwanted and very angry. I said that I understood the appeal of the comic zone – but he and I knew we could not ignore these feelings; they mattered too much for him not to go away – and they were here in the therapy room.

He was quiet for a while and at one point left the room to go to the toilet. When he returned, he suddenly started to talk quite movingly about the friend he had had at primary school who had moved away. He remembered feeling very confused about it at the time – he just couldn't understand why his friend had had to go. He had felt very let down and hurt – and his mother being ill and his father being away left him feeling even more abandoned and confused than before. As he left the session, he apologised for yelling at me – he said he felt 'bad' about that and he hoped that I was not too upset.

Therapy continued for eight months after that session. He returned for a while to the 'comic zone' and didn't give up his 'songs' of hatred about other people for a while. He held onto these, however, with less tenacity than before and, although always resistant, he did begin to think about 'changing my life'. He talked more about his childhood friend and with greater candour than before, he recalled his lack of friends at school, the bullying he had been victim to, and the overriding sense of betrayal he felt in general. The idea of seeking revenge on all those who had let him down excited him still – and he could talk animatedly of the tales of vengeance that occurred in the comic stories. He was more amenable to my raising the destructive and self-destructive consequences of such revenge – and he at least could begin to reconsider whether or not his parents 'deserved it'. There was no prospect as far as he was concerned, however, of 'letting up' on his father, but he was opening up to the possibility of getting out of the home more – rather than 'digging himself' in all of his hatred.

In the last period of therapy, Ronald seemed to 'grow up'. He seemed more ready to leave his comic zone and develop more his interest in computers. He seemed less fraught and more able to laugh at himself 'the loony in the attic' – and even express some concern about his mother's health. He finally found himself a job in a computer firm which he could actually allow himself to say he enjoyed. He felt that 'therapy had worked' but, partly because of his new working hours and travel, and partly because he felt 'he'd had enough for the time being', he decided to finish therapy.

Discussion

This boy preferred a world of his own. His immersion in his 'comic zone' insulated him from intolerable tensions in the external world and provided him with a wealth of possibility in fantasy that he felt was unattainable in reality. Adolescence for him was not a pleasurable or exciting time. He found it overwhelming and frightening – a predominantly frustrating and humiliating experience. He was, as far as he could see, safer and stronger by himself.

Perhaps most disturbing – and most disruptive of his adolescence – was the hostility that he carried into his adolescence from his childhood. This was not necessarily manifest in his late childhood, but a growing sense of resentment seemed to characterise his early adolescence. His petty delinquency, truancy and underachievement at school were indications that things were not right for him. His eventual isolation and evident rebuke of, and periodic attacks, on his parents were stronger, more trenchant expressions of discontent and anger. People in his family were made to suffer – to be left in the dark and uneasy. And people outside the family were avoided – for fear of what they might do (mess him about) and what he might do ('kill 'em'). 'em = 'them'

His self-imposed exile (he banished himself from the outside world, and he banished others from his) seemed ever-increasingly complete, almost fortress-like. He effectively snarled at all those outside whom he saw as traitors and persecutors; his contempt and denigration and exclusion of others gave vent to his hostility and equally preserved his illusion of his inviolability. He had, he felt, no need of others; he had no feelings, no desire or yearning that could be hurt or thwarted. His safety was himself – and his pleasure was within himself. In many ways, it was true that he truly loved himself. His comic characters gave solace and fortitude. They had all of the powers and attractions which he felt he lacked and which he could catch hold of through identification. These characters were unhurtable and invincible; they were also powerful – they could hurt and wreak havoc. Through their super-abilities, they could set things right – many of them triumphed *over* villains – and this had its own particular appeal to his own sense of injustice in his actual life.

This major narcissistic retrenchment served him well in many respects. Not only did it provide him with a place of safety, albeit illusory, but it also opened up a world in which he could feel good and enjoy a sense of control and strength. It was a plastic world in which he could elaborate fantasies of all sorts, not least of revenge and aggression. It could be said that in this elaboration, within the private confines of his room, he found an 'acceptable' way of expressing his violence. It was a form of self-containment. At the same time, it cocked a snook at those he wished to defy.

All of this suited him, both in his pathway through adolescence and in his own particular protest at his parents. His narcissistic retreat had both a developmental and individual significance – it served to deal with adolescent anxieties in general and with the *revived* feelings of hurt and resentment that he brought forward from his childhood. The intensity of these feelings (and thus of the degree of narcissistic defensive response) is difficult to fully understand from the knowledge of the history given – but there are indications to suggest that he was from the beginning a sensitive 'difficult' infant, who may have encountered early obstacles to the attachment to his mother. He later endured levels of stress in his family and in the parental marriage which may in turn have been confusing and frightening and proved more than he could understand or cope with. His unusually close relationship to his school friend may have been a sign of this stress and represented a pre-adolescent narcissistic defence against loss of faith in his parents – through devotion to an idealised friend. In these circumstances, the loss of his friend for reasons beyond his control may have constituted a major trauma in latency – that overlay earlier trauma.

This boy was a reluctant entrant to psychotherapy. There were many reasons – not least the many advantages accruing from his narcissistic defensive retreat – why he would not be motivated to change. He was in effect pushed into psychotherapy by his mother – and therapy therefore was something instantly to be resisted. The only possibility of any therapeutic movement could arise through his own recognition of the inadequacy of his narcissistic solution. Clearly, at some level, he was already aware of its limitations before he came to therapy – his life was restricted, he had few friends, the world he perceived as frightening. But through his denunciation of the outside world and his involvement in his inner world, he could hold off the reality, at least for the time being.

Psychotherapy had to proceed slowly in acknowledgement of this ambiguity – and for much of the beginning period of therapy took place according to the dictates of this boy's narcissistic requirements. To have pressed 'reality' on him prematurely

would have been to have risked his further retrenchment – either culminating in
the termination of therapy on his part or leading to a form of false compliance.
Time had to be taken to follow his lead and to relate to the world that he was so
interested in. It was important to play – not only in the Winnicottian sense of establishing a necessary transitional area for personal exchange, but also in the spirit of
adolescence – attending to both childlike and adult-like facets of his personality.
The admixture of boyish delight and, as it were, manly severity was a striking feature of psychotherapy with this boy.

Within this broad setting, the psychotherapy took many forms – at times absorbed
in the details and manoeuvrings of the various comic characters and the impressive
facts of computer literacy, and at other times, struggling with the feelings and sensibilities that he had about himself and about his parents and others in his life. There
were aspects of the transference that clearly reflected his defiance of his father and
disappointment in his mother; he fought not to be taken over and he resisted any
hint of dependency for fear of being let down. But what was most prominent as the
therapy moved on was the development of more primitive narcissistic transferences.
As he opened up his 'comic zone' so increasingly he sought to secure me within it as
an admiring and devoted audience. His narcissistic need was to have me in attendance, following and affirming – and effectively mirroring benignly his achievements.
Within this transference, I did not have the sense that I was other than what he wanted
me to be – a part of his world – a 'self-object' (Kohut 1972). His manner became
quite imperious and arrogant – and the facets of himself that he so dreaded – his use-
lessness, his impotence, his stupidity – were conveniently projected on to me.

This was the mode that was set for much of the therapy, particularly in its middle
phase. It was a way of proceeding that he effectively insisted upon in accordance
with the demands of his narcissism. Psychotherapy could not have proceeded without passing through it – without some basis of his sense of affirmation and positive regard from me. Equally, it could not have progressed without his narcissistic
retrenchment being challenged.

As much as he avoided or resisted, and with however much violence, he could
not entirely *evade* the encroachments of the external world – the rebuff of his peers,
the failure of his exam efforts and of course the criticism of his parents. No matter
how much protection his narcissistic world offered, it could never be enough to
withstand the pressure of the external world – and these pressures were inevitably
experienced in therapy. Psychotherapy consisted of a constant tension between his
narcissistic insularity and the demands of the outside world (much of which of
course he internalised). The phone calls from his mother into my office were part of
these demands – they literally sounded the bell. Moments occurred in therapy that
were unavoidably fraught and desperate and made more poignant – as effectively,
I was perceived as no longer part of his narcissistic milieu but different, separate
and thereby threatening and betraying. These moments, though alarming, were not
in fact destructive – in the context of the whole therapy – but were on the contrary
productive of change. What was striking in the midst of these moments and in their
aftermath was his increased acknowledgement of his vulnerability, of his 'hurt'

feelings and of his fears – and most notably of the loss of his childhood friend who stood for so much in his early life to do with loyalty and attachment. The therapy was able to move on, on the basis of the insights of these moments towards greater integration and an acknowledgement of the demands of reality. Clearly by the end of therapy, this process had not been completed – but enough had been achieved to facilitate this adolescent to join up in the mainstream of life. He of course did not relinquish all of his fantasies and preoccupations – but effectively they interfered less with his ordinary adaptation to ordinary life and the development of his abilities in relation to other people. He himself thought 'therapy had worked'.

Summary

Adolescence is a time of change and uncertainty. Its development is characterised by a range of anxieties associated with changes in the body and the processes of separation and individuation. These anxieties give rise developmentally to a state of vulnerability that needs to be contained. It is inevitable that adolescence will be peculiarly preoccupied with issues of self-worth and self-coherence. These are fundamental narcissistic concerns and they form the basis of adolescent experience.

Narcissistic regressive processes are an integral part of adolescent development. They serve to defend against the developmental anxieties and to provide stimulus and direction to the emergence of the self. In adolescents who bring from their childhoods particular insecurities and unresolved conflicts, these narcissistic processes may predominate and interfere significantly with the adolescent's adaptation to the reality of his own limitations and of others. Adolescent disturbance in its many forms can be understood in terms of the effects of narcissistic retrenchment – leading to excessive preoccupation with the self and as in the case illustration, to extreme forms of social isolation.

References

Blos, P. (1962) *On Adolescence: A Psychoanalytic Interpretation*, New York: Free Press.
Greenberg, H. (1975) 'The widening gyre: transformations of the omnipotent quest during adolescence', *The International Review of Psychoanalysis* 2: 231–244.
Kohut, H. (1972) 'Thoughts on narcissism and narcissisms rage', *Psychoanalytic Study of the Child* 27: 360–400.
Kohut, H. (1977) *The Restoration of the Self*, New York: International Universities Press.
Phillips, A. (1994) *On Flirtation*, London: Faber.
Wilson, P. (1988) 'The impact of cultural changes on the internal experience of the adolescent', *Journal of Adolescence* 11: 271–286.

Chapter 7

Me loves me: what is this thing called narcissism?

Resistance in adolescent psychotherapy

Presentation at a Conference of the Limbus Foundation, Dartington, Devon, UK (2019). Unpublished.

Me loves Me. This is the title of this chapter. Stark, to the point. This is the point: Me. This is what I want to highlight in what we might want to call the compelling world of the 'Meedom' that we live in today – a 'me' generation, a world of the 'Me Too'.

And then, if we take a look at our politicians who cavort in front of us on our streets and screens and in our ever-widening social media, we are overrun with the rejoicings of those who glorify themselves. Trump of course trumps them all. On Thanksgiving Day, for example, he hailed his ever-adoring audiences to give thanks, not to the hardy saviours and pioneers of a great country, but, guess what, to Him. Thank Me, he said. And now, our very own Boris. On the day of his inauguration as Prime Minister, the first three lines of a Guardian article read 'Me, Me, Me', The Spectator magazine added to this with a front cover, full of identical little bobbing hair Borises with the caption 'The Boris Team'. Finally, we can take a look at two recent book titles in the admittedly self-engrossed world of auto biography. One by the endearingly and appositely named writer, Will Self. He entitled his autobiography *Will*. Elton John topped this. His was simply *Me*.

To put all this in another word, what I am talking about is a thing called narcissism. Cole Porter sang his immortal song 'What is this thing called Love' and I amend simply 'What is this thing called Narcissism (Self Love)'. He and I call it a thing because in many ways, it is something that is so difficult to fully get a hold of. Are we talking about vanity, pride, dignity, self-assurance and forthrightness? Or do we have in mind someone who is self-engrossed, conceited, nothing less than a raving, vainglorious megalomaniac too big for his or her own boots? The word carries all sorts of meanings and nuances and, in many ways, it can be applied to all of us, to every Tom, Dick and Harry amongst us.

Whatever it is, there is no doubt in my mind that it refers to something so very fundamental in our human nature and in our everyday clinical practice. Freud of course highlighted sexuality in his 1905 'Three essays on the Theory of Sexuality', as a central pulse in the very essence of our being. But it was not all that much later – only nine years – in his writing that he came to appreciate the importance of narcissism as a basic general human attitude and as a stage of emotional development in which we favour ourselves in our emerging relation to others.

DOI: 10.4324/9781003680437-8

Briefly, in his introductory paper *On Narcissism* (Freud 1914), he came to acknowledge that people find ways of withdrawing from whatever it is that is disagreeably required of them in external reality and as experienced internally. Most dramatically, he saw schizophrenics disappearing within their own internal delusional and hallucinatory worlds, seemingly in flight from overwhelming external and internal stimuli. He saw people in sleep as effectively retreating within themselves from their waking life and people in physical pain losing interest in other people, not least in making love to them. Freud quoted, with a twinkle in his eye, the German poet Wilhelm Busch who was musing on suffering from toothache. He put it succinctly: 'Concentrated is his soul in his molar's narrow hole'. And finally, he saw children, in the midst of their omnipotent assumptions about their place in the world, believing that that they are at the centre of everything (that for example, if their parents are angry or upset or divorcing, it is their fault). It was from these observations that Freud developed his ideas on narcissism as an over-riding self-preoccupation. It is also worthy of mentioning that in the very midst of the Three Essays, he was becoming interested in the way the libido moved back and forwards from what he called object libido to ego libido, what he called 'narcissistic libido'. He concluded that there were two kinds of love, that is, we love ourselves and we love the mother who nurses us.

Within narcissism itself, he suggested that there were two levels – what he referred to as a primary narcissism and a secondary narcissism. The first he imagined as a force stirring as it were from within the individual in a very rudimentary sense, that this is so say, from the sheer inherent biological pressure to assert and to express life. This he thought could in turn be celebrated secondarily from the acceptance and admiration of one's self by other people. Let me give you an example – may I offer a 'me' example – I play the piano for my own pleasure; I sit alone and what I do comes from just Me. I don't look for anyone to hear it; it's sufficient that I find my own expression. But when I play in public for performance, I am delighted to be recognised and appreciated.

In all of these enquiries and theoretical ideas, I believe that what Freud was trying to do was to figure out how we, as human beings, can progress from an initial undifferentiated state of infantile bodily tension, what he called 'auto eroticism', to the most developed mature adult state in which the individual is able to fully appreciate the existence of another person to be loved in his or her own right. He saw narcissism as a necessary step in this direction in childhood and throughout life.

Following on from Freud, and keeping in mind the Greek myth of Narcissus, the young man who became so besotted by the image of himself in the water that he eventually drowned, a great deal of interest developed over the years among psychoanalysts in the whole phenomenon of narcissism. I shall highlight the work of Heinz Kohut (Kohut 1968, 1972), who explored a new theoretical conception of narcissism. He came to prominence in Chicago in the 1960s and 1970s at a time when there was a general sociological concern that the United States was being taken over by a 'Culture of Narcissism' (Lasch 1979) – that is a culture in which individualism and self-seeking prevailed in a predominantly capitalistic, consumerist society. Kohut and another psychoanalyst, Otto Kernberg (Kernberg 1985), built up a lively controversy between the two of them, as to how to understand narcissism and how to treat narcissistically disturbed individuals – or more accurately how to understand what they called pathological or malignant narcissism.

Kohut recognised of course that we are all narcissistic in one way or other in how we care for ourselves and others and how we all strive to improve and better ourselves. He saw nothing wrong in that – in what we can call 'normal' or 'healthy' narcissism. This was in keeping with various philosophical ideas, such as from Baruch Spinoza, the seventeenth century Dutch philosopher, that all of our emotions are a sort of register of our attempts to hold ourselves together – to fend off threats to our survival and cohesion and to live integrated lives (Edwin 1985–2016). Kohut in effect focused on people who had been unable to cope with such threats. He saw these people whom he described as suffering from a severe narcissistic disturbance, as having experienced in their early childhoods what he called narcissistic trauma – that is to say, experiences in which they had been rendered terrified, confused and helpless.

These experiences he understood to have happened of course in the hands of adults and parents who, for one reason or another, had been for the most part neglectful, abusive and, perhaps worst of all, highly ambivalent in their dealings with their children. I refer to such ambivalence later, when I make use of a phrase, the 'balm and startle' of the experiences of many children faced with the tormenting perplexity of extreme parental inconsistency – that is to say, children growing up for example in a peculiarly overly intense intimacy with parents who, themselves wrought and equivocal, alternate between periods of lovingness and of hatred towards their children.

How do children such as these live in such turmoil? Kohut suggested two fundamental intrapsychic defensive processes with which such children magically seek respite from such trauma – either through the creation of an internal fantasy of what he called the 'grandiose self' or through the creation of what he termed the 'idealised parental imago'. In other words, to deal with the underlying feelings of terror, humiliation and utter helplessness, they create within their minds the conviction that "I am perfect (and no longer vulnerable)" or 'You are Perfect (of which I am a part and thus again no longer vulnerable)'.

It may be of interest that I wrote a paper many years ago in which I drew on Kohut's ideas to put forward a rather grand quasi-sociological theory about the adolescents of the day (Wilson 1988) based on my making three prominent observations: firstly that teenagers were increasingly getting caught up in the entertaining 'balm' of the television; secondly and simultaneously that they were being terrified and 'startled' by the horrific images of war and potential nuclear travesty; and thirdly that they increasingly lack support and containment in their attempts to manage their lives in an increasingly loose libertarian and anti-authority culture. Bringing all this altogether at that time, I saw a new kind of 'me' generation, a new breed of highly narcissistic teenagers, faced with cultural inconstancies and the absence of coherent authority.

Since then, we might suggest that the situation has become further exaggerated in the light of the growing expanse of social media, the increasing awareness of potential global catastrophe and a general fragmentation in the social order. The appeal of a retreat into individual narcissistic fantasies of grandiosity or of the blind narcissistic devotion of revered politicians, celebrities, musicians, 'gods' of one sort or another may contribute to an even worsening of the prevailing cultural situation.

However, at this point in my talk, I don't want to dwell any further on these theoretical and speculative ideas. For the moment, I think it is time for me to talk about adolescence in general and about some of the adolescents that I have seen in recent years. There is no question in my own mind that an understanding of narcissism has played a very significant part in my trying to make sense of the contemporary adolescent predicament and what I have found useful in psychotherapy with adolescents.

A few years ago, I wrote a chapter on 'Narcissism and Adolescence' (Wilson 1995). I began by saying something obvious. Adolescents. I said, are 'peculiarly bothered about themselves'. There is after all 'a great deal going on'. I described at some length the enormous impact of the biological revolution going on in their bodies (called puberty) and the unrelenting demands of the developmental separation/individuation process – both of which could lead to what I called the 'very distinctive insularity' and fragility in the adolescent experience.

The adolescent in other words is in a precarious developmental state – no longer cared for as a child and increasingly left exposed to the uncertain and daunting prospects of adult life. Again, remembering Kohut's ideas, grandiose and idealising fantasies are very much a necessary part of this experience, in what Greenberg described as the 'omnipotent quest during adolescence' (Greenberg 1975). Greenberg saw the teenager dealing with what he referred to as a development 'void' (in the separation/individuation process) with the use of various kinds of defences (or, as he put it, 'magical manoeuvres'). Some adolescents buttress themselves in close friendships: others look to peer groups or older young people or adults to give them the sense of being cared for, yet others in their devotion to various kinds of heroes whom they think have almighty power to save them. There are others who retreat into their own narcissistic reveries in which they can hold the illusion of their perfection, inviolability and sense of total control.

Adolescents: the frenetics and the isolates

I want now to tell you about some of these more disturbed adolescents whom I have tried to deal with over the years. I am not going to pull out straightaway the *DSM* categories to give you an idea of what they were like because as we well know now they throw little light on the complex nature of the problems they are trying to categorise. Instead, I am going to use my own descriptive terms to cover the kind of adolescents that I have been involved with in psychotherapy. I have in mind two groups, one of which I will call the 'Frenetics' and the others the 'Isolates'.

The word 'frenetic' carries with it an image of something wild, outward going, uncontained and frantic. Interestingly the word comes from the Greek *phrenitis* meaning the 'inflammation of the brain'. The word 'isolate' on the other hand, is pretty well self-explanatory, with connotations of withdrawal, insulation and indeed seclusion – in effect keeping apart from others. Needless to say, these are not discrete entities – within the isolate there are frenetic goings on in their minds, and in the minds of the frenetics, there is an inner sense of isolation. However, they will do to paint a picture of how I saw them.

In the following account of four adolescents, I shall begin with a brief description of how each presented themselves in psychotherapy with me and how I experienced them. I shall later think about how I tried to help them.

For the most part, I saw these adolescents in psychotherapy on a once weekly basis. The duration of psychotherapy was on average two years.

The names used for these adolescents are pseudonyms.

Two adolescents; the frenetics

Sarah: the frenetic

Sarah was a 16-year-old girl who seemed to live a life that was in perpetual chaotic motion, interspersed with times of morose inertia. Her mother was on tenterhooks wondering what would happen next. Her older brother was furious with her for being so 'bloody irresponsible' and her closest friend described her as 'desperate'. Sarah meanwhile seemed not to care. She danced; she raved; she stayed out late at night; she drank; she took drugs. She was 'mad' about a man much older than herself who was a leader and singer in a band she thought was 'awesome'. She literally flung herself into reckless, wild and often dangerous situations. Her schoolwork deteriorated and her health became precarious, often undernourished by erratic feeding or overstimulated by drugs unknown. She was in many respects beside herself. Occasionally she collapsed exhausted in her room tearful, angry, scratchy.

Her therapy with me in the beginning was for the most part a kind of race. She sort of hurled her way through the sessions, full of endless accounts of new clubs that she had been to, of boyfriends that she had and of hair-raising incidents that she had put herself through. Unusually, she seemed totally unconcerned about recounting all of this; it was all very much in the open, 'a blast', a boast. For many weeks, I found it impossible to establish any real contact with her, to acknowledge with her what indeed she might be concerned about. Everyone, including she and I, was at sea and the question forever grew as to where were we all going! Sarah seemed to be in full flight in a world of defiance, in masterly denial. In such almighty command, she made it clear that she 'knew' that she was alright – that the dangers she encountered were harmless, that the people she knew were fantastic and that her mother and brother were 'just fine' or 'wrong'. There existed no problem. Her enduring refrain was 'I know' what 'I am doing'. 'You lot are stupid, you don't understand, you never will understand, I don't need to listen to you. I'm sorted'.

Charlie: the frenetic

Let's now to turn to Charlie. Charlie too was 16. He was in many respects in his patch, Jack the Lad. He saw himself as one of the most able and popular boys at school and he boasted of a large group of friends all of whom he thought looked up to him. He fancied himself as an authority on music. He did indeed have a vast knowledge of all the major bands in the music world and he had a particular interest in two local bands for whom he saw himself as 'manager'. He himself had no particular musical talent, but this did not deter him in promoting himself as someone who could help build musical careers. He was a particular fan of one of the most popular and prominent bands of his time and he attended most of their gigs, all over the country. He just knew that they were the most fantastic band of all time and he set about to know everything about the band's members and the music they wrote and performed.

His life was very much taken up with all this activity. He attended school but he had no time for study. He knew more than most teachers about pretty well everything and he treated their concern with contempt. He had no need to study. He would pass anyway. And besides, he knew the teachers either liked him or feared him. He reckoned he could get away with anything. He was smart and needing no one.

His therapy with me in the beginning was little more than a glorified performance. He effectively controlled me and demanded my approval and admiration. He saw no need to see me – he was only seeing me because his mother, in his view, was needlessly on his back. In those early sessions, he would often suddenly interrupt his flow and say 'Why am I here'? There is nothing wrong with me'. His disdain for me was very similar to Sarah's.

Two adolescents; the isolates

Damien: the isolate

Damien, aged 17, was described by his mother as miserable, withdrawn and angry all the time. He didn't go to college. He was abusive to his younger sisters and at times he was physically violent with his father. He spent much of his time in his room on his computer. He rarely went out of the house; when he did so, he went late in the evening without any explanation to anyone. He didn't eat with the family, choosing to make his own sandwiches and eat them in his room. He had no friends and he showed little interest in studying. He was contemptuous of school, making it clear that they had nothing to teach him. They were imbeciles and he had no need of them. He didn't care about their silly examinations.

However, he did have one interest – and this was to do with the protection of animals. He was in thought and sympathy (but not yet in action) an animal rights protestor. He knew a lot about all the laboratory experiments that were carried out on animals. And he knew a great deal about all the various species in the world that were being made extinct because of the greedy and selfish behaviour of human beings. About all of this, he spoke with passion and sheer rage – 'I hate them all'. He said that when he goes out he found himself wanting to murder 'pesty' children and fat, flabby and bossy women, all of them 'slags'.

His therapy was rarely comfortable. He had been seen by several eminent psychiatrists before he came to see me.

He made it clear that they were all useless and that he hated them. He couldn't see how I could possibly be any different. He generally dismissed me as 'pointless' like all those other fuckers. He thought I knew nothing and certainly not him. He didn't need any understanding. The only person who understood him was 'me'. The only person who could teach him anything was 'me'. He often sat in silence and then would criticise me: 'If you don't say something in the next five minutes, I am buggering off'. 'I don't think you have a clue what you are doing ... and stop staring at me like that'. The only reprieve to any of this was when he spoke about the protection of animals and the species. He spoke admiringly of some of the leading animal rights protestors and of the injustice of what is happening to defenceless animals. For the most part, he basically talked to himself with me as a captive audience, with little opportunity to respond in any way.

Ronald: the 'isolate'

My fourth case, Ronald, was similarly isolated as Damien though with less venom. He too was 17. Much to his mother's consternation, he, as she put it 'does nothing'. He spent his time almost entirely at home, watching television in the living room and in the evening locking himself into his room. His mother thought he read comics and played computer games. He, like Damien, occasionally went out at night but no one knew where or what he did. For the most part, Ronald made sure that he was not seen by the rest of the family. He mostly ignored some of them, including his father, but to others such as to his mother and sisters, he was openly contemptuous and offensive. The only affection he showed was towards his dog. He had in early adolescence been part of a group of boys, but he had since broken away out of disappointment and anger – he talked of how they often excluded him from their activities, ridiculed him for his childish interest in comics and dismissed him as a geek and a weirdo. He found all this deeply humiliating and cut himself from them with loathsome contempt – to put it in one word, they were just 'wankers'.

It became increasingly clear that his private life was filled with excitement in the world of comics and computer games. He referred to this world as including various 'zones' of activity – zones in which he was in full control and in which he could manipulate characters in the plots in any way he wished. In this world, he ruled supreme. He had no need for education; he knew all he needed to know about computers and anyway he saw himself as a master in writing comics. He knew he could make a living writing comics. People simply did not know what he knew – and he had no intention of letting them know anyway.

His therapy was not so much uncomfortable as tortuous and trying. He was rarely silent but for the most part he was relentlessly preoccupied with his computers and in particular with his comics – in particular, drawing and making up new comic characters. He did in fact talk a lot about all of this, but not so much to share as to parade his remarkable knowledge and secure my due admiration. He required little of me, other than to pay attention. He often mocked me for my ignorance and accused me of wanting to 'hoodwink' him just like his father had done over the years. For the most part, he was flippant and ridiculed me for being 'mad'. At times, however, he could be much harsher, berating me for not remembering all the details of his comic and computer world, and for my 'smart ass' attempts to think about his feelings in the family.

The four adolescents: common themes

These are my four cases, the two frenetics, Sarah (everything is 'a blast'). Charlie (the 'Jack the lad', the 'manager') and the two isolates Damien ('I hate them all') and Ronald (the comic and computer man), all in their mid-adolescence. So, what can we learn from them. What common themes emerged from their behaviour and their therapeutic experience with me that throws any kind of light on whatever it was that was the matter with them.

First of all, they were all referred to me by their mothers, all of whom were at the end of their tether. I can't go into any detail about their histories, but it is fair to say that none had had an easy ride towards adolescence. In one way or another their latency years had been unsettled, whether because of trauma in infancy and early childhood (for example, growing up with a depressed mother or under the threat of a frightening father) or because of disillusionment in childhood (for example, experiencing a heartfelt loss of a beloved parent or a sense of betrayal by a father or a painful disappointment in a close friend). It was Winnicott who once said that "Sanity is essential in the latency phase and the child who in this phase cannot maintain sanity is clinically very ill" (Winnicott 1958). All four were already vulnerable as they encountered the turbulence of puberty and the task of individuation.

Against the background of their lives and the changes in their bodies, they desperately defended themselves against such vulnerability through various entrenched narcissistic manoeuvres. In different ways, they insisted on their certainties; they glorified themselves in their sense of control and mastery and they fortified themselves through a withering disdain for anyone else (except those they idealised). Above all, they knew that they knew everything and that they didn't need anybody. Their grandiosity protected themselves from the reality of their neediness. And their idealisation of others, whether of individuals or groups, provided them with some form of almighty illusion of comfort and security.

If we are to think of them diagnostically, the widespread and fashionable labels of autistic spectrum disorder or ADHD did not for me carry much weight. If anything, I found myself more inclined to view them in the *DSM* category of Narcissistic Personality Disorder. I am aware, of course, that that such a diagnosis should not be applied to children or adolescents, since they are still in the process of development. However, I did see their disturbance as profoundly narcissistic in origin and behaviour and with all the ingrained and pervasive quality of a personality disturbance. They were not suffering from any pronounced difficulty in eating, nor exhibited any significant phobic or obsessional preoccupations.

Whatever the diagnosis, the pressing question remained as to what treatment was to be recommended – or indeed what psychotherapy.

I, of course, cannot spell out here in this chapter in detail the unique complexity of these adolescent lives and their psychotherapeutic experiences. However, in brief, what I set out to do was to 'meet' them (a much-undervalued word) rather than to judge them (as almost everybody else did in their lives). I sought to create some kind of atmosphere in our developing relationship in which they might begin to find it interesting or worthwhile (or indeed narcissistically gratifying) enough to bother to come to see me. And so I steadfastly listened and observed and tried to imagine the way it was to be them. I did not seek to chivvy them along, hurry them up, make them see the folly of their ways. As it so happened, and this is an important point, I myself didn't have too much of a narcissistic urge on my part to assure myself of my therapeutic potency. I just sat and received what they wanted to talk about or show me – Sally's goings on, Charlie's performances, Damian's hatreds, Ronald's comics.

Throughout all of these endeavours on my part, however, I met with various resistances to getting better. Most of these adolescents were not consciously motivated to change; it was overwhelmingly their mothers who were desperate for things to be different. I should add here, though, that despite their outward indifference and indeed defiance and attack, I did trade on the assumption that somewhere within them all they did know that things were not right – and in fact they missed very few sessions with me.

In thinking about the nature of their resistances, I was aware of course of what Freud termed the repression and transference resistances. Theses adolescents were often loathe to open up with any hint of candour, and so much of their perception of me was far from positive, coloured by their past lives with their parents, experienced variously as intrusive, judgemental, neglectful, punitive, mistrustful, disappointing and full of a sense of betrayal.

However, beyond these kind of resistances, I think there prevailed a more fundamental, almost more insidious, form of resistance – that form of resistance which arises in the narcissistic or mirror transference. This may be a feature in all psychotherapies with adolescents, but it is something that I do think applies to these particular adolescents that I have described in this chapter. Because of their self-absorbed experience of others as essentially extensions of themselves, they did not in general take in others as separate or different from them. They fundamentally expected and required others to meet their narcissistic assumptions, namely to obey and admire them. And so, I don't think I was basically regarded as a person in my own right by them but as some form of reflection of their own narcissistic state. So much of the early months of my therapy with them consisted essentially of my compliance with their expectation of admiration or proper attention to what they had to say. To have been otherwise would have almost certainly brought about an abrupt termination of psychotherapy on their part. In this, I was particularly influenced by Kohut's therapeutic approach. Unlike some other psychoanalysts in his time, such as Otto Kernberg, he saw no gain to be made in basically challenging the grandiose assertions of his patients. Instead, he took the view that it was most helpful to essentially provide the affirmations his patients demanded, not simply to provide a corrective emotional experience, but to explore further the nature of their vulnerabilities and to work through their sensitivities in the interest of greater understanding and integration. To take a challenging approach in his view would only lead to an entrenched narcissistic position in the patient.

As I draw closer to the end of this chapter, what I would like to highlight is this idea of an additional form of resistance in work with adolescents – perhaps with all adolescents but certainly with the kind of adolescents I have been writing about in this chapter. Young people, in other words who are so unprepared to renounce their grandiose ideas about themselves will simply not allow the psychotherapist any sense of agency, of potency or of countenance, any sort of implied criticism or disrespect of their omnipotent solutions.

With this kind of mirror transference in mind, I am aware that I take my time in my psychotherapy work with them. The relationships with them could not be rushed. Basically, I held off and waited until timely moments of clarification, even interpretation, might occur later on in psychotherapy. And interestingly, in all these cases, such moments did come to pass. My experience was that, if I waited patiently enough, through a kind of attentive inattention that Adam Phillips writes about in his most recent book, *Attention Seeking* (Phillips 2019), these moments had a way of turning up – sometimes of their own accord in the course of psychotherapy and sometimes significantly as a result of some kind of external intrusion that effectively shakes up the modus vivendi of that course of psychotherapy

After several months in therapy, for example, Sarah's friend wrote to me telling me of her concern that Sarah had been crying uncontrollably and talking of suicide. Charlie's mother wrote to let me know that his school was considering expelling him; Ronald's mother rang me to make it clear that unless he pulled himself together, she and her husband were going to throw him out of the house. The only exception to these external interventions was in the case of Damien, although something very unusual did happen in the course of the therapy that seemed to have a similar and profound effect on him. This was the most unusual moment when my cat somehow suddenly idled into the consulting room and immediately sat on his lap! I cannot go into the ins and outs of that particular moment, other than to speculate that in the context of his animal rights passion, hatred became mediated by a love he had strenuously tried to suppress. But of the other three, these uninvited intrusions into the privacy of the therapeutic experience by worried mothers and a friend had a powerful effect. Of course, Sarah, Charlie and Ronald were initially furious that these people were poking their noses into their business. However, they were suddenly confronted in a particularly unique way by the realities of reality, the very realities that they had sought to avoid in their narcissistic reveries. And they found themselves having to face their pain and fear in my presence. You could say my patience had paid off because, as a result of the growing trust in our relationship, they were able to feel safe enough with me sufficiently to share their underlying vulnerability and desperation and to gain some beginning understanding of their narcissistically defensive way of surviving. These were extraordinary moments, I even venture to say mutative. Two cried desperately and one just about hid his tears. And Damien's smile as the cat sat on his lap was as much a cry as he could allow.

You will of course ask for outcomes. It is my view that, faced with the deep-seated nature of their narcissistic retrenchments, no grand transformation could be expected. But I did notice subtle movements over time, not least a gradual relinquishment of their narcissistic rigidity that in turn enabled them to relate to reality in a more realistic way. Sarah's significant achievement was to move from 'knowing' everything to **not** 'knowing' everything – in other words a greater acceptance of her vulnerability, of her true feelings and in effect of her 'ordinariness'. Charlie, as he so aptly put it, gradually 'tempered' his omnipotence so that he could accept his imperfections and the unreality of some of his dreams. He came slowly to realise his potential to sustain his grandiosity in forms of living that were actually achievable – not to be a super-rich manager of a fantastic international band, but to be a regular player in the music world that could value his knowledge of the business and his wish to succeed. Damien had a long way to go, so hard was his conviction of his own superiority that he could barely tolerate any difference at all in himself or other people, but he did find a job and he did manage to moderate some of his contempt for his family. I did think that he might find his way into an occupation working with animals, perhaps in an animal hospital in which he might find a possibility of loving that he had gradually found in therapy beyond his hatreds. And Ronald at the end seemed to 'grow up' and move on beyond his devotion to comics; he seemed less fraught and more able to laugh at himself (as he put it, 'the loony in the attic'). He found himself a job in a computer firm which he could actually allow himself to enjoy. He even expressed concern about his mother's health.

Conclusion

What I have tried to do in this chapter is to encourage us to think about the central role narcissism plays in our lives – in all our lives. We are all of course narcissistic – we hopefully love ourselves. As one of the key Christian commandments makes clear, you should 'love your neighbour as yourself'. So, don't knock narcissism – we all want the best for ourselves, we all want to somehow safeguard our private sense of well-being in the midst of life's inevitable disappointments and imperfections. We all have our own ideals and ambitions. But like so many other mental phenomena, everything is on a spectrum and we find ourselves confronted with what we and others regard as 'normal' or 'healthy' narcissism, and for want of a better term, 'malignant' or 'pathological' narcissism.

And to return to how I began in this chapter, our leaders may well have their more than fair share of narcissistic dosage in their desire for fame and fortune; so many carry out their missions with absolute belief in themselves combined with super confidence and a sense of rightness. They seem driven by an inordinate compulsion to possess power and prestige. Elisabeth Lunbeck (2014) has an interesting passage in her book *The Americanisation of Narcissism* on the rise of leaders in organisations. She writes:

'An appealing grandiosity eases their organisational ascent, as they dazzle investors, enchant fellow employees and charm the media with their charisma and seemingly unlimited strategic acumen'. This phrase carries remarkable prescience, particularly since it was written several years before the arrival of Trump as President of the United States! But wait, let us hear her next sentence: 'Then all too often stunning bouts of folly and recklessness ensue and flagrant rule or law breaking' (Lunbeck 2014: 260).

And finally, is there anything new in all of my preoccupation with this whole thing called narcissism? There can be little doubt that most of the people who have achieved notoriety over the centuries have been very narcissistic in their views of themselves and in their preoccupations. And I might well include 'the hero' Freud in this. As Ernest Jones (1958) makes clear in his biography, '(Freud) was possessed at times of a sense of greatness about himself and he was determinedly ambitious in pursuit of his ideals. He also had little time for those who disagreed with him and who asserted their separateness and difference'. And, as far as cultures in general are concerned, we might ask ourselves do we live in a particularly narcissistic culture now? As I mentioned earlier, Christopher Lasch cited and condemned all the sins of individualism and capitalism, an excess of self-interest and promotion, an excess of vanity and sense of entitlement. Many would say much the same about today. And indeed, it is embedded in the core of neoliberalism that our economy is best advanced through the free expression of self-seeking enterprise.

And finally, I can't finish without a cartoon. We are in a consulting room in which the Psychiatrist faces the adolescent.

The Psychiatrist says, "I think you may have a Narcissistic Personality Disorder".

The Adolescent replies, "I bet I'm the only person in the world who's got it".

References

Edwin, C. (1985–2016) *The Collected Works of Spinoza*, Princeton, NJ: Princeton University Press.

Freud, S. (1905) Three Essays on Sexuality *Standard Edition* Vol. VII, London: Hogarth Press.

Freud, S. (1914) On Narcissism: An Introduction *Standard Edition* Vol.X1V, London: Hogarth Press.

Greenberg, H. R. (1975) 'The widening gyre: transformations of the omnipotent quest during adolescence', *International Review of Psychoanalysis* 2: 231–244.

Jones, E. (1958) *The Life and Work of Sigmund Freud Vol 2. Years of Maturity 1901–1919*, London: Hogarth Press.

Kernberg, O. (1985) 'Normal and abnormal narcissism'. In *Borderline Condition and Pathological Narcissism*, Northvale NJ & London: Jason Aronson.

Kohut, H. (1968) 'The psychoanalytic treatment of narcissistic personality disorders - outline of a systematic approach', *Psychoanalytic Study of the Child* 23: 86–113.

Kohut, H. (1972) 'Thoughts on narcissism and narcissistic rage', *Psychoanalytic Study of the Child* 27: 360–400.

Lasch, C. (1979) *The Culture of Narcissism: American Life in an Age of Diminishing Expectations*, New York: Norton.

Lunbeck, E. (2014) *The Americanization of Narcissism*, Cambridge, MA: Harvard University Press.

Phillips, A. (2019) *Attention Seeking*, Harmondsworth: Penguin.

Wilson, P. (1988) 'The impact of cultural changes on the internal experience of the adolescent', *Journal of Adolescence* 11: 271–286.

Wilson, P. (1995) 'Narcissism and adolescence'. In J Cooper and N Maxwell (eds) *Narcissistic Wounds*, London: Whurr.

Winnicott, D. (1958) 'Child analysis in the latency period'. In *The Maturational Process and the Facilitating Environment*, Madison, CT: International Universities Press. pp.115–123. 1965.

Chapter 8

The adolescent, the psychoanalyst and the working alliance

Unpublished paper presented at the Winter Conference, IPCAPA/BPF, London 2021.

The adolescent

I have written various papers exploring the emotional development and experience of the individual adolescent in the context of psychoanalytic psychotherapy. Much of this is included in earlier chapters of this book (in Chapters 3–7). A more broadly based paper which I wrote in 1988 attempted to encompass the cultural context in which young people in general were struggling to deal with adolescence:

> There are something like 10 million human beings aged 16 to 24 in Britain. They live in many communities with wide cultural and economic differences - north and south, inner and outer city, unemployed and employed. The deadening inertia of the unemployed in the north of England and the jaunty cavorting of the yuppie in the smarter parts of London bear little resemblance. Nor, too, the drug-defeated inner cities and the gymkhana delights of fashionable parts of suburbia. There is on the face of it little connection.
>
> Whatever their regional allegiances, their everyday ways of living and making sense of their lives are increasingly fashioned within the swirl of cultural forces that are worldwide in influence. The awesome prospect of nuclear war, the uneasy anticipation of Aids, the revolutionary impact of the oral contraceptive, all these enter everyone's experience everywhere, their implications affecting fundamental assumptions about life and death and challenging the local rules, customs and conventions and rituals.
>
> (Wilson 1988)

In the light of what has developed in the context of today's society, I would add much more. The sheer number of young people in this country is bigger; the divide between the poor and the wealthy, larger; the global perspective, wider; and the penetration of social media much deeper. I could go on and on, what with the formless dreads of Covid (more so now than AIDS), of climate change, of potential unimaginable wars and, not least, the cultural narcissism that pervades our society and politics – in capitalism, neoliberalism, Trumpism and much more. There is now a much-heightened awareness of racism, sexism and homophobia. Within all

DOI: 10.4324/9781003680437-9

this, we encounter all manner of differences in family composition and the way children are brought up and adolescents dealt with.

Beneath the sheer weight of all these cultural forces, the adolescent has to find his or her own ways of coping, endeavouring to make his or her way often against the odds. Inherent in this endeavour are the two fundamental developmental tasks of adolescence – the task of integrating the impact of the truly revolutionary pubertal changes in the adolescent body and the task of separation and individuation with its implicit challenge of facing loss and seeking new identity. I would add, too, the heightened force of narcissism to deal with the essential transitional vulnerability of this period of life, associated with all the above external and internal anxieties. As I put it in the opening paragraph of my paper on Narcissism and Adolescence, 'it can be of no surprise that adolescents are peculiarly bothered about themselves. There is a great deal going on.... The adolescent lives in a state of new physical tension, with sharper awareness and broader understanding'. In a similar vein, I have dwelt unreservedly in my other writings on the extraordinariness – indeed, the mysteriousness – of adolescence in order to sharpen and heighten our own awareness and appreciation of adolescence.

It is this period of life which is so much in the process of transition, caught in the throes of puberty and facing all the demands of growing up, forging relationships and finding some sense of self and individuality. It is so different from childhood or adulthood which by and large contain greater stability and certainty. I am always reminded of Anna Freud in 1958 when she observed that 'adolescence is a neglected period [in psychoanalytic writings], a stepchild where analytic thinking is concerned'. She wrote:

> the analytic study of adolescence is not a happy one and especially unsatisfactory when compared with that of early childhood. With the latter period we feel sure of our ground and in possession of a wealth of material and information which enables us to assume authority and apply analytic findings to the practical problems accordingly. When it comes to adolescence, we feel hesitant.....
>
> (Freud 1958)

The psychoanalyst and the psychoanalytic psychotherapist

(*Note:* for the rest of this chapter, the terms 'psychotherapy' or 'psychotherapist' will be used to denote 'psychoanalytic psychotherapist' in the interests of simplified style. The terms 'psychoanalysis and psychoanalyst' are retained. Psychoanalysis is seen as an integral part of the psychotherapy referred to in this chapter.)

Now, where does the psychoanalyst sit with all this. What does he or she do? How does he or she do it? What is indeed his 'therapeutic approach and attitude'? Well, of course, there is no straightforward answer to any of these questions. Psychoanalysts, like adolescents, are not a homogeneous lot, no matter how much they may subscribe to the one main theory. They practice in their own idiosyncratic ways. For the sake of brevity, however, it might be helpful to simply think of two broad groups of psychoanalysts – for want of better terms, the classical and the 'modern'.

The classical psychoanalyst works within a rich understanding of human nature and behaviour. Whatever differences there may be in the wide terrain of psychoanalysis, there is a basic grounding in the key concepts of the unconscious, psychosexuality, psychic determinism, the structural model and anxiety, conflict, defence and symptom formation. The classical psychoanalytic therapeutic practice takes in a full appreciation of the dynamics of transference and counter transference in the psychoanalytic relationship and emphasises the value of verbal interpretation of the unconscious and the process of free association. Its practice works within a consistently held frame, bounded by clear personal and professional boundaries. The classical psychoanalytic process is generally a stringent affair, with limited social interaction and direction and is reliant on the patient's readiness to speak without restraint of his experiences and to tolerate silence. In many ways, it is quite an exacting process and requires a clear understanding and readiness on the part of the patient to commit himself or herself to the experience.

This is of course a brave summary of the essence of psychoanalysis. However, as I have written it, I want to stress that classical psychoanalysis stands for something that sets high standards and ideals within its regime. It is a serious, thoughtful and thorough undertaking and is well suited to the needs of some adults. However, whether or not it is used with most adolescents is another matter. Most importantly and of particular relevance to our discussion of the working alliance, it holds reign in many of the minds of our aspirant psychoanalysts who strive to reassure themselves that they are indeed psychoanalysts. They too often feel obliged to follow the imagined strictures of classical analytic technique to the detriment of their allowing themselves to relate appropriately and ordinarily enough to adolescents. They labour beneath the oversight of what is known as their psychoanalytic 'superego'.

At the other end of the spectrum from the classical psychoanalytic is the other broad group which I have called the more 'modern'. There are many variations and modifications of the evolution of this group and clearly too numerous to cover here. However, again for the sake of brevity, I would like to refer to a very thoughtful book, entitled *Winnicott and the Psychoanalytic Tradition; Interpretation and Other Psychoanalytic Issues* edited by Lesley Caldwell (Caldwell 2007). As the title suggests, the place of interpretation in the psychoanalytic process is under scrutiny. A number of prominent psychoanalysts have written chapters in this book – notably Ogden, Bollas, Barossa – and it is striking how much in agreement they are in challenging the cardinal importance of interpretation of the unconscious in psychoanalysis. I shall just quote from one chapter by Ken Wright, an English psychoanalyst, intriguingly entitled 'The Suppressed Madness of Sane Analysts'. He spoke of his 'relief and pleasure when I read of his [Winnicott's] writing down interpretations instead of giving them to the patient, What a relief from the tyranny of the interpretation'. But this left Wright with the question – 'if not giving interpretations', what was he going to do instead? He describes how, in the later years of his clinical work, his approach became more 'conversational in line with the findings of contemporary infant research......In my experience, an interpretation often cuts the emotional flow of the session and brings things to a halt....'

It is interesting that Wright is talking about a striking sense of liberation, as if released from a kind of subservient loyalty to the almighty authority of classical psychoanalysis. I do not know if he treated adolescents but his use of that term 'conversation' (a term I note of increasing use in contemporary psychotherapy writings) suggested a very different therapeutic approach from the classical one – one that does not abandon the basic tenets of psychoanalysis but may well be more acceptable to many adolescents.

The working alliance

All of the above discussion has a bearing on the nature of the working alliance. Of course, no two working alliances are the same, so many different adolescents, so many different psychoanalysts, so many different problems and stories that adolescents bring. With adults in general, psychoanalysis proceeds on the basis of trust and an explicit agreement to enter into the therapeutic process. In this sense, both psychoanalyst and patient work in alliance with each other. The situation with adolescents, particularly the more disturbed and extreme, is for the most part very different. More often than not, they in effect tumble into our lives, all too often with no expectation, no acknowledgement that they have a problem, no understanding or indeed concern of what might be wrong. For the most part, they are plonked in front of us with desperate requirements on us from parents or caring authorities to stop or 'cure' the troublesome (to them) behaviour or symptomatology. It is at this point when we are challenged to form what is called a working alliance – particularly in the beginning of contact but also to be sustained throughout should psychotherapy catch hold. In all of the cases which I have described in this book, it could hardly be said that they were in any sense allied with me in their perception and anticipation of psychotherapy.

Does the term 'alliance' ring true when we are thinking about the nature of our relationship with so many of the adolescents we see? In an attempt to answer that question, I think it is necessary to take into consideration a number of key characteristics of adolescents that fundamentally do not justify the use of the term, 'alliance'. Three characteristics stand out as important – the maturity of the ego in adolescence, the essential narcissism of adolescence and the prevalence of 'I don't know' (Chapter 3 in this volume) in adolescence. To put it simply, how can someone, still unsure of his or her capacity to cope, who is so engrossed in himself or herself and who often doesn't know clearly what he or she thinks, how can that person, an adolescent, readily enter into the relative formality of an alliance with an adult psychoanalytic psychotherapist?

Taking into consideration the first characteristic, the ego, it is as well to remind ourselves of what is at stake. The ego is that agency of the mind that deals with reality testing, thinking, impulse control, defences against anxiety, problem solving and self-reflection. In adolescence, developmentally, the ego may well be not securely held or strong. Anna Freud spoke of the inordinate pressures that prevail upon the ego during the process of separating from parents, buffeted by pressures from the super ego, external reality and the forces of the id, not least regressive incestuous yearnings. In many respects, she and others (e.g. Greenberg 1995) have viewed the adolescent predicament as precarious, a time of vulnerability. We know what we know from brain research that the pre-frontal cortex, closely associated with our conception of the ego, is still very much in the process of maturation.

I have written at length about the two other characteristics of adolescence – the prevailing narcissism to counter underlying vulnerability in the process of transition (Chapter 6) and the complexity of the familiar communication of 'I don't know' (Chapter 3). All of these characteristics have to be taken into account by anyone seeking to establish a therapeutic relationship with an adolescent, most particularly with one very disturbed, angry, frightened and wary.

Our attention therefore needs to be paid to how people with weak egos – how adolescents – are best approached in psychotherapy. I am very much taken by what Michael Balint had to say in treating patients suffering the effects of what he called the basic fault (Balint 1968). He was preoccupied with patients who in their early childhood had experienced trauma arising from a fundamental 'lack of fit', a primary disconnection and disordering of experience in childhood. His emphasis in treating such patients was to facilitate an emotional regression to the early state of disturbance and to support them to build their ego and create what he called 'a new beginning'. I am not of course suggesting that all adolescents suffer from a basic fault nor indeed that they are required to regress so much in their psychotherapy. But it is how Balint understands the nature of the fragility of egos and how he sets about to treat that fragility which I find interesting. Putting it baldly, he was discouraging interpretation, seeing it as being all too often oppressive; similarly, he was wary of transference interpretation, seeing it as evoking a sense of the mighty psychoanalyst diminishing the insignificant patient. He warned against the psychoanalyst being omnipotent and asserting that he or she understood everything. I think we might profitably take counsel from this when recognising the ego vulnerability of the adolescent in his relationship to the psychotherapist.

Balint goes on to talk of the capacity of the psychoanalyst to be receptive to the disparate elements of experience in order to help bring about a sense of cohesion. Much depends on the psychoanalyst's capacity to hold emotional tensions and readiness to tolerate not knowing. He wrote, 'Not knowing becomes hard to tolerate and the analyst then falls into premature knowing in order to escape not knowing. Interpretations in this context are often given out of the analyst's need for his own sanity, fortifying and fortified by his theory at the cost of truly following the patient'.

In relation to the force of adolescent narcissism, the psychotherapist needs to appreciate the adolescent's hypersensitivity about his or her sense of dignity. In the psychotherapy situation, they are wary of being scrutinised, of losing their sense of pride or self-cohesion, no matter how precarious that may be. In narcissistic terms it is as if they have to keep their ends up, to fight off any threat of impingement or conquest. As I put in my chapter on 'I don't know':

> .. they are so unprepared to renounce their grandiose ideas about themselves that they will not allow the psychotherapist any sense of agency or potency or countenance any sort of implied criticism or disrespect of their omnipotent solutions.
>
> (Wilson 2001/2025)

The idea of forming an 'alliance' (involving sharing or connecting) with anybody is in many ways anathema. The psychotherapist also has to bear in mind that the adolescent may be so caught up in his or her narcissistic preoccupation with him or herself, that he or she barely experiences the psychotherapist in his or her own right, outside the experience of his or her own interests or preoccupations. The four adolescents whom I described in Chapter 7 were so frenetically caught up with themselves and their antics or so immersed in their splendid isolation that they often seemed far away from any sense of their engagement, let alone alliance, with me, the therapist.

Once again, if the psychotherapist is to ever establish some kind of therapeutic experience with an adolescent, he or she has to find ways of going along with the adolescent, of being prepared for much of the time to affirm rather than to confront, to imagine the adolescent life, rather than analyse it – always in full recognition that there would be limitations to the therapeutic enterprise. As I put it in relation to myself, 'I didn't have too much of a narcissistic urge on my part to assure myself of my therapeutic potency' (Wilson 1995). Similarly, the psychoanalytic psychotherapist has to exercise patience and humility in his desire to encourage the adolescent to express himself or herself In the same chapter, I give an example of an adolescent submerged in a stream of 'I don't knows'. My plea to the psychotherapist was to take the oft-repeated phrase of 'I don't know' seriously – to see it 'as an expression of the adolescents inherent inarticulacy in the midst of the sheer newness, confusion, unpredictability and complexity of the adolescent experience' (Chapter 6). The adolescent needs time to be ready to make any commitment or engage with any psychotherapeutic enquiry.

Conclusion

There are of course some adolescents, more so in late adolescence and with less disrupted internal lives, who are curious about themselves and who are motivated for a classical psychoanalysis. They are I believe in a minority, and they are also in danger of being treated as mini-adults in denial of their adolescence. By and large, I do not believe that classical psychoanalysis is an appropriate treatment for disturbed adolescents. Psychoanalytic understanding that informs and guides modern forms of psychoanalytic psychotherapy is very much appropriate and indeed necessary. Certainly, in the beginning phases and sustainably throughout the course of psychotherapy, a less exacting approach than the classical needs to be adopted. Greater flexibility and dare I say playfulness needs to be adopted. A greater, more active readiness to engage in an interaction, in a conversation with the adolescent, may be more appropriate and less constraining. The overall aim of psychotherapy is to find a way of talking with the adolescent, a way of being with him or her in what is now often referred to as a 'relational' approach – sufficient to leave the adolescent with a greater sense of hope and willingness to keep on turning up, despite his or her difficulties. This approach is not as easy as it might sound and can often feel very muddled, full of mistakes and uncertainties about what is happening and where it is going. But I think it is an approach that is more in tune with where the adolescent is, without losing the psychoanalytic purpose of gaining insight and awareness.

I do not think it necessary to be opaque as a person in psychotherapy nor to leave long silences, waiting for the material to unfold as is often customary in classical psychoanalysis. I think it is important for the psychotherapist to present himself or herself as what I might call a recognisable human being rather than a someone more remote as in classical psychoanalysis, someone who is available to be related to and listened to. Similarly, I do not think it outrageous when presented with a question from the adolescent to answer it – within reason (for fear of suspending analytic neutrality, disturbing free association or being overly gratifying).

It is difficult to catch the gist of what I have in mind in describing this more facilitating, 'modern' psychoanalytic approach. I am aware that such an approach carries with it more risks, the psychotherapist becoming more exposed without the protection of the classical frame. He or she is more prey to the subtleties of transferences. The angry defiance and opposition of some adolescents may evoke unexpectedly hostile and overly defensive reactions towards the psychotherapist, leading inadvertently to the premature closure of the case. Or more precipitately affectionate feelings may have the effect of drawing in the psychotherapist's positive, more caring and overly protective responses, leading to the dangers of collusion and/or needless disappointment.

These matters are important. More pressing, however, is the nature of what is called 'the working alliance'. In the two case presentations that I have written in Chapters 3 and 4, the adolescents concerned certainly entertained the prospect of psychotherapy with either an array of ambivalence, defiance, contempt, denial and defensiveness or a fog of not knowing anything. In both cases, they were more or less plonked in front of me by parents or caring authorities to just 'stop' or 'cure' the behaviour that was troubling them, the parents. At the same time, beneath all of this pressure, the adolescent knows something is not right about him or herself, however much he or she wants to disown their concern. At best, there is a curiosity and a readiness for something new and hence an underlying interest in psychotherapy, notwithstanding their mistrust. There is enough here to make something positive happen. Whether it is possible to describe this as a possibility for an 'alliance' to take place is less clear. At the heart of its definition are a collection of feelings about connectedness, co-operation, sharing and joining together. Its etymology is from the Latin, 'alligante', to bind or to tie. The word simply does not have the right connotations – all too ponderous, too neat, too rational, too grown up – as in the world of organisational (national or corporate) deals, pacts or treaties. Its most common usage is in a military or political sense whereby armies or countries combine with a common interest often in a competitive or combative enterprise. The adolescent by contrast enters into a therapeutic relationship with less clarity and less determination; the idea of a 'contract' is, in all of its sense of purpose, initially alien. It may well be more accurate to use, instead of 'working alliance', the term 'developing co-operation', indicating something less decided, more open to whatsoever might emerge. Adult psychotherapists are in danger of deluding themselves that they have a more mature, sensible, definitive agreement with the adolescent, holding unrealistic expectations and lacking appreciation of the more slowly evolving sense of co-operation. Far better to leave open the possibility of a relationship developing as a kind of dance, keeping it light (though not flippant), getting alongside, allowing for possibilities, finding a way of being with each other, talking with each other. Winnicott suggested (1966) that adolescents 'eschew psychoanalysis though they are interested in psychoanalytic theories' because their preservation of personal isolation is part of the search for identity'

References

Balint, M. (1968) *The Basic Fault,* London: Tavistock Publications.

Bollas, C. (1999) *Hysteria,* London & New York: Routledge.

Caldwell, L (ed.). (2007) *Winnicott and the Psychoanalytic Tradition: Interpretation and Other Psychoanalytic Issues,* London: Karnac.

Freud, A. (1958) 'Adolescence', *The Psychoanalytic Study of the Child* 13, New York: International Universities Press, Inc. pp. 268–233.

Greenberg, H. (1995) 'The widening gyre: transformations of the omnipotent quest during adolescence', *International Review of Psychoanalysis* 2: 231–244.

Laufer, M. (1976) 'The central masturbation fantasy: the final sexual organisation and adolescence', *The Psychoanalytic Study of the Child* 31: 297–316.

Wilson, P. (1988) 'The impact of cultural changes on the internal experience of the adolescent', *Journal of Adolescence* 11: 271–286.

Wilson, P. (1991) 'psychotherapy with adolescents'. In J Holmes (ed.)'. In J. Holmes (ed) *Textbook of Psychotherapy in Psychiatric Practice*, London: Churchill Livingstone. pp. 443–467.

Wilson, P. (1995) 'Narcissism and adolescence'. In J. Cooper and N. Maxwell (eds) *Narcissistic Wounds,* London: Whurr. pp. 51–63.

Wilson, P. (2001) 'I don't know', *Journal of the British Association of Psychotherapists* 39(2).

Wilson, P. (2019) *Me Loves Me; What is this thing called Narcissism: Resistance in Adolescent Psychotherapy,* Unpublished conference paper here published as chapter 7.

Winnicott, D. W. (1971) *Playing and Reality,* London: Tavistock.

Chapter 9

People meet in a classroom and say 'hello'

Previously published in D. Colley & P. Cooper (eds) Attachment and Emotional Development in the Classroom: Theory and Practice. London: Jessica Kingsley (2017).

The learning experience in the classroom can be strongly influenced by a range of emotional tensions and conflicts that reside within the teacher/student relationship. Many of these are irrational and unconscious and can have a disturbing effect on how learning takes place. In this chapter, an illustration is given of this which highlights a particular 'meeting' between one teacher (Mrs Parker) and one student (Jimmy) in which they say, in effect, 'hello' to each other – from widely different backgrounds and perspectives.

The concepts of 'transference' and 'countertransference' in psychoanalytic theory and the concept of the 'internal working model' in Attachment Theory are used to help throw light on the quality of interaction between the two. Misunderstandings and misperceptions can be more fully understood with reference to the experience of both individuals outside the classroom and from the past. The importance of support for both is underlined, not least for the teacher in the form of work discussion groups and consultations in which all kinds of feelings and sensibilities can be expressed, shared and thought about.

'Mrs. Parker' and 'Jimmy' in this account are two fictitious characters, composites of similar teacher/student interactions.

The teacher

I'm Mrs Parker, 35 years old, happily married with two young children. And it was Monday.

The weekend had been busy. On Saturday, we had a birthday party for one of my children and we went out for dinner in the evening. On Sunday, we visited my parents for lunch. This was fine but my youngest brother refused to join us which upset my mother. We then did some shopping. By 9 o'clock, I was exhausted. But marking and preparation had to be done for the week ahead.

By and large, I had a good day on Monday. But at the end of it, things went wrong. I had a Year seven class for English. They were restless and fidgety from the start. I thought I was well prepared and I tried to create as safe and well-structured an atmosphere as possible in the classroom.

DOI: 10.4324/9781003680437-10

Despite all my efforts, however, two boys would not stop giggling and playing about at the back of the class. They seemed to enjoy flicking bits of paper at each other. I told them to stop and attend to their work, but after a few moments, they carried on just as before. I reprimanded them as straightforwardly as I could, but to no avail. They ignored me and, worse, one of the boys, Jimmy, the bigger and bulkier of the two, started laughing out loud and making farting noises which got the whole class going.

I decided to separate them and bring one of them down to sit at the front, close to me. For a moment, I thought this might work. But much to my annoyance, he sat with his arms folded, smirking and staring at me, ignoring what he was supposed to be doing and continuing to make the farty noises right in front of me. I tried very hard to be patient and firm but with no success. He then started to walk around the class 'accidently' knocking off the paperwork of the other children.

It is at that point that I lost it. I'd had enough. I shouted at him to behave and eventually I told him to leave the class and report to the Year Head. At first, he just grinned but, as he got up to go, he called me 'a fucking, stuck up bitch' and a 'use-less teacher'. His grin had gone and for a moment I felt scared of him.

After he had gone, I couldn't settle the class and I was left feeling furious but defeated. I had lost control of myself, I had excluded a child from my class and I had not managed to create the safe atmosphere I intended. Furthermore, I doubted whether I had properly covered the syllabus. I was 'a useless teacher' – just as Jimmy had said. I thought I should quit.

The student

I'm a student. I'm Jimmy, 12 years old and big for my age. I live with mum and dad, two older brothers and two younger sisters. And it was Monday.

Saturday had been boring and on Sunday I stayed in bed all morning. I had to stay in for lunch because my gran and uncle were coming over. All right I suppose, but in the evening, things went mad. My dad got drunk and brought a couple of his mates over. Soon he and my mum were screaming at each other. My sisters were crying and my brother had a go at him which ended up in a fight. The best I could do was to get out of the house. I found a couple of mates and just hung about until real late.

There are always rows at home. My dad drinks too much and he keeps on losing down the betting shop. He's got a nasty temper, takes it out on my mum and me. He's alright sometimes, especially when he's got some money in his pocket, but for most of the time, he's a pain in the neck and I don't like him. What really gets me though is that my mum lets him get away with it.

I don't really get her. Sometimes, she can be really nice and gives us treats and even cuddles. But she has always been sad and this is getting worse. She drinks too much too, and on some days she can stay in bed all day and not lift a finger for anyone. My brother says she's got mental problems, whatever that means. But he tells me she has to take pills for it.

Anyway, back at school and I was sort of relieved not to be at home. School's alright. I've got a lot of mates there and we can have a laugh. But the teachers don't leave you alone. You can be just minding your own business, larking about and then bang, just like at home, some bloke is having a go at you. That sports teacher is the worst. Fat big bugger, full of himself, reminds me of my dad. Sod him.

And then there are all these other teachers. I can't make them out most of the time. But on Monday, I got really pissed off. We've got these English lessons, all about verbs and things and books. Fair enough, but in walked this English teacher. We've had her before. Posh cow, fat arse. She took no notice of me. She's got her favourites and as far as I can see couldn't care less about me and my mates. So I thought, if she's going to be that way, I wasn't going to be bothered to listen to her. So, I decided to have just a little chat with my friend. We flicked a few bits of paper about and really we were just minding our own business.

The next thing I knew was that she was telling me to sit in the front of the class. That annoyed me but I put up with it. But she kept on having a go and then suddenly out of the blue, she just lost her rag and started yelling at me, calling me all sorts of names. I couldn't believe it. It was completely out of order. And then she told me to go the Year Head. Well, that was it. I'd had enough. I told her she was a useless teacher and right stuck up.

Not a good day. Good to be out of the house. But at the end of it all, I felt crap. Shouted at and pushed around, no one really taking any interest in me. So, to hell with it. They are all like that. Just interested in themselves. Why bother? Who cares? I'll do what I want to do….

Teacher and student: the meeting

So, here we are at the end of an ordinary Monday in an ordinary school. Two worlds colliding and two people at odds with one another: both, in their own ways, left feeling devalued, angry and wanting to give up. And the upshot? No cooperation, no enjoyment and no learning.

What on earth went wrong between these two people?

A whole range of factors might well have played a part – but common to them all in one way or another was perhaps the most pervasive, the emotional factor, that is to say, the experience of strong feelings that can so easily consume people's minds and have such a powerful impact on behaviour and attitude.

When we read of the impasse between 'Mrs. Parker' and 'Jimmy', we are witnessing something very intense and irrational. There was a kind of 'madness' going on between the two of them in which neither could make full sense of themselves or the other. They were in the midst of an emotional muddle that was clouding their vision and judgement. Many perspectives on human behaviour can be drawn upon to make sense of this muddle. But, two in particular need to be taken into account, the one residing in psychoanalysis, the other, in Attachment Theory – both contributing to a substantial body of knowledge that is built on extensive clinical insights and empirical research.

Psychoanalysis and Attachment Theory

Psychoanalysis refers to a body of theory drawn from a particular kind of clinical practice. It consists of a wide range of ideas and concepts that have emerged from the clinical experience and theoretical thinking of many psychoanalysts across the world since Freud began it all at the beginning of the twentieth century (Ellman 2010; Freud 1910). These ideas and concepts have been attempts essentially to build an understanding of the complexity of human nature and behaviour. Psychoanalysis is viewed with suspicion by some who regard it as unscientific, even fanciful (Spence 1994). The fact that it highlights the existence of the unconscious – that is to say, that so much of what we do and think takes place outside the province of our conscious life and that we are moved and driven by forces of which we are not aware – does not add to its popularity (it being seen as an affront to our conscious rationality). Nevertheless, there is so much that it can offer to throw light on what goes on between people emotionally that it would be a pity if this were to be overlooked.

Like many other schools of thought, it places great emphasis on the influence of infant and child experience on later life (Fonagy 2001). How well a child, or an adult in later life, can trust and care for other people, how well he or she can be curious and free to learn, how well he or she is able to cope with frustration and adversity – so much of this is determined by what has gone before.

Following on from this, psychoanalysis highlights the concept of 'transference' and 'countertransference'.

Transference refers to how feelings and thoughts can be so readily 'transferred' from one person to another (Freud 1912, 1914; Lanyado and Horne 1999; Rycroft 1968). A child or an adolescent, for example, may behave towards a teacher in a similar way as he or she has behaved towards a parent in his or past, or continues do so in the present. Basically, what transference means is that our early experiences can become revived, repeated and acted out in the ways we relate and behave with other people in the present. This is not to say that all our current relationships are affected in this way. Far from it. But in particular circumstances and in some people (usually at times of stress), transference can play a particularly significant part. We become more inclined to relate to other people not as they actually are but more as we imagine them to be, according to our past experience. For example, if a child's father was cruel and frightening when he or she was a child, it is likely that with certain men in authority, the child may well be inclined to perceive them in a similar way as the child experienced his or her father – and either defy them or flee from them.

The flip side of transference is 'countertransference' which refers to the emotional response of the person who is in receipt of the impact of these transference expectations. So, if an adult in a position of authority is aggressively challenged by a male student like 'Jimmy' who, as a child, experienced the kind of father that he did, then the adult may well react with indignation at being seen as someone other than who they feel that they are. The adult may thus become impatient, punitive or just walk away.

Attachment theory has evolved from the research and writings of many psychoanalytic theorists. Its founder, John Bowlby (Bowlby 1988, 1969), himself a psychoanalyst, re-emphasised, in the 1950s and 1960s, the importance of early childhood experience for the mental health of children and adults. His theories underwent extensive empirical scientific scrutiny from the 1960s onwards (see Ainsworth 1969, 1978: Main et al. 1995), and it is now well accepted that the experience of security in childhood is key to the well-being and emotional development of children (Holmes 2009).

At the centre of Bowlby's theory is the concept of an 'internal working model'… Bowlby conceived of this as a fundamental structure in the mind, built up during the course of numerous infantile and childhood experiences in relationships with their parents. He saw how children 'internalise' the patterns of attachment which their parents create with them and how this forms the basis of their personalities, their views of themselves and their perception of others. Juliet Hopkins, an experienced child psychotherapist illustrates this most clearly.

'For example, if a child has experienced reliably responsive caregiving he will construct a working model of the self as competent and lovable, but if he has experienced much rebuff, he will construct a model of the self as unworthy of help and comfort' (Hopkins 2015: 61).

The concept of an internal working model is not dissimilar to that of transference. What has been set as routine and familiar in the founding years of a human being's life finds a way of perpetuating itself in current relationships, colouring and flavouring the perception the child has of him or herself and his expectations of others.

Applications of theory in the classroom

So, how can these theories be of any help to the teacher, Mrs. Parker?

In recent years, there has been a growing interest in applying attachment theory to a greater understanding of school life. Heath Geddes (Geddes 2006), Louise Bomber (Bomber 2007) and Marie Delaney (Delaney 2009) for example, have written with great clarity about the tensions that can exist in the classroom and have offered positive practical suggestions to help teachers better cope with the difficulties they encounter.

The psychoanalytic concepts of transference and countertransference can be of considerable value in this regard.

If Mrs. Parker, for example, could have figured out a bit more clearly what it was about Jimmy that distressed her so much and if she could have extended herself as far as possible to imagine where Jimmy was coming from emotionally, then maybe there could have been a greater chance that what turned out to be so stressful could have been handled without the same degree of animosity and confusion. This is not to suggest that the conflict and tension between the two would have been 'cured' or that Jimmy would somehow have become transformed in his behaviour. It is likely, however, that greater flexibility would have been found to take the edge off the tension between them – that is to say, cumulatively, bit by bit and over time, the moments of harshness and resentment might become less strident, thus allowing for a more co-operative learning experience to take place.

The teacher, Mrs. Parker

We can only speculate what might have been behind all this for Mrs Parker. This is not to question her integrity or competence as a teacher. But in the context of her own life, it is important to wonder what it was about Jimmy that got under her skin? Who did he represent in her mind? For example, did he arouse in her similar feelings she had for her own younger brother? Was there something wild and delinquent in him that both excited and repelled her? Was there even something sexual in his general manner of taunting her, making her feel at times oddly uncomfortable? Was there something in the way he made her feel so impotent that challenged the part of herself that needed to prove that she was, in fact, a much needed and valued human being?

In asking questions such as these, the purpose is not to undermine Mrs Parker in any way but rather to explore and understand an experience that was, for that moment, intensely emotional and irrational. She, like all of us, is none other than a mortal human being with all kinds of strengths and sensibilities. It matters that she could make sense of what was on reflection an overreaction to Jimmy. With understanding and self-awareness, there is always the possibility of doing things differently and hopefully more constructively.

The student, Jimmy

If we now turn to Jimmy, we can see more clearly what was driving him in his way of being in the classroom. From what he tells us, home was not a safe place. Above all, he lived with fear of his father and sadness in relation to his mother.

His father sounded violent, erratic and overbearing while his mother, depressed. Simply in terms of his current life, Jimmy felt scared, neglected and angry. We can only speculate again on whether he had lived with these feelings all his life. Families do change and function differently according to changed circumstances. But too often, they do not, and it may well have been the case that Jimmy had experienced considerable insecurity from early on, growing up with an overwhelmed mother in a turbulent and unpredictable family atmosphere.

With this behind him, it is not unlikely that his 'internal working model' was such that he believed himself to be unworthy and others to be uncaring and attacking. And so, in effect, he brought this into his current life in the classroom situation.

Such was the nature of his transference that he tended to anticipate being attacked by male authority figures and ignored by female teachers. So strong were these anticipations that he unwittingly acted in such a way as to bring about confirmation of his worst fears – to be angrily censured and excluded by the adults in school.

In a most extraordinary and unconscious way, he seemed ready to provoke the very destiny he dreaded – evoking such a strong countertransference in Mrs. Parker that she found herself responding so punitively to him, which was so out of character.

To be succinct, Mrs Parker was not seen by Jimmy for what she thought she actually was, but much more in terms of what he had made of her in his mind, based on his childhood experience.

'Hello'

One way of thinking about transference and the living of the internal working model in the school setting is to imagine how children say in effect 'hello' when they come into school – not just hello in words but much more broadly in their behaviour, demeanour and attitude (Wilson 2003). It is as if they present themselves as they believe themselves to be and as they anticipate what will happen.

Let us take the following example from a child, not unlike Jimmy, a girl, 13 years old, struggling with the emotional abuse meted out by her father.

> Hello, my dad is horrible to me
> Sometimes he's nice but then he puts me down and ignores me
> He laughs at me, at my clothes and says I am rubbish
> I feel scared of him and humiliated
> I feel bad and stupid; and I feel guilty and confused.
> All this must be my fault
> Now when I meet you, Mr Teacher, I expect you to laugh at me the same way that he does, because that is what happens, see.
> I think you think I am rubbish
> And so, I might do something to get you to take the piss out of me, just as I expect
> But
> I don't like the way things are because it's not right.
> So, I could just give in. Who cares? let him (and you) say whatever. Not much I can do about it. I'll treat myself as useless, not eat, go dirty. Even run away, leave school, sleep rough, become a slag.
> Or I could make a fuss. Turn the table on you.
> Tell you to piss off. Not to get near me. Not to taunt me
> I might call you names, ridicule you in front of everyone
> I could do these things to make you feel as scared and as helpless as I do.
> I could get my own back and make you feel as low and embarrassed as I do
> This way I could make you feel how awful I feel
> – and so, get to feel a bit more in control of my life.

There is so much sadness and anger in this 'hello' that it can be of no surprise that teachers are left fielding the full force of its intensity and anguish. They may find themselves experiencing a whole range of feelings – attacked, abused, ignored – as if they were the student himself or herself; or indeed attacking, abusing, ignoring, as if they were the parent. These feelings and reflections are profoundly disturbing and potentially undermining. They are not, for the most part, of the teacher's own making but aroused through the pressure of their student's transference expectations onto them.

Final thoughts

This chapter has focused on one particular distressing encounter between a teacher and student. Of course, in the large group context of the whole school, this kind of difficulty can only be amplified and complicated in a wide range of comparable situations. Schools are places in which people of all kinds and ages come together and say their 'hellos' to each other. All kinds of agendas are brought in – academic, vocational and social and so too, the emotional. Everyone brings to the party so much of their childhoods and family circumstances that affect their relationships with each other. Teachers and students alike carry the brunt of each other's wishes and fears, the more pronounced in some relationships than in others. Their own personal vulnerabilities can so easily be augmented by the effects of each other's vulnerabilities.

Attention needs to be paid. Students need a range of supports, including counselling for the more troubled. And teachers need the time and the space to reflect on their experiences in the classroom. They need to find ways of keeping themselves aware and alert to what is going on in their relationships with their students. It is important that the confusing and disturbing feelings they are often left with from their students are shared through teacher support structures.

How practical it might be to provide the opportunities for this kind of teacher support to occur – for example, through work discussion groups, consultations or supervision – is not clear. Some schools may regard such support to be an indulgence and irrelevant to the teacher's task. After all, there is no tradition of supervision as part of the working practice in schools as there is, for example, in the psychotherapy/counselling professions. Such an attitude, however, is misguided because teachers need to feel safe and free enough to explore and learn from their doubts and uncertainties about their work without fear of censure or accusation of incompetence. Indeed, the Roberts chapter in the book by Colley and Cooper (see 'The importance of professional supervision for all staff in schools') makes a strong case for supervision for all staff in schools. The poor retention rates currently in the teaching profession testify to the importance of this need for teacher support which is too often absent.

To end on a more positive note, it is as well to remember that not all children in a classroom prevail upon teachers in the same way as do children like Jimmy. Nor do most children feel prevailed upon by the teachers, as did Jimmy. The majority of children are less torn by their family experiences. They do not bring strife into the classroom. Instead, they are likely to bring positive expectations and goodwill which in turn invites more goodwill. Here is a 14-year-old girl who has enjoyed throughout her life a secure and loving attachment experiences with her parents.

Hello
I've been loved by my mum and dad
I've felt secure and I've known where I stood
I just feel good and valued
I expect you to like me just like my parents love me
I like you and I am not afraid
I trust you and I want to learn from you
Too good to be true? Romantic? Silly? Maybe.
I want to be here in school and do well with you

But not impossible nor, in fact, uncommon. This 'hello' makes its point. It simply matters that teachers and students feel appreciated and want to come to school to teach and learn together.

References

Ainsworth, M. D. S. and Whiting, B. A. (1969) In B. M. Foss (ed) *Attachment and Exploratory Behaviour of One-Year-Olds in a Strange Situation*, London: Methuen.

Ainsworth, M. D. S., Blehar, M. C, Waters, E. and Wall, S. (1978) *Patterns of Attachment: A Psychological Study of the Strange Situation*, Hillsdale, NJ: Erlbaum.

Bomber, L. M. (2007) *Inside I'm Hurting: Practical Strategies for Supporting Children with Attachment Difficulties in School*, London: Worth Publishing.

Bowlby, J. (1969) *Attachment and Loss, Vol.1: Attachment*, London: Hogarth Press and the Institute of Psycho-Analysis.

Bowlby, J. (1988) *A Secure Base: Clinical Applications of Attachment Theory*, London: Routledge.

Delaney, M. (2009) *Teaching the Unteachable: Practical Ideas to Give Teachers Hope and Help When Behaviour Management Strategies Fail*, London: Worth Publishing.

Ellman, S. J. (2010) *When Theories Touch*, London: Karnac Books.

Fonagy, P. (2001) 'Introduction to attachment theory'. *Chapter 1 Attachment Theory and Psychoanalysis*, London: Karnac.

Freud, S. (1910) 'Five lectures on psychoanalysis', *Standard Edition* 11: 3–36.

Freud, S. (1912) 'The dynamics of transference', *Standard Edition* 12: 99–108.

Freud, S. (1914) 'Remembering, repeating and working through', *Standard Edition* 12: 145–156.

Geddes, H. (2006) *Attachment in the Classroom: The Links between Children's Early Experience, Emotional Well-Being and Performance in School*, London: Worth Publishing.

Holmes, J. (2009) *Exploring in Security: Towards an Attachment-Informed Psychoanalytic Psychotherapy*, London: Routledge.

Hopkins, J. (1990) 'The observed infant of attachment theory *British Journal of Psychotherapy*. Reprinted in A. Horne and M. Lanyado (eds) 2015 *An Independent Mind: Collected Papers of Juliet Hopkins*, Hove & New York: Routledge. pp. 53–63.

Lanyado, M. and Horne, A. (1999) 'The therapeutic relationship and process'. Chapter 5 in M Lanyado & A Horne' (eds) *The Handbook of Child and Adolescent Psychotherapy*, London: Routledge. pp. 55–72.

Main, M. (1995) 'Recent studies in attachment: overview, with selected implications for clinical work'. In S. Goldberg, R. Muir and J. Kerr (eds) *Attachment Theory: Social, Developmental and Clinical Perspectives*, Hillsdale, NJ: Analytic Press. pp. 407–474.

Rycroft, C. (1968) *A Critical Dictionary of Psychoanalysis*, London: Nelson.

Spence, D. (1994) *The Rhetorical Voice of Psychoanalysis*, Cambridge, MA: Harvard University Press.

Wilson, P. (2003) *Young Minds in Our Schools*, London: YoungMinds.

Chapter 10

Why can't an adolescent be more like an adult?

The relationship between adolescent and adult psychoanalytic psychotherapist

Unpublished paper given at a joint conference of Brent Centre for Young People and Westminster School, London 2013.

I came to this title because I had long been amused by the words of a song in an old musical, 'My Fair Lady' – 'Why can't a woman be more like a man?' I should add this musical was set in Edwardian times. In the musical, it is sung by the leading man, Professor Henry Higgins, a male professor of phonetics who is trying to educate a working-class young woman, Eliza Dolittle, to speak properly in an elegant posh upper-class accent. His are the words of sheer incomprehension and exasperation – the ultimate cry of the narcissist. In other words, 'Why can't you be me or be like me? On no account be different or separate from me and thus be in anyway a threat to me'. The poor professor, so frightfully eminent, professorial, so knowledgeable and above all so perfectly rational and reasonable – why should he have to endure the obduracy of such a recalcitrant young woman, a waif like Eliza Doolittle, with such a resounding cockney accent? His expertise demanded deference and compliance with his insistent procedures. But he did not receive this with any of the willingness or appreciation that he had assumed he would receive.

Similarly, we could say, any professional of some seniority, an adult psychoanalyst or a teacher, for example, might find himself or herself in a comparable predicament, faced with – or as too often the case, not faced with – the indifference and unresponsiveness of an uncooperative adolescent, resistant to his or her formidable classical and above all, rational ideas. They may well cry 'Oh, why can't an adolescent be more like an adult?' – their sights similarly lofty and their methods, their unique methods, so irreproachable. Beyond all protestations, both are made to conclude that there is a lot they don't know – and indeed that they may prefer not to know.

In this chapter, I want to emphasise one basic observation – that adolescents are, as far as I can make out, very different from adults – they are not grown-up children nor are they mini adults. I wrote this chapter, initially, with the relationship between adolescents and adult psychoanalysts particularly in mind. I believed that adult psychoanalysts or psychoanalytic psychotherapists need to change the customary ways in which they work with adult patients and to adapt what they know to reach the developmental ways of adolescents if they are to make any kind of therapeutic rapport with them. I think much the same kind of adaptation needs

DOI: 10.4324/9781003680437-11

to be made by most adult professionals, such as teachers, if they are to establish more meaningful and comprehensible conversations with the adolescents they are dealing with. Whatever their worthy and rational adult ideas and ideals might be of what they believe to be 'in the best interests' of young people, it may well be that they get a reception not quite in synch with what they intended or hoped for. They may find themselves a bit at odds with the particular adolescents in front of them – and they may well have to adapt what they think is right for them, the adolescents, if they want to find some kind of meaningful connection.

Of course, adolescents vary in their degrees of maturity, reasonableness, and receptivity. But by and large, they often behave in ways beyond the comprehension of mature, reasonable, and receptive adults. And it is this that strains whatever notion of normality an adult might hope for. Only the other day, a dear colleague joined me for morning coffee, staggering and gasping into the cafe in which we met having gone through what she described as 'ten rounds' with Cathy, her endearing but 'impossible' daughter who had just driven her round the bend. Here is what she, a beloved parent, had to say, 'I thought I had nailed this whole parenting thing but then she throws in some great curve balls and leaves me thinking how on earth did we get from O.K. to whatever this is in a couple of minutes?'

In this chapter, I want to dwell on what I shall call 'the sheer force of mental tension', of the tension deriving from the unyielding vigour of differences, differences of all kinds – differences in thoughts and feelings, in preoccupations, in ways of going about things, in certainties; and, more specifically between the worlds of the young and the adult, and especially between the worlds of adolescents and adult psychoanalysts. Without becoming entangled in the difficulties of defining exactly what an adult is, I am wanting to explore the major differences between the adolescent and the adult, not least in the world of psychoanalytic psychotherapy.

I have been particularly struck by how Carl Jung captured the essence of the two major stages of life that I am interested in – on the one hand, the archetype of what he called the Puer Aeternus, the spirit of eternal life, immersed in the present. Moore (1979), an American Jungian analyst, elaborated on this in a particularly vivid way: 'Whenever new movements of the soul come to life, stir and press upon consciousness, Puer may constellate. One is then close to virgin soil, flailed perhaps with the spirit of adventure, excited, nervous and unsteady – like a colt on shaky legs, eager to run but awkward and unpredictable'. And on the other hand, the archetype of the Senex, the holder of maturity, gravity, settlement and authority, representing order, continuity, time and history, the past.

How the two, the Puer and the Senex, live with each other is perhaps one of the most critical issues that arise in the way any society manages to work. At best, the two live in a kind of dynamic harmony, with the young looking for guidance and affirmation; and the old, essentially generative, celebrating the energy, the idealism, the beauty of the young and, as Moore puts it, their 'unbridled creativity and unbounded potency'. At worst, the two languish in inglorious battle, the young, defiant, rebellious and dismissive and the old, profoundly contemptuous, in a defensive denunciation of the young threatening chaos, anarchy, revolt, disrespect, ignorance and superficiality. Several years ago, the Barnardo's charity carried out a survey of British Attitudes to Young People, entitled 'The Shame of Britain: Intolerance of Children' (2008) (by children, they meant young people under the age of 18). The survey sprouted a long row of statistical findings. Here are just a few: 54% of adults think that British children are beginning to behave like animals; 49% agree that children are increasingly a danger to each other and to adults; 45% agree that people refer to children as feral because of their behaviour; 41% agree that something has to be done to protect them, the adults, from young people. And I cannot resist the passionate words of the vicar of St. Giles in London in 1621 who is reported to have said: 'this coming generation will bring in such a torrent of vice and corruption as will overrun the world with rudeness, lewdness and extreme barbarity'.

400 years ago. Plus ça change, plus ç'est la meme chose. There is inherent in this everlasting tension between the adolescent and the adult both positive and negative possibilities. Under favourable conditions, such tension can be so fruitful, welding the best of the old and the new. However, forever lurking, a darker, more compelling and destructive dimension may emerge. Basically, this latter hinges on fear and wariness on both sides, though particularly so on the adult side – including the side of adult psychoanalytic psychotherapists. I think I am right in thinking that the majority of adult psychoanalysts prefer to work with adults; and child psychoanalysts, with children in early childhood and latency. As Anna Freud observed in her seminal paper on 'Adolescence', 'the position with regard to the analytic study of adolescence is not a happy one, especially when compared with that of early childhood... One can hear it said frequently that adolescence is a neglected period, a stepchild where analytic thinking is concerned' (1958). Considering how important the state of the adolescent mind is for the future of enjoyment and achievement in later life, I have wondered why so many adult psychoanalytic psychoanalysts choose to seemingly dodge adolescents as best they can in their practice. It has often crossed my mind that they too, in keeping with their age, are frightened of young people – and that their insistence on holding the sacred 'frame', the fundamental condition of the psychoanalytic experience, may be a vital means of protecting themselves from the sheer potency and unpredictability of the adolescent force. It may well be too that they deny the adolescence in those adolescent patients, who stay the course of psychoanalysis with them. They are inclined to treat them not as adolescents but more assuredly as mini adults, which I strongly believe adolescents are not.

So, let's take another look at what we understand about this thing called adolescence. What is it about it that differentiates it from adulthood? For brevity's sake, I shall simply say that I am thinking of people in their teenage years, running through into their early twenties. There is of course much written about all this and there is a whole range of perspectives that need to be taken into account in order to capture the full complexity of the adolescent experience. Family dynamics of course play a critical role in how the adolescents can find their own way of life beyond the orbit of their families. Social and cultural factors clearly play an important part in establishing environments with differing values and customs which adolescents are expected to assimilate. The influences of social media are both invasive and pervasive and crowd the minds of adolescents in quite unprecedented and imperative ways. Issues relating to racism, sexism, homophobia and gender place further demands on the adolescents' approach to adulthood, let alone the grotesque politics of our time.

However, for my purposes of this chapter here, I shall concentrate on the internal, biological life of the adolescent, the fundamental essence which I believe too often is at risk of being overlooked. At the centre of all this is, of course, puberty – a familiar and comfortable enough little word that I believe we all too readily take for granted. It is often said, for example, that 'adolescence is the psychic counterpart of the physical process of puberty' – true enough, but all too often declared without the emphasis that I think is needed to properly register the extraordinariness of what is going on. Puberty is none less than a biological revolution. When now I give lectures on the psychology of adolescence, I start unequivocally with the basic biology of adolescent bodies.

Puberty is not a single event. It can last for several years and, for the first time after a relative period of steady growth in childhood, it involves remarkably dramatic changes in the anatomy, the physiology and the physical appearance of the adolescent body. Above all, the adolescent becomes capable of reproduction – to impregnate and to be impregnated; (significantly, the prefix, 'pu' in the word 'puberty' comes from the Latin 'to beget'). The endocrine system is a highly complex and refined collection of glands releasing the many movements of so many hormones throughout the body. It is all of this that comprises the bodily system and which has such a powerful impact on mental and behavioural functioning.

The volume and intensity of puberty is quite frankly staggering. To make my point, I want to simply quote the following extract from a textbook entitled *Adolescence and Emerging Adulthood: A Cultural Approach* by J.J. Arnett, second edition (2004). This is not a biology or psychoanalytic textbook but one written by a well-respected and authoritative American writer in the field on adolescence in general. Although most of the book is preoccupied with cultural issues, Chapter 2 is entitled the 'biological foundation'. He writes as follows:

Females for example are born with about 400,000 immature eggs, called follicles, in each ovary. By puberty, this number has declined to about 80,000 in each ovary. Once a girl reaches menarche (her first menstrual period) and begins having menstrual cycles, one follicle develops into a mature egg, or ovum, every 28 days or so. Females release about 400 eggs over the course of their reproductive lives. In the male, once spermarche arrives on average at age 12, boys produce sperm in astonishing quantities – there are between 30 and 500 million sperm in the typical male ejaculation which means the average male produces millions of sperm every day …. the female immune system registers sperm as foreign bodies and begins attacking them immediately. One further fact – the growth spurt in puberty. 'By mid-teens in girls, oestradiol is 8 times higher than in childhood. In boys, testosterone is 20 times higher'.

(Arnett 2004)

I want to steam ahead with this for a few more moments with a quotation from my earlier paper, 'I don't know':

> Within adolescents, pubertal bodies startle in all of their mysterious ways: some begin earlier than others; others become bigger than others. But at the heart of the matter, fears of the sheer physical power of these changes, of losing control of new internal pressures, and of the dread of growing onward without limit into some sort of monster or freak remain. There is of course excitement, empowerment, exhilaration – but uncertainties persist and the shadowy underside continues to torment. Compelling images of monumental and desirable men and women may fill teenage screens, preen their fantasies, and shape their imitations. But beyond all of this, in the aloneness of the bedroom or toilet, the shape of the nose, the size and touch of the breast, the size and hardness of the penis, the flow of the menses or semen, the countless other encounters with the phenomena of the body remind them of the vivid unprecedented newness of growing up and too often of the inadequacy of words to account for it all. In the fumbling and wandering forays into early conversations, there remains, for most, an inarticulateness in catching hold of the things that are novel, fascinating but essentially unknown and yet to be discovered.
>
> (2001; Chapter 3 this volume)

What on earth do adults make of this knowledge? What do they have to say about it? Have I gone over the top, too far-fetched? There is much to digest and maybe I have veered off into overstatement. But the more I think about, I stay with it. One comment I came across recently on a greeting card maybe suffices for the moment: 'Puberty is when your parents start turning really weird'.

Whilst we stay in the physical domain, we have to keep in mind too what is going on in the brain of the adolescent. I, of course, am not a neuroscientist and I do not pretend to know what I am talking about when it comes to the intricate workings of the brain. But what I have increasingly gleaned with greater confidence in recent years from the ample literature that is available is that there is a general agreement amongst neuroscientists that the pre-frontal cortex in the adolescent brain is still in a relatively immature state. It is still developing and is not surely established – certainly not during the teenage years but also ongoing well into the mid-twenties.

This part of the brain I have often seen as akin to the psychoanalytic concept of the ego. The ego is not something that can be identified or seen in the brain. It is no more than a concept, a concept that Freud drew up to make sense of how we humans deal with the complexities of living. Essentially, he saw the human mind besieged by pressures both from 'within' and 'without'. From within, he referred to the Id, a kind of biological powerhouse of all kinds of bodily urges, primarily sexual, which he called the drives and which pressed imperatively for release and discharge. And from 'without', primarily what he called the Superego, the repository of all the social constraints and requirements, internalised and imposed in family upbringing set in different layers of culture and society. And there in between Id and Superego sits the Ego, trying in one way or another to broker the conflicting forces, managing and moderating as best it can. With this in mind, I see the pre-frontal cortex of the brain as serving in effect these basic functions.

It is now well known that this part of the brain is seen to be responsible for the development of a range of skills, including organising plans and ideas, adapting to reality and to social environmental pressures. It includes all those faculties, so essential for everyday living, such as setting priorities, forming strategies, balancing short-term rewards and long-term goals. Piaget's ideas on the development of formal operation thought in adolescence sit well alongside these understandings of the developments in the brain. The adolescent in effect possesses greater but not complete capacities to think logically and abstractly with more complex problems, and to conceptualise what is beyond the immediate to the wider perspective – but still not fully.

So much for the body. The other major concern of adolescence is essentially to do with relationships, not least with the task of separation and individuation from childhood dependence on parents and family. This is no easy business and again, I think there is a tendency to overlook its importance or at least to pass over it as some kind of a cliché. Separation means loss – the loss of something that has gone before – under favourable conditions, with supportive family back up, the loss of the familiar assumptions and assurances, the loss of the relative reliance for safety and protection, the loss of the comfort in believing that everything that has been known is known for sure. Adolescents are driven onwards beyond this by the sheer maturation of the body that we have spoken about and by the implicit requirement, as I see it, in the individualistic culture that pervades our Western society – the requirement to individuate, to achieve difference through separation, to find a sense of self that has distinction and coherence and that draws recognition from others.

All of this may be all very well but as Harvey Greenberg points out in his excellent paper on adolescence in 1977, it leads inevitably to the adolescent finding himself in a kind of limbo or of what he calls a 'developmental void'. The way forward is uncertain, the question of who one is, or for that matter who anybody is, the undefined sense of what being an adult is supposed to mean – all of this, with less, as it were, to fall back on, fills the adolescent with an abiding state of anxiety, a state of tension that has to be dealt with in some way to get through it.

It is here that I see a retreat to narcissism as setting in – in other words into an inner retreat to which adolescents succumb, leading to an exaggerated self-love and self-preoccupation that in turn fortifies their sense of competence and self-reliance. This amounts to a regressive process by which adolescents counter their newly encountered experience of instability and unsureness. They build themselves up with an inner assertion of, or an illusory belief in, their own superior strength and power. Greenberg understands this process very well, adolescents bolstering their fragile and isolated self through an immersion in fantasy and periodic acting out in devotion to all kinds of intimacies. As Greenberg makes clear, some adolescents buttress themselves, particularly in early adolescence in the intensity of close and mutually reassuring friendships: others look to peer groups or adults to whom they give themselves over for the provision of imagined protection and courage. Some devote themselves to various kinds of all powerful heroes, upon whom they bestow extraordinary powers to elevate and save them. There are others who recoil into their own narcissistic reveries in which they can hold onto the illusion of their perfection, omnipotence and sense of total control.

A few years ago, I wrote a chapter on Narcissism and Adolescence (1995; Chapter 6 in this volume). I began by saying that adolescents are 'peculiarly bothered about themselves' in view of all that I have emphasised in this chapter. Inevitably, this leads to what I called a 'very distinctive insularity and fragility' in the adolescent experience. The adolescent in other words is in a precarious developmental state – no longer cared for in the same way as a child might be and increasingly left exposed to the uncertain and daunting prospects of adult life. I refer as always to the psychoanalytic writer, Heinz Kohut's (1977) concepts of the grandiose self and the idealising parental imago to make sense of what Greenberg (1975) describes as the 'omnipotent quest during adolescence'. Greenberg referred to what he called 'magical manoeuvres', that is to say certain kinds of defence mechanisms that employ illusory thinking to deal with this development predicament – it is as if the adolescent is saying, as a way of denying his or her insecurity or sense of helplessness, 'I am perfect and omnipotent; or you are perfect and omnipotent and so I am inviolable, no longer impotent, always to be protected and never to be vanquished'.

It may be that some of you may think I am making a right old meal of all this business of adolescence, chanting out so loudly from old textbooks. However, I insist that this kind of magnification is necessary in order to ride against a general level of complacency or blindness about the peculiarities of adolescence. I repeat, in my view, adolescents are not mini adults nor grown-up children to be treated in the same way as either in their own right. They have their own peculiarities. This is an interesting word, a word that I have come to use more frequently to capture the gist of what I am thinking about when I think about adolescence. To quote from the dictionaries, something 'peculiar' is a 'strange or unusual feature of someone or place'; it is a 'characteristic that is distinctive about a particular person or place'; it is 'something different or unusual'; or even further 'something eccentric, unusual, even weird' (how much this last word crops up when adolescents describe the oddness of others or indeed in themselves). In this respect, I have to quote Anna Freud again in her paper on Adolescence as she addresses the problem of deciding whether an adolescent's worrying behaviour can be judged to be no more than a normal expression of the peculiarities of his or her age or whether it indicates a more serious and entrenched mental health problem. 'The adolescent manifestations come close to the symptom formation of the neurotic, psychotic or dis-social order and merge almost imperceptibly into borderline states, initial, frustrated or fully fledged forms of almost all the mental illnesses. Consequently, the differential diagnosis between the adolescent upset and true pathology becomes a difficult task' (Freud 1958).

We might finally add to this bodily and heady concoction two other peculiarities – the sheer changeability of the adolescent's moods, feelings, states of being that are a part and parcel of the urgencies of the adolescent's puberty and the limitations within the adolescent's brain to handle this urgency, to regulate emotion and thought. It is no surprise that the adolescent is often known for his or her impulsivity, a propulsion to act and to do before to reflect and to think. The other peculiarity, related, but different, is one that I have written about in the chapter that I have already referred to 'I don't know' (2001; Chapter 3 this volume). This chapter emerged after years of my sitting down as a therapist in therapy sessions with adolescents of all kinds with all the eager and hopeful psychotherapeutic vigour and curiosity that I could muster – only to be greeted by an all too familiar response, so deafening and dispiriting in its resonance – 'I don't know'. At first I was cross about this – after all, I was giving of myself with all my new-found knowledge to 'explore' and 'help' – but only to be blunted with what seemed a deliberate defiance and a cussed refusal to co-operate. Over the years, however, I have come to understand this phrase not so much as a defensive resistance, but more of a developmental resistance – a demonstration of the adolescent's vital need to push against the parent/adult psychotherapist's control as well as an expression of the adolescent's familiar confusion or fear or wariness or indeed of sheer inarticulacy ('I feel crap but I just can't find the words'). It is as if the adolescent is conveying many different meanings that lay behind the 'I don't know': 'I haven't yet learnt how to put into words whatever it is that I know or whatever it is that I am feeling. I can't figure out what I know or don't know: I am supposed not to know and if I told you what I am not supposed to know, I don't know what you will think of me: and anyway, what is mine is for me to know, it is not for you or anybody else to know'. Of course, there is much paradox in the adolescent state – to be understood, to not be understood; to be given licence, but clear boundaries; to be cared for as a child and to be left alone as an adult. It is all very befuddling.

And so again what on earth do adults make of all this – these puberties, these sexual imperatives, these bodily discoveries, these physical forces, these varying brain capacities, these struggles for individuation, these narcissistic retreats, these peculiarities, these moodinesses, these inconsistencies, these not knowings....? Isn't it here, in this quagmire, that adults encounter the true mysteriousness of adolescents? Isn't it here that the fundamental differences between adolescents and adults reside?

I began this lecture by drawing a parallel between a distinguished phonetics professor, befoxed by a recalcitrant cockney girl and an eminent adult psychoanalyst befuddled by an uncooperative adolescent. Both the adult and adolescent didn't match too easily with each other, the psychoanalyst so enwrapped in his or her precise speciality, and deeply loyal to the tradition in which he or she had trained. Can psychoanalysts properly extend themselves beyond their professional fortresses to encompass an alien creature, the adolescent? 'Why' indeed might they cry 'can't an adolescent be more like an adult', or, more to the point, 'be like me?' I think we are all, all of us adults, left flummoxed by the many peculiarities of adolescence, by its differences from the child or adult state of mind.

In the world of psychoanalytic psychotherapy, two fundamental questions arise. What kind of working relationship can be formed between the adolescent and adult psychoanalytic psychotherapist, and what can be achieved in psychoanalytic psychotherapy with an adolescent? With regard to the first question, can adult psychoanalytic psychotherapists really reassure themselves that they have secured with an adolescent what is commonly called a 'working alliance'? I have written about this (Chapter 8) and suggest that the term 'alliance' implies a level of mature formal co-operation that actually does not exist in therapeutic relationships with many adolescent patients; that the word conjures up something of a more hopeful, wishful fantasy on the part of the adult. Can it really be the case that the adolescent is capable of such grown-up agreements – in view of what I have described as the adolescent really being so absorbed with him or herself as to be relatively indifferent to the requirements of any other; similarly, as being so unclear what he or she thinks at any one moment and as being so unsure what he knows anyway, can the adult expect the adolescent to be other than relatively unready for psychotherapeutic commitment? As I see it, the psychoanalytic therapeutic relationship that more realistically exists between the adult and the adolescent is by and large a more fluid, more unformed, more chancy one – a more evolving relationship that develops in a less orderly way, especially in the early stage of contact.

With regard to the second question – what can be achieved in psychoanalytic psychotherapy with an adolescent? What in fact is the nature of the relationship between psychoanalysis and adolescence? A distinction has to be made between, in my view, for want of better terms, 'classical' and 'modern' psychoanalysis. In the first, there is a clear insistence on well-established procedures. Suffice to say that great emphasis is placed on the 'frame' of the therapeutic setting, the preservation of constant and clear boundaries which serve to provide a safe and containing environment in which the psychoanalytic relationship can proceed. Within this setting, there is the provision of time, space, patience and silence, qualities which allow the analysand to lie back and relax, sufficiently unfettered by the personal intrusions of the psychoanalyst and sufficiently encouraged to freely associate in relation to his dreams and fantasies and the events of his past and present life. The primary purpose of all this is for the analytic pair to gain a greater understanding of the unconscious, largely through interpretation in the transference.

This classical psychoanalysis works for some well-motivated troubled adults. The question is, does it do so for similarly afflicted adolescents? Some adult psychoanalysts think it does – and in doing so, they stay loyal to their belief in psychoanalysis proper, regardless of whether it is appropriate for most of the adolescents they may see. I personally am not happy about that kind of thinking – basically because it relies on what in effect is a false compliance on the adolescent's part to fit in with the expectations of the adult psychoanalyst at the cost of the emergence of the adolescent's own independent and authentic development.

What clearly needs to be developed in work with adolescents, as I see it, is an adaptation of the psychoanalytic procedure. I am not talking about a renunciation of psychoanalysis. Holding the frame that I have spoken about is unquestionably fundamental, though at times, this can be held seemly too rigidly tight and overcontrolling for many adolescents. Silence, listening, waiting, not barging in is similarly crucial but can at times seem rejecting and/or persecutory. In my view, there has to be a preparedness on the part of the adult psychoanalytic psychotherapist to enter into a more active interaction with the adolescent, an involved exchange which captures the curiosity and excitement of the adolescent. This of course can be risky for the psychotherapist, floundering in a particular kind of familiarity without the sure rules and professional constraints.

I would like at this point to give an illustration of what I have in mind by sharing with you an excerpt from one particular session in which an adolescent and the adult psychotherapist were engaged in psychoanalytic psychotherapy. This session was contributed by an adult working as a child and adolescent psychotherapist. The adolescent in this case is Harry (a pseudonym) who was seen in once weekly psychotherapy for three years in the middle years of his adolescence. He was referred for depression and he came with a history of disruptive behaviour in his childhood. This session occurred in the second year of his psychoanalytic psychotherapy. I should add this is a relatively condensed version of the session, a session which occurred in the context of a series of similar sessions during the course of the psychotherapy. This session is written in the first person by the psychotherapist.

The session began in a fairly typical manner in which Harry half played around with his smart phone, sometimes looking at it, sometimes using it as a toy to push around like a model car. He seemed tired, lethargic and seemingly not wanting to be in the session. He sighed and said 'I don' know' to any overture or question to him made by the psychotherapist. Eventually, he suddenly looked at me and said 'wow, you look different'. He seems amused and I feel a bit off guard. It turns out that he has noticed that I am wearing a different, brighter coloured jumper. He says it is his favourite colour...... This exchange feels playful but also a little awkward and I am not sure where he is going or even coming from.... I wait a bit and then decide to ask him again 'How have you been? 'Oh me?' I say 'Yes, you...it has been a couple of weeks since we last met hasn't it and things were quite eventful when I last saw you.' 'Ah yeah, school is kind of a pain.' I ask in what way and he tells me that no one is talking to him anymore and that he has lost all his friends. 'So that's kind of boring'. He corrects himself quickly and says that actually three people are still with him and they were good friends before, so that's alright. He thinks the others will come round eventually. 'I'm kind of working on it'. It sounds quite mature and reassuring but I say, 'But that's not Fred' (a friend he has been talking about recently). Harry looks very serious and agrees: 'no, *not* Fred' with emphasis.

We talk about Fred and what kind of friend he is. I track Harry's descriptions as closely as I can with one or two comments that I think highlight his main points. Harry rewards me with an emphatic 'exactly' or 'that's it' every now and then. This way I find out that Fred's quite a callous figure who is primarily concerned with his social status, that he uses girls and is only out for himself. Harry says he has known this about Fred for some time, but chose to hang out with him because he was very popular. Also, Harry says he was quite impressed that there is a side of Fred that is more genuine. Fred had let Harry know something more vulnerable about himself as he confided that there were things that upset him 'and stuff'. Harry explains that this was why he thought he had an important connection with Fred. However, later in the session, he talks about sending text messages to Fred but only getting responses from him that were empty and lacking any enjoyment. So I comment that it is a real shame not having that friendship anymore and Harry agrees. There is a brief silence and I go on making educated guesses about different types of messages he may have received from Fred. Harry says 'that's exactly it' with visible relief. I then make a misstep in my next comment in referring to something 'intimate' about his friendship with Fred. Harry frowns at this and I correct myself, 'maybe that's not the word that sounds good; maybe 'real' is better'. He nods and we call something good between people as 'real' from then on.

With ten minutes left to the session, I comment that Harry hadn't talked about his family. There is a lull in the conversation but with Harry periodically looking at me. Eventually, he scowls and grumbles that things are pretty much the same as always. When I wondered whether things had in fact got better, he reacted sharply – 'What do you mean? .... Well, my parents are just the same, so not really...yeah, so what can I do, they are just the same'. He yawns and I ask him if he is tired. He says 'yeah' with a meaningful look. I ask if he is still having late nights. He exclaims 'Yea.... I get to sleep at 4 pm'.

What I think this session highlights is the very intimacy of the exchange between the two. The psychotherapist is above all attentive and sensitive, honest about herself and ready to take her time with the flow of the session. She acknowledges that she is in effect in the dark, mostly unsure, guessing and finding the right words. There is so much she doesn't know about this boy's life at home or at school – and, initially, it can hardly be said that the adolescent experiences the psychotherapist as an ally. There is a typical beginning wariness, and what I would call a narcissistic aloofness, but it is encouraging to see that a gradual development takes place in the session in which a sense of co-operation between the two – a certain kind of trust that had grown out of the ongoing nature of the many weekly meetings between the two. Matters of some importance are suddenly openly addressed – Harry's view of himself, his confusion about himself in friendships, his sense of isolation, his awareness of vulnerability, concealed by bravado (in Fred and implicitly in himself), his anger and despair about his parents. The psychotherapeutic experience has enlivened Harry's curiosity in himself. Moments such as this that are encountered in this one session are likely to accumulate during the course of the psychotherapy and build up towards a greater understanding on the part of the adolescent that in turn may enable him or her to be less scared, hurt or angry and thus more free to enjoy his or her life.

Some, of course, will say 'Well, is this it? Is this what you call psychoanalytic?' And, indeed, on the face of it in this one excerpt of one particular session, criticism could well be levelled at those, such as myself, who believe that this kind of work is realistic and within the bounds of what most adolescents can manage. It of course is not of the same order as that achieved by classical psychoanalysts with neurotic adults. But the classical model in most cases falls short, I believe, in simply reaching and engaging the adolescent. The psychoanalytic experience that I am talking about is a more collaborative one, more a kind of conversation, more to and fro. This may slip into all kinds of goings on between psychotherapist and adolescent – weaving and bopping, parrying, sparring even, dancing in the face of all the resistance – not at all unlike was the case with Harry at the beginning of his session. This may sound flippant, tricky, risky and of course, there are many pitfalls – but I believe a psychoanalytic knowledge and awareness of the familiar adolescent preoccupation with himself or herself and an appreciation of the adolescent resistance to too much scrutiny may allow a psychoanalytic experience to be achieved with an adolescent. But throughout, the intention is to provide a regular place in which the adolescent may become sufficiently engaged with the adult psychoanalytic psychotherapist to turn up, to continue and to carry on learning about his or her self.

Winnicott (1971) described the state of adolescence as

a few years in which the individual has no way out except to wait and to do this without awareness of what is going on. In this phase, the child does not know whether he or she is homosexual, heterosexual or narcissistic. There is no established identity and no certain way of life that shapes the future and makes sense of graduating exams. There is not yet the capacity to identify with parent figures without loss of personal identity.

He goes on to say:

There is only one cure for adolescence ant this is the passage of time and the passing on of the adolescent into the adult state.... We hold on, playing for time, instead of offering distractions and cures.

It is indeed tempting to share such a sigh. But I believe that most adolescents, despite their resistances, are sufficiently and narcissistically fascinated about themselves and indeed concerned about themselves to be quite strongly motivated for psychotherapeutic treatment. The critical factor resides not so much in the adolescent as in the psychoanalytic psychotherapist. His or her interest in the mysteriousness of adolescence and acknowledgement of the uncertainties inherent in the psychotherapeutic process is crucial and sufficient to engage their psychoanalytic knowledge in response to the needs of their adolescents who are not adults.

Perhaps, we should reverse our opening question: 'Why can't an adult be more like an adolescent?'

References

Arnett, J. J. (ed) (2004) 'Biological foundations'. In *Adolescence and Emerging Adulthood: A Cultural Approach*, 2nd Edition, Hoboken, NJ: Prentice Hall.

Barnardo's. (2008) *British Attitudes to Young People: 'The Shame of Britain's Intolerance of Children'*, Barnardo's press release.

Freud, A. (1958) 'Adolescence', *Psychoanalytic Study of the Child* 13: 255–278. New York: International Universities Press.

Greenberg, H. (1975) 'The widening gyre: transformations of the omnipotent quest during adolescence', *International Review of Psychoanalysis* 2: 231–244.

Kohut, H. (1972) 'Thoughts on narcissism and narcissistic rage', *Psychoanalytic Study of the Child* 27: 360–400.

Moore, T. (1979) 'Artemis and puer'. In *Puer Papers*, Dallas: Spring publications.

Wilson, P. (1995) 'Narcissism and adolescence'. In J. Cooper and N. Maxwell (eds) *Narcissistic Wounds; Clinical Perspectives*, London: Whurr. pp. 51–63.

Winnicott, D. W. (1968) 'Adolescence: struggling through the doldrums'. In *The Family and Individual Development*, London: Routledge.

Appendix

Publications and papers

2018   The Porn Retreat: Narcissism and Adolescence *Psychodynamic Practice* 24 (3): 235–235

2017   People Meet in a Classroom and Say Hello. In D Colley & P Cooper (eds.) *Attachment and Emotional Development in the Classroom: Theory and Practice* London: Jessica Kingsley

2016   What Evidence Works for Whom? In S Campbell, D Morley & R Catchpole (eds.) *Critical Issues in Child and Adolescent Mental Health* London: Palgrave

2014   Hatred and Helping: Working With Our Fear and Narcissistic Rage. In M J Spelman & F Thomson-Salo (eds.) *The Winnicott Traditions* London: Karnac

2003   *Young Minds in Our Schools* London: YoungMinds

2003   Supervision and Consultation. In A Ward, K Kasinski, J Pooley & A Worthington (eds.) *Therapeutic Communities for Children and Young People* London: Jessica Kingsley

2002   Child Mental Health. In K White (ed.) *Reframing Children's Services* NCVCCO *Annual Review Journal No. 3* London: NCVCCO

2001   I Don't Know. Psychotherapy with Adolescents Special Section *Journal of the British Association of Psychotherapists* 39 (2)

1999   Therapy and Consultation in Residential Care. In M Lanyado & A Horne (eds.) *The Handbook of Child and Adolescent Psychotherapy: Psychoanalytic Approaches* London & New York: Routledge

1999   Delinquency. In M Lanyado & A Horne (eds.) *The Handbook of Child and Adolescent Psychotherapy: Psychoanalytic Approaches* London & New York: Routledge

1998   Development and Mental Health: The Issue of Difference in Atypical Gender Identity Development. In D Di Ceglie (ed.) *A Stranger in My Own Body* London: Karnac Books

1997   The Problem of Helping in Relation to Developmental Breakdown in Adolescence. In M Laufer (ed.) *Adolescent Breakdown and Beyond* London: Karnac Books

1997   The Energy of Hatred and the Relationship with Violence *Medicine, Conflict and Survival* 113 (1)

1996   *Mental Health in Your School* London: Jessica Kingsley

1996   Working with Adolescent Delinquents. In C Cordess & M Cox (eds.) *Crime, Psychodynamics and the Offender Patient* Vol 2: *Mainly Practice* London: Jessica Kingsley

1995   Time to Think. In E Smith (ed.) *Mental Health in the Market Place* London & New York: Routledge

1995   Narcissism and Adolescence. In J Cooper & N Maxwell (eds.) *Narcissistic Wounds: Clinical Perspectives* London: Whurr

1993   Consultation to Institutions: Questions of Role and Orientation. In S Ramsden (ed.) *Psychotherapy Pure and Applied* ACPP Occasional Papers No. 6 London: Association for Child Psychology and Psychiatry

1991   Adolescence. In J Holmes (ed.) *A Textbook of Psychotherapy in Psychiatric Practice* London: Churchill Livingstone

1989   Latency and Certainty *Journal of Child Psychotherapy* 15 (2)

1988   Multi-Disciplinary Work: The Emotional Problem for the Professional Worker *Maladjustment and Therapeutic Education* 6 (2)

1988   The Psychoanalytic Treatment of a Boy Dominated by Omnipotent Fantasies *Journal of Child Psychotherapy* 14 (2)

1988   Therapeutic Intervention through the Nursery School *Bulletin of the Anna Freud Centre* 11

1988   The Impact of Cultural Changes on the Internal Experience of the Adolescent *Journal of Adolescence* 11: 271–286

1987   Psychoanalytic Therapy and the Young Adolescent *Bulletin of the Anna Freud Centre* 10

1986   Psychoanalytic Therapy and the Young Adolescent *Maladjustment and Therapeutic Education* 4 (2)

1986   Individual Psychotherapy in a Residential Setting. In D Steinberg (ed.) *The Adolescent Unit* London: Wiley

1985   Wilson, P & Hersov, L Individual and Group Psychotherapy. In M Rutter & L Hersov (eds.) *Child Psychiatry: Modern Approaches* 2nd edition London: Blackwell

1982   'Don't Help Me!': The Troubled Adolescent's Dilemma in Accepting Help. In Monograph No. 8 London: Brent Consultation Centre

1980   The Use of Observation in Hampstead Clinic Nursery School *Bulletin of the Hampstead Clinic* 3 (1)

1980   Wilson, P & Bottomley, V The Emotional Climate in the Classroom: The Interaction Between Adult Teacher and Early Adolescent Students. In G Upton & A Gobell (eds.) *Behaviour Problems in the Comprehensive School* Cardiff: Faculty of Education, University College Cardiff

1978   Psychoanalytic Thinking about Problems in Education *Bulletin of the Hampstead Clinic* 1 (4)

1978   The Influence of Sexuality. *Monograph 7* London: Brent Consultation Centre

1977   The Referral of Nursery School Children for Treatment *Psychoanalytic Study of the Child* 32

Public Lectures

2024   Me loves me.
        Brent Centre for Young People's International Online Seminar

2023   Why can't an adolescent be more like an adult? The relationship between adolescent and adult psychoanalytic psychotherapist.
Joint Conference Brent Centre for Young People and Westminster School

2021   The adolescent, the psychoanalyst and the working alliance.
Winter Conference of IPCAPA (the Independent Psychoanalytic Child and Adolescent Association at the British Psychotherapy Foundation)

2019   Me loves Me.
Limbus Foundation, Dartington, Devon

2018   Whence Anna Freud: and Whereto?
Introductory Lecture, Annual Colloquium, Anna Freud National Centre for Children and Families

2013   Youthful misbehaviour: to condemn or understand?
Jane Blom-Cooper Memorial Lecture, Place2Be, London

2003   The psychoanalyst and the delinquent.
Edward Glover Memorial Lecture, Portman Clinic, London

2003   The Place of Adolescent Services.
Dean's Annual Lecture, City University, London

2002   Today's adolescents: towards becoming an adult.
David Astor Annual Lecture, Thomas Coram, London

2001   A fear of growing up: the adolescent challenge.
Lionel Monteith memorial Lecture, St George's Hospital, London

Index

For Product Safety Concerns and Information please contact our EU
representative GPSR@taylorandfrancis.com
Taylor & Francis Verlag GmbH, Kaufingerstraße 24, 80331 München, Germany

www.ingramcontent.com/pod-product-compliance
Lightning Source LLC
Chambersburg PA
CBHW050611280326
41932CB00016B/3005

9 781041 156291